ONTACT HOLLAND "

ay 1942

20 MAART

24 MAART

20 NOV.

NOV.

11 MEI

17/18 JAN.

23/24 FEB.

9 DEC.

25/26 NOV..

29 SE

IJMUIDEN

A'DAM

NOORDWIJK

KATWIJK

SCHEVENINGEN

DEN HAAG

ROTTERDAM

CALAIS

2nd-Lt. Spec. Serv.

SOLDIER
of
ORANGE

SOLDIER
of
ORANGE

by

Erik Hazelhoff

HODDER AND STOUGHTON
LONDON SYDNEY AUCKLAND TORONTO

All the people in this book,
with one exception, appear
under their real names.

E.H.

FOREWORD

*by His Royal Highness Prince Bernhard
of the Netherlands, Prince of Orange.*

At first glance *Soldier of Orange* struck me as an odd title for the war
memoirs of Erik Hazelhoff. He was by any conventional standard an impossible soldier and furthermore only conditionally
"of Orange". The military mentality was alien to him and he
consistently displayed a striking lack of enthusiasm for its disci-
plinary aspects, to an extent which finally landed him before a
court martial. As far as the venerable House of Orange was concerned he also set his own standards, as he himself makes quite
clear in this book: "We judged everybody solely on his record in
the fight against the Nazis and whoever in our opinion fell short,
even had she been the Queen herself, we dismissed contemptuously."

In spite, or maybe because, of his refusal to be awed by rank and
position he finished the war, knighted and decorated, as A.D.C. to
my mother-in-law, Queen Wilhelmina of the Netherlands, after
having experienced World War II from more angles than perhaps
any other Dutchman. His story, although a highly personal one,
contains much which hitherto was known only to a very few and
thereby throws new light on our little country's role in that great
conflict.

7

I imagine that many a reader, especially from the younger generation, will ask himself with a certain amount of bewilderment: "Can it really have been like this?"

It so happens that I am in a position to answer that question: "I was there, and this is how it was."

ILLUSTRATIONS

Between pages

Leyden 1937   48–49

Traditionally required bald heads

Minerva, Leyden's hallowed students' club

Paul Renardel

Jean Mesritz

Rejected for military service

Count B

They all turned up, including Mia

Contraption to cross the North Sea

Students vote to strike

Frits van der Schrieck

Lobo van Hamel, Holland's first secret agent

"Orange Hotel"

St. Cergue

Our little H.Q.   96–97

General van't Sant

77 Chester Square

Stratton House

The "Mews": Peter, Erik, Chris

This enemy shore

M.G.B. 320

9

I typed up my own letter of appointment
Dutch Prime Minister Gerbrandy
Colonel Euan Rabagliatti, M.C., A.F.C.
Bob Goodfellow
Gerard Dogger
Frans Goedhart
Louis Baron d'Aulnis de Bourrouill
Secret transmitter ready for action   144–145
German E-boats tracked us down
I was recommended for trial by court-martial
Goodbye to Holland
I had the recurrent notion of being one world war behind
Robert Bergmann
Erik Michielsen
Supernumerary officers
We got our wings
Little Cohen
We bounced our bombs in through the front door
139 (Pathfinder) Squadron, R.A.F. Upwood, 1944
Ben Hein
De Havilland Mosquito
We crowded around the battle-order
It was forbidden to photograph briefings   192–193
I had an emergency map in my boot
The aiming-point photo showing the target
We hardly saw the "Pike and Eel"
Mozzie, R.A.F. Pathfinder
The first step back on Holland's soil
We gazed out over the multitudes
A SHAEF pass opened all doors
Two generations of Queens turned on me
The Packard rolled into my old stomping-grounds

I

AT FOUR A.M. ON 10 MAY 1940, QUEEN WILHELMINA OF THE Netherlands awakened her daughter, Princess Juliana, with the words: "They have come." She did not bother to elaborate as to who "they" were; she had been expecting the Nazis for a long time. In this she was almost alone in Holland. Even after Austria, Czechoslovakia, Poland, Denmark, Norway — none of us believed that we would be next. Hadn't the Kaiser by-passed our country in World War I? Then why not Hitler now? Ever since 3 September our little speck of land, squeezed between Germany and the North Sea, had been surrounded by violence on an epic scale, yet it conducted its business as usual, as if World War II were some foreign product unsuited to the Dutch market-place. When the war came, it was like no other war before or since.

I had spent the night at my parents' house in Wassenaar, a suburb of The Hague. In a dream someone seemed to be banging on the heating pipes, banging fast and loud. I awoke to the strong, sweet smell of hyacinths wafting in through the open windows from the bulb fields along the dunes. I got up and looked out; the sky, never quite dark in May, was limpid with the first light of another brilliant day. The noise I had heard came from the meadow across the street, behind the nursery school. I recognised the bark of anti-aircraft cannon, but could only see cows running through the grass with their tails in the air. Then my bedside radio informed me that, without warning or declaration of war,

German forces had crossed our common border and fighting was in progress.

Back at the window I saw a Junkers transport plane lumbering low over the edge of town, dropping parachutes like larvae from its tail. "They're out to get the Queen," I thought, knowing that the Royal Family was staying at Huis ten Bosch, a mile or two away. Then, for want of anything better to do, I went downstairs and made a big pot of coffee.

My guess was accurate, though for reasons that I could not know. Adolf Hitler, like most foreigners, misjudged the character of the Dutch people. He should have remembered that Holland had fought for eighty consecutive years to wrest her independence from the Spanish empire, in a war which the American philosopher and historian Will Durant has called "the longest, bravest and most cruel struggle for freedom in all history". Instead, he considered only our nation's Germanic origin, ignoring its racial and spiritual amalgamation with centuries of refugees from every kind of oppression, and cherished the vain hope of ultimately winning the Netherlands for the Nazi cause. But about Queen Wilhelmina he harboured no such illusions. She was a Princess of Orange-Nassau, the family which has guided the fortunes of Holland ever since its Declaration of Independence from Spain in 1581 in the midst of a revolution led by her ancestor William the Silent, Prince of Orange, and she had now been Queen of the Netherlands for forty-two years. In spite of the fact that both her mother and husband had been German, she steadfastly refused to have anything to do with the Third Reich ("an immoral system") or to accommodate its leaders ("those bandits") in any way. Clearly, she interfered with their dream of a Greater Germanic society, the *Herrenvolk*. She must be captured, and subsequently subdued or eliminated. For her part, she had frequently stated that, rather than fall into Hitler's hands alive, she would kill herself.

The parachute division commanded by S.S. General Student, which in the early hours of 10 May landed all around The Hague, had been assigned to take care of the Queen, in addition to occupying airfields, disrupting the government and sowing confusion behind the lines. Meanwhile the Wehrmacht, rolling in from the east, was to crush all military resistance in "honourable battle", employing a force sufficiently superior in men and equipment to save the Dutch army's face and preclude any bitterness which might stand in the way of ultimate brotherhood between the two nations. For the same reason this victory had to be achieved "without alienating the Netherlands people". Despite the treachery of their surprise attack and the accompanying assault on vital bridges by specialists previously smuggled into Holland and dressed in Dutch uniforms, despite the later horror of the bombing of Rotterdam, the German forces were actually under orders that violence was to go hand in hand with "correct behaviour" and "good manners". The paratroopers who at that moment were dropping by their hundreds into the dunes and meadows behind my home had been issued not only with bullets and grenades for killing Dutch soldiers, but also guilders with which to pay Dutch shopkeepers for refreshments and souvenirs, as well as little hand-books of friendly and polite Dutch phrases —

We sat drinking coffee and listening to the radio, expecting God knows what to happen, when I heard the familiar purr of Chris' BMW coming down the street. It was only six o'clock but it felt like noon. When the motor-bike turned into our driveway I poured a large cup, lots of sugar, no cream.

"What's up?"

"War," he grinned. "Would you believe it?" He gulped down his coffee. "Come on, let's go, before the roads are cut."

"Where are we going?" Already we were outside. It was terribly quiet. The guns behind the school had been silent for some time. The only sound in the warm, fragrant air came from the nightingales; they had been unbelievable this spring, singing day and night without interruption. I looked suspiciously at the thick foliage all around. "Aren't we going to get bumped off?"

"I could see them right from my balcony," Chris said, fluttering the carburettor. "In the meadow at the back, near the tram depot. Crawling in ditches, shooting rifles, everything. They were pushing south, this way, towards The Hague, I guess. But along the edge of the woods, near Rijksdorp, there are a lot of Dutch soldiers, facing towards Haagse Schouw — you know, that café where they sell Bokma jenever. Nobody seemed to be making much headway."

"How about Park de Kieviet?" That's where we were, a lush section of comfortable villas and large gardens at the foot of the dunes.

"Well, on my way here I didn't see any. They say that some landed very close by, in the dunes. If so, perhaps they're hiding, waiting for others to get through. If and when. Come on, let's go."

"Where are we going?" I asked again, hopping on the back of his bike. We tore out of the drive; I caught a glimpse of my mother at the window.

"Join up. What else?"

The streets were deserted. We went as fast as we could, bent into the wind, huddled together. The empty gardens bright with flowers, the mounds of rhododendrons, the silent stretches of thick under-brush, all so familiar yesterday, now made our skins crawl. We looked neither left nor right. We were going to join up, what else? And then what would happen? Were we going to die? Very suddenly, with a weird, whispering, whistling roar, a plane flashed by overhead, scraping the tree-tops. My heart pounded in my throat. Chris sat up and turned his head to speak to me. "Ah well," he said, "at least it looks as if that bloody exam next week is down the drain."

I had to laugh. Chris under pressure was quite something. I poked him in the ribs, immensely pleased, and remembered the first time we met. . . .

It was on 26 September 1937, less than three years before. A new crop of freshmen, bald as eggs as tradition required, reported for induction into the Student Corps at Leyden, Holland's oldest and most famous university, ten miles north of Wassenaar on the road to Amsterdam. I pushed the heavy door ajar and wished I hadn't. The noise was terrifying. Instinctively I backed away — too late. With triumphant shouts they dragged me down the dark hallway. It smelled of stale beer, jenever, wet rain-coats and sweat. At an entrance to the right I dug in, as a matter of principle, which cost me a sleeve and all the buttons of my shirt. A powerful brute picked me up from behind and shoved me into the air. For a moment I had a fine view of the scene at my feet, before crashing into it like a sack of potatoes.

I saw a large, rectangular room with high ceilings and graceful windows. Red plush curtains screened out the afternoon, chandeliers lit the spectacle. Between the bar at one end and a fireplace at the other, pandemonium reigned: a heaving, yelling, sweating sea of humanity in which bald heads bobbed about forlornly like little white buoys in a storm. I caught a glimpse of a sad-eyed character sitting in the sink with water streaming down his shiny pate, flapping his arms like a demented duck. Then I tumbled into the debris of overturned tables and chairs. It was the first day of Initiation, 1937, and I had landed on the floor of "Minerva", Leyden's hallowed students' club.

The first hour or so I had it easy, discussing Dutch colonial policy with an erudite senior, a perfectly pleasant conversation marred only by the fact that I was lying flat on my back on the floor with his foot planted firmly in my stomach. After he left me I was set upon by a gaggle of sophomores, who proceeded to make my life miserable. They slapped my scalp until it tingled, then cooled it off by pouring gallons of beer on it, meanwhile forcing me into a tenacious defence of my great-great-granduncle, a colonel in Napoleon's army, whom they accused of losing the battle of Waterloo. Finally I took advantage of a moment's confusion to scoot on all fours underneath a table, unseen, determined to hide until dinner. Sitting in the dirt and broken glass, legs all around me, beer trickling down my spine, I became aware of another bald presence in the gloom. "Krediet," he whispered, courteously introducing himself. "Chris Krediet."

"Any relation to Dr. Krediet, of Wassenaar?" Put two Netherlanders together for the first time, no matter what the circumstances, and they will doggedly mention names until they hit upon a common acquaintance. Holland being the size it is, sooner or later they always do.

"My father. You from Wassenaar?"

I nodded and introduced myself. Now we knew where we stood. We shook hands with a certain amount of formality, careful not to disturb our tormentors around the table above us. Then we settled down to explore each other's antecedents.

We were both born in the Netherlands East Indies, precursor of Indonesia, Chris on the island of Sumatra, I in Surabaya, Java. We had come "home" to Holland in time for school. With our blue eyes and fair complexions it would have been impossible to tell us from other Hollanders; Chris, especially, looked like an advertisement for Dutch cheese, apple-cheeks and all. Yet we immediately sensed the affinity of our common birthplace, peculiar to "Indies" Dutchmen who had spent their childhood in those enchanted islands. Chris was already twenty-one, a year older than I. Between school and Leyden he had gone off to Brazil, and he told me about a gigantic dam he had built, somewhere in the Minais Gerais, for a local "fazendero" who had entrusted him with all the engineering calculations. Undaunted by his rudimentary knowledge of mathematics Chris had supervised two hundred labourers for four months to complete the dam, which had vanished tracelessly after the first rain of the monsoon, closely followed by Chris himself. I recognised the syndrome: Chris was an Indies boy, like me, and every so often Holland became too small for us. Then we burst its seams to blow off steam abroad. But we always returned to our little frog-patch between Germany and the North Sea.

In the safety of our hiding-place, shielded from the noise and violence by a ring of grey-flannelled legs, we whispered earnestly as if we had known each other all our lives. "Let me tell you something," I started, wagging my finger for emphasis. At this moment the table above our heads keeled over. There was a resounding crash, glasses shattered, chairs toppled, seniors jumped about swearing and yelling at the culprit and there we were, suddenly revealed at the core of the commotion. I got out of there fast. But Chris Krediet couldn't be bothered. When I looked back from a safe distance he still sat cross-legged in the ruins, my new friend, straight and bald, motionless, like a strange idol of some unknown culture just uncovered.

*   *   *

The invasion of the Netherlands across our common border was entrusted to the German Sixth Army. It attacked in overwhelming force, especially in tanks and aircraft. Dutch units in the eastern part of the country fought desperately for time to prepare the "Fortress Holland", comprising the western provinces – except Zeeland – which contained the major cities of Amsterdam, Rotterdam, The Hague and Utrecht, as well as Leyden. On three sides it was bound by water: the North Sea, the Zuider Zee and to the south the big rivers Rhine, Waal and Meuse. All the principal bridges across these rivers were surprised at dawn by groups of Nazi specialists in Dutch uniforms. Only a few fell intact to the enemy, but these included the vital Meuse bridges of Rotterdam where German assault-troops landed by seaplane in the heart of the city. The fourth

16

side of "Fortress Holland" was secured by the main Netherlands defence system, the Water Line. Its inundations, in conjunction with the Grebbe Line across the Veluwe hills to the south, were stoutly held and proved an unexpectedly formidable barrier to the Wehrmacht.

Amongst the Dutch forces marching up to the Grebbe Line in the early morning of 10 May 1940, was my close friend and fellow Leydener, Alexander Rowerth. Tall, handsome, aristocratic, he looked totally out of place in the uniform of an ordinary private. He bore a striking resemblance to the American film star Robert Taylor, but even this handicap had failed to affect his popularity in Leyden. Alexander was a great guy, funny, alive, always up to something spectacular. We loved him. He was the Student with a capital S.

To my knowledge he was also the only Leydener who had volunteered for military service, on 3 September 1939, the day Germany attacked Poland and World War II broke out. I was still asleep the next morning when my landlady banged on the door. "Sir! Quick, come and look, that crazy Mr. Rowerth."

I dashed to the window and out, on to the little balcony above the cigar shop, in my pyjamas. A platoon of soldiers was marching by, and there at the very end was Alexander, towering above the rest. As soon as he saw me he shook his hands above his head, exuberantly, like a boxer. The sergeant in charge barked at him, but Alexander – who was studying Law, like myself – pointed at me and promptly began to argue his case. After a while the sergeant, clearly discouraged, shrugged his shoulders. Now they were right below me.

"What the hell!" I shouted; Alexander beamed up at me. "Come and tell us about it. When can you come?"

"This afternoon," he called back, ignoring the sergeant who glared at him. "After lunch!" And off he went, one, two, one, two, occasionally turning round to wave.

At noon I had the gang together in my room, Chris Krediet, Paul Renardel, Jacques Maasland and I. Only Alexander was missing, but he was on his way, strolling leisurely down the Rapenburg which curved stiff and silent on both sides of the canal, once the city moat; I could see him coming towards us from my window on the corner of the Kloksteeg. It was a still, grey day. Somewhere a caril-

lon chimed the hour to its conclusion, an introverted little tune
which sank absentmindedly into the streets and squares of the old
university town. Behind us we could hear the barges chugging down
the Zwarte Water, past the town hall and the weighing station,
their decks well above the streets on either side. Alexander had
stopped to chat with someone, but when a cyclist approached he
cut the conversation short and crossed the nearest bridge, nonchal-
antly but not without haste. I recognised the man on the bike: our
tailor, known to carry bills on his person. From across the water
Alexander waved at him in jovial greeting. Now he strolled past
the university building, a sombre hulk opposite my room. One
more little bridge and we heard him stomping up the stairs.
"Christ!" he said, standing dramatically in the doorway in his
uniform. "To think that I may have to go to war with this bunch
of nitwits."

We ignored him. I grabbed my cane, which as a Junior I was
finally entitled to carry, and tapped on the floor — a series of taps to
attract the landlady's attention, then one tap for each cup of coffee.
Alexander flopped down on the couch and put his feet on the table.
Paul Renardel picked up my *Laws of the Netherlands* and threw it
against the pot-bellied stove to shake up the coals. The stove
sputtered. The landlady came in and put the tray on the table,
next to Alexander's feet; the room sagged so badly that the coffee
nearly slopped out of the cups. Alexander pinched her bottom; she
whacked his hand and slammed the door coyly. "Well," Chris said
at last. "What's this all about?"

"There comes a time," Alexander declared, "when we must be
ready to lay down our lives for our country."

"Cut that crap," Chris replied, pointedly. I chuckled. I knew that
he was heavily engaged in the noble art of draft-dodging, anything
legal considered. I myself had nothing to worry about, my eyes were
bad. I had been drafted and subsequently rejected for all military
service.

We argued endlessly in our usual, desultory manner which ultimately reduced every subject to a joke. The sounds outside reflected
the passing of the day; students on their way to class, their steps
echoing sharply in the narrow Kloksteeg, then flattening out on the
Rapenburg and up the hump-backed bridge. Now and then we
recognised someone by a single word, a laugh. Canes rapped the

cobblestones, followed by periods of quiet when our more dedicated colleagues had disappeared into the building across the canal, "Leyden", the medieval presence which since 1574 had looked down on our forefathers, our fathers, ourselves. In no time at all the day was done. We said good night, nothing solved.

I stepped out on the little balcony, four feet square and perched almost above the bridge. Leyden slumbered against the sky. The wet night air smelt of coal-stoves and canals. Somewhere a barge puff-puff-puffed down the Old Rhine. Behind me the Pieters Church, chiming the hour, dropped its notes into the alleys at its feet, gently, for the houses were old and leaned to each other for support. The voices of my friends faded away along the Rapenburg, until gradually I could only hear the tapping of their canes across the water. Then silence.

Alexander Rowerth was a patriotic fool. But he had nothing to worry about. War was inconceivable —

That was only eight months ago. Now he marched in full battle-order up to the Grebbe Line, through a spring morning of unbeliev-able beauty. When the regiment got to Utrecht, his home town, he sneaked away during a short rest and found a telephone in a near-by café. His mother was German born, and he just wanted to make sure that she'd be all right. He dialled his home.

"Police Inspector Dunger speaking."

Alexander thought he had got a wrong number. He pressed the coin-release button and put the coin back in the slot. This time he dialled very carefully.

"Police Inspector Dunger speaking."

"Where are Mr. and Mrs. Rowerth? What's wrong?"

"Nothing wrong. Quislings. We're holding them at the station. Who's calling?" Alexander hung up.

He left the café by the back door and walked to the police station. He stuck his rifle in a corner. His parents were sitting on wooden benches along the wall, together with a score of other suspects. A soldier stood guard over them, bayonet fixed. They were badly frightened, pale and tearful, and told him how they had been roused from their beds in the middle of the night and given ten minutes to dress. "Mark my words," his father whispered. "Nobody can stop Germany. And when it's over, someone is going to pay for this."

They sat together for a while, silently, Alexander holding his mother's hand. Then he got up, kissed them and walked out. He didn't take his rifle.

*   *   *

Initially the situation around The Hague looked serious. General Student's parachute division continued to land in the surrounding countryside and advanced on the city from several collection zones, mounting separate attacks on the near-by airfields of Valkenburg, Ypenburg and Ockenburg, as well as striking south to occupy Rotterdam's airbase of Waalhaven. Small groups of paratroopers, detached from the main body by design or accident, created great confusion by their real or imagined presence behind the lines, and this was compounded by the persistent rumours of German soldiers disguised in anything from Dutch uniforms to nuns' habits. The Netherlands forces, including some hurriedly recalled from the Grebbe Line, gave a good account of themselves once in contact with the enemy, but the tension and uncertainty in non-combat areas perplexed many of the green troops. Their nervous suspicion of friend or foe added to the state of near-chaos in the city itself, where limited bombings by the Luftwaffe had destroyed several barracks as well as sundry unrelated buildings including a hospital, causing casualties for whom no provisions existed. Thousands of civilians milled aimlessly about and blocked military movement, leading to immense traffic jams which also entangled the Royal Family during their transfer from exposed Huis ten Bosch to the relative safety of Noordeinde Palace, in the heart of the town. The Queen, unimpressed by reports of skirmishes in many streets, was in a towering rage because these prevented her from visiting wounded soldiers, who now began to fill the hospitals and schools in increasing numbers. Her mood was not improved by her inability to contact the cabinet ministers, hardly the most militant sector of the Netherlands nation at that time, who were deeply ensconced in various bomb shelters. Only towards the close of the first day, with all airfields except Waalhaven recaptured, the paratroopers contained everywhere and the surprise attack on The Hague a failure, did a semblance of order return to Holland's seat of government.

When Chris and I arrived at the army recruiting post the place was packed. We had to stand in line for three hours to join up.

"You'll hear from us soon," the corporal behind the desk said, when we finally got to him.

"What's soon?"

"A week. Ten days." That seemed reasonably soon. A radio blaring through the building had just interrupted various instructions to announce a Dutch counter-attack somewhere in Brabant, and furthermore the British would surely be arriving at any moment now. Then we'd show those bloody *Moffen*!*

Seeing that we were in The Hague anyway, we decided to drop in on Jacques Maasland. His father was a judge and they lived in a big house on the edge of town. We pushed and honked our way through the crowds and ran up the stairs. Clearly, we had interrupted something. Jacques stood at the window, his parents sat around stiffly. Mrs. Maasland glared at us when we told of joining up.

"As long as he does the correct thing," the judge said to his wife.

Silence. What was going on? Jacques stared outside, where a white pattern of flak suddenly exploded against the bright blue sky. As always he looked immaculate. "Do you think it would be incorrect if I . . . sort of sit tight for a couple of days until there's more to go on?" – His father didn't answer.

"I think that I'll sit tight for a few days, until there's more to go on." Without looking our way Jacques went to a desk, took out some books and stalked from the room. War or no war, life went on. You had to set your sails to the wind. Holland had been invaded, but there was obviously little he could do about this unfortunate turn of events; he might as well go back to work. Without a word to anyone we got the hell out.

We rode back to Wassenaar. Half-way along the Schouwweg shots suddenly rang out, right next to us, and more further down the road; we almost fell off the bike. Chris braked as hard as he could and we jumped behind a tree, dropping the BMW where it landed. In the garden across the street automatic rifles blasted away, or perhaps machine-guns. Shaking with fright, we pressed together as tightly as possible, holding on to each other, peeking around the tree-trunk only to make sure it covered us. The firing was coming from dense bushes of oak and evergreens on either side of a long, sloping lawn. We saw no one. Then, from a little grass-covered mound in a corner

* *Mof* (plural: *Moffen*) was a derogatory term for a German used widely by Hollanders during World War II.

21

of the garden, a hand came out and waved a white handkerchief. Gradually the shooting died down. When all was quiet a very old lady climbed out of the bomb-shelter, ever so slowly, followed by a maid in uniform. The girl kept glancing around but the old lady looked neither left nor right as they tottered across the lawn to the house in the background. Undoubtedly she was summoned by some urgent physical necessity which she refused to perform elsewhere. They disappeared into the house and the shooting resumed.

I backed away from the tree, keeping it between me and the garden as long as possible, then turned and ran. I could trust Chris to get out of there by his own devices. I kept running long after I had turned a corner. When I reached Park de Kieviet I was stopped by a Dutch lieutenant, who stood arguing with a milkman. "You can't go any further," he said. "Park de Kieviet is in German hands."

"Come on, captain," the milkman protested. "I'm only a milkman. I've got to make my rounds. I want no part of all this business." The lieutenant shrugged his shoulders.

We entered Park de Kieviet, the milkman and I. A few hundred yards from my home six German paratroopers stepped out of the rhododendrons. With a shock I saw that they were boys, like Chris and Paul and me. They bought four bottles of milk, paying the exact amount with Dutch money. "*Auf Wiedersehen,*" they mumbled politely, as they faded back into the bushes.

I climbed the highest dune behind our house. To the west stretched the North Sea, steel-blue, silver-scaled, rimmed by a ribbon of surf. The beach shimmered in the sun, all the way from Scheveningen in the south, past Katwijk, to the knotty point of Noordwijk in the north. Behind the dunes lay Holland, a strip of pastel colours dwarfed by sky, green polders, here and there the glint of water, little steeples and the arms of windmills pencilled on the haze, reds and yellows where the tulips bloomed.

Then I went home.

II

"OTHERS GO TO BATTLE," THE ROMAN HISTORIAN TACITUS WROTE, "these go to war." He was referring to the Batavians, who lived in a small triangle of land at the mouths of Europe's great rivers. Their descendants, the Hollanders, defeated Spain in eighty years of bloodshed to become a nation, known as the Netherlands. As a leading power in the Western world they fought nine major wars between 1650 and 1800. Overseas meanwhile they engaged in trade and piracy establishing themselves by force in America, Brazil, the Caribbean, South Africa, Ceylon, Malacca and what came to be known as the Dutch East Indies, a 4,000 mile chain of giant islands stretching from Burma to Australia. Due to their small numbers — about $2\frac{1}{2}$ million at the start of the nineteenth century — their power gradually waned, but when finally forced to relinquish their pugnacious role, having lost many of their far-flung strongholds, the Dutch still maintained possession of the richest prize, the East Indies, a colonial treasure-chest second only to the British Empire. An unprecedented era of peace followed, during which they applied their restless energies to the development of commercial and industrial enterprises, with so much success that at the outbreak of World War II Holland was rich and fat, and enjoyed the highest standard of living in Europe. She had a superiority complex to match. All of us, although usually too well-mannered to admit it to foreigners, in our hearts considered the Netherlanders superior in almost all respects to every other nation in the world. This delusion did not exclude the military sphere in which, as the progeny of corsairs and conquerors, we believed ourselves to be anybody's equal. To Queen Wilhelmina fell the traumatic necessity of puncturing the balloon. On the morning of 14 May, the fifth day of hostilities, it was announced on the radio that she had left our country and arrived in England. "Why, the bitch!" I exploded, not unlike most Hollanders who heard the news. "The yellow bloody bitch!"

Up to that moment I thought the war was going pretty well. General Student's parachute division had been effectively dealt with, its tough young soldiers mostly killed or captured, restoring an air of normality to The Hague and surroundings. We knew little about the situation in the rest of the country, but newspapers and radio, by the tone of their reporting, contributed to the hopeful mood which held no inkling of impending disaster. Occasionally a headline might puzzle us, such as 'Fighting in Rotterdam Continues'. Rotterdam? Inside the Fortress Holland? But then the story itself would concentrate on the skill and prowess of our marines – obviously things were well in hand. True, we had learned by the grapevine that Crown Princess Juliana with her two little daughters, the Princesses Beatrix and Irene, had been taken to safety by her husband, Prince Bernhard; that made sense. But the Queen?

I had to talk with Chris about it. While we waited for our call-up from the army we busied ourselves as dispatch-riders for the local Civil Defence, and he was off on an errand. After lunch I got on my motor-bike and set out to find him. The road to Leyden, cut off for several days by paratroopers, had been re-opened. I rode by all the likely places, eventually ending up in Minerva, but failed to locate him. After a beer or two I decided to return home for dinner. The weather continued to be unbelievably beautiful. Purring along placidly on the road to Wassenaar, amid sunshine and bird-song and cows in the meadows, I noticed a curious cloud. It towered to a great height in the otherwise flawless sky, churning russet at its base, then bulging upwards in rose-coloured convolutions to a snow-white crest well above 30,000 feet – a giant strawberry sundae. I slowed down to look and estimate its position: south, about twenty miles away. Rotterdam.

Just then my attention was diverted by a column of Royal Netherlands Grenadiers which emerged from the tram depot at Deyleroord, wheeled into the road ahead and moved towards me.

Something about it held me spell-bound. The column came down the middle of the highway, forcing whatever little traffic there was on to the verges and bicycle-paths. Suddenly I knew what struck me: never had I seen soldiers march like this, so rigidly, so stiff with pride. They all stood ten feet tall, legs moving with brutal precision, arms chopping harshly, chests out to bursting, shoulders flung back, heads high as if they were looking straight at God. Only when I had come quite close did I see that tears were streaming down their faces. I raced home and burst into the kitchen.

"What happened?"

It was all over. From the beginning Rotterdam, at the confluence of the big rivers, had emerged as the key to the military situation. Its bridges had fallen intact to the treacherous pre-dawn assault on 10 May and though its airfield, Waalhaven, held against repeated Dutch counter-attacks, enemy reinforcements continued to flow into the battle. Meanwhile General Von Kuechler's Eighteenth Army ground its way from the south-east into the southern part of the city, until only the Meuse bridges prevented it from breaking out into the Fortress Holland. But though efforts to recapture or destroy the bridges had failed, Dutch troops put up a fierce and effective resistance at their northern end, containing the enemy in a narrow and precarious bridgehead. Time was of the essence to Von Kuechler, already behind schedule in relation to General Von Rundstedt's giant offensive against France and the British Expeditionary Force. Rather than slug it out, the German High Command decided to forget about "correct behaviour" and "good manners", and at 13:20 hours on 14 May presented its Dutch counterpart with an ultimatum to cease all resistance within three hours or see Rotterdam subjected to unlimited attack from the air. Long before the ultimatum expired the first Heinkels and Junkers appeared over the city. Subsequently the Luftwaffe, unopposed since the small Netherlands Air Force had fought itself to extinction in the first two days of war, obliterated the heart of Rotterdam in twenty minutes of leisurely low-level area-bombing. Confronted with indications that a similar fate awaited Utrecht, then Amsterdam and other cities, the Dutch commander-in-chief, rather than prolong the hopeless struggle for at best a few days, had signed the capitulation of Holland's armed forces that same afternoon.

"You'd better destroy your wines," my uncle from Brussels said.

25

We were all sitting in the kitchen around the radio. "In Belgium, in 1914. . . ." He pulled a lugubrious face.

My father and I went to the wine-cellar and systematically emptied every bottle down the drain; at least it gave us the illusion that we were doing something to protect our loved ones from the Hun hordes. We felt very badly about it, however, and from most of the better vintages we took a melancholy swig or two. After a while we were both completely sloshed. I staggered out into the garden and threw up all over the primulae. Then I stood against a tree and thought. A breeze stirred the warm smells of evening, and in the lilac-bush near the gate sang a nightingale.

Surrender.

Suddenly I began to cry. I sobbed deeply for a long time, not quite understanding why, but somehow in concert with the singing bird, the smell of flowers, the trees, the Dutch earth on which I stood and the night around me. Twenty-three years I had been myself, nothing more. Now all at once I knew myself to be a part, infinitely small, of something boundless which poured its grief from many eyes besides mine. The moment was like death, the end of what had gone before. Inexorably birth would follow, a new beginning of whatever lay ahead, but as yet I could not bring myself to cross the dubious threshold. I clung to time without substance, my mind rejecting all thoughts of where I was going, and groping back to where I had been. . . .

Childhood. Suddenly I'm in the Indies once again, growing up amongst people who reject Western concepts of reality. Fishing in Lake Sarangan, high up in Central Java, apologizing to the fish as the little red float goes down, down, down. Banging on a hollowed tree-trunk to bring back the moon during an eclipse, taking turns with the natives around the fire. When I'm sick Babu blows on my belly to drive out the evil spirit. Lying awake at night I tensely listen to the gekkos for portents of things to come . . . Then "home" to Holland. I take with me a smooth stone for luck. "A big boy like you will barely fit into this little country," my father laughs as the ship nears Rotterdam. I try to become as small as I can, but it makes me splutter and cough. . . . In Holland, people believe that things are what they seem. A bicycle is a bicycle and a cheese is a cheese—could that be all there is to reality? It's very confusing to me. One day we are to see the Queen in her Golden

Carriage. I perch halfway up a lamp-post for a better view. Here she comes! She is small and round and she bounces back and forth against the back-rest like a toy, back, forth, bowing to the crowds, back, forth, back, forth – now surely she can't be real? . . .

The memory brought me back to the present and I stopped crying as abruptly as I had started. Somewhere in my mental meanderings I must have crossed the threshold, for better or for worse. I was quite sober and, everything considered, felt pretty good. So we had capitulated and were now occupied by Nazi Germany. I looked about me with interest. The world seemed clear and taut, starker than before, less complicated. The horizon, always vague and distant, had been laced in and curved close around. Within it, reality was flat and sharp as a photograph, without depth. No mysteries here, no doubts, no questions without answers, no shades of grey to temper black and white, no confusion. The reality was war, the enemy Germany, Holland my country and every Hollander my brother.

I searched for a stone, the nightingale in the lilac began to bore me. Finally I picked up a handful of dirt and threw it at him with all my might. It zipped through the leaves like shrapnel. The song broke off on a tremulous note, leaving a hole in the night. I chuckled in the dark. Life was really very simple.

III

THE GERMAN OCCUPATION KILLED MORE PEOPLE IN HOLLAND THAN in any other country of Western Europe. One reason stood out: there was nowhere else for the people to go. Squeezed between Germany and the sea Holland lay furthest from the neutral sanctuaries of World War II – Sweden, Switzerland, Spain and Portugal. The way to England and freedom was blocked by more than a hundred miles of statistically the most deadly body of water in the world, the North Sea. Some of its more famous storms wrecked the Armada and on occasion all but sank the Netherlands itself, and even now dozens of ships perish every year in its unpredictable gales which come roaring down the funnel from the Atlantic and Arctic Oceans.

Within this isolation no area was less suited for a resistance movement. Small, flat, highly cultivated, densely populated, it offered no natural hiding-places. No room here for any of the familiar features of the "Underground" – the band of armed desperadoes, the hidden cave, the safe redoubt in swamp or mountain, the camp-fire meeting. Holland's secret struggle took place in a café full of people, a quiet board-room, a busy shipyard, a cellar, a dark city street, and always under the only cover available: everyday life.

As a result the outward appearance of the Netherlands – until the battle of Arnhem in September 1944 and the subsequent "Hunger winter" – was one of normality. Every member of the Underground led a double life; the more normal it seemed, the safer his secret.

The Nazis reinforced this situation by their mulish efforts to win the Dutch for their Greater Germanic ideas, dismissing the five-day war and the bombing of Rotterdam as regrettable incidents between friends. On the other hand, anyone who by words or deeds defied this obscene dream they destroyed without mercy. As the mere sight of a German uniform sufficed to infuriate the average Hollander, it was only a matter of months before the jails filled up and executions began to take place.

Consequently, except for the Jews, the choice of existence in Holland during most of the Occupation lay between extremes. One could either live in comparative safety and comfort by complying with the authorities, or in mortal danger by defying them. As a member of the Resistance you enjoyed life quite normally, in your home, with your friends, in your job, on the beach, at football-games and cinemas and parties, until you were beaten, kicked or shot to death. And once in trouble, you were on your own. The coast stretched straight and bare as a speedway – no hidden coves for sneak approaches by Allied submarines, as in Norway. The land lay open and crowded – no improvised airstrips marked with flash-lights for fast pick-ups by R.A.F. planes, as in France. The only two-way contact with the free world existed via secret wireless-transmitters, possessed on pain of certain death. Once the German armies had crushed the Netherlands and wheeled south into Belgium and France, Holland was a trap. By the time we regained our senses, we were caught in it.

Each of us had weathered in his own way the stunning blow of the capitulation. Chris' reaction had been to move to a new room, so small that to let down his hide-away bed he first had to put his chair and table out in the hall. If anything, it served to shut out as much of the world as possible. He didn't tell us his new address, not even me. I tracked him down, however, and found him moping around in a scarlet robe, thumbing through Kant, Kierkegaard and *Yachting Magazine*. He stared for a long time at a picture of a yacht in some Caribbean bay. When I asked for coffee he snarled. He hadn't shaved since the surrender.

Paul spent most of his time drinking beer in Minerva, as if he were afraid to go home and be alone.

Jacques had probably buried himself in his law books, I didn't go looking for him. Alexander Rowerth was a different matter. He had called me from Utrecht right after the capitulation and told me in great detail how he had discovered his parents being held at the police station as potential collaborators with the enemy, where they had subsequently been locked up until liberated by the Germans. He himself had quit the war cold, on the spot, and simply gone home. Then he said: "Can't you come down and stay with us for a day or two?"

There followed a long, embarrassed silence. Of course I considered Alexander one of my very best friends, but Christ! I wasn't going to stay in the same house as a couple of collaborators, real or suspected. I'd rather push them into a deep, dark canal. He really should know better than to invite me to his home under these circumstances. "No, I can't possibly get away right now," I finally lied. "Why don't you come to Wassenaar instead?"

He had laughed and hung up on me, without a word. It was a strange reaction. Stranger still, Chris went through exactly the same experience with him. "Alexander is a hell of a nice chap," I said, when we discussed the matter. "He can't help it that his parents are lousy quislings. Rough on him. But good God, surely he can't expect from us . . .?" We decided to forget Alexander for a while.

I myself had wandered through the dunes at Wassenaar for weeks, returning home only to sleep, obsessed by the notion that I had made an ass of myself over the capitulation. So we lost the war, so the Germans now occupied us, so what? I had survived, hadn't I, what else could be so important? Let's forget that we only lasted five days, let's forget everything. I couldn't face the truth: I was ashamed of my country. Five days . . .!

But Belgium fell, and loud-mouthed France, with its genius and *élan* and marvellous Maginot Line, in a matter of weeks. Well now, how about that? Next Great Britain, proud and powerful, had to scurry off the Continent at Dunkerque in a most undignified manner. Tough, but then, our own battle at the Grebbe Line had not been so pleasant either. I began to feel much better.

Then there was the Queen. She had been proved right in leaving the country in the nick of time, and we were all ashamed of our violent reaction to the news. We should have known better. Even before the advent of Hitler she had distrusted the Germans intensely and ever since 1934, the year in which the Austrian chancellor Dollfuss was murdered by the Nazis, she had felt the war coming, even predicting that in Holland it would open with a massive parachute attack.

Simultaneously she realised that in the event of an invasion her position in north-western Holland would quickly become untenable. She flatly refused to consider the possibility of any compromise with National Socialism or "that bandit" Adolf Hitler personally, and if she could not stay out of his clutches she preferred death. In February 1940, three months before the German attack, she discussed with her Foreign Minister, Eelco van Kleffens, the possibility of falling back on the province of Zeeland, south of the river Scheldt – "if necessary over the ice", she added. "I still have a white fur coat somewhere." She also made early arrangements for the departure of her daughter, Princess Juliana, and her grand-daughters, thereby safeguarding the legitimate succession within the House of Orange. She was, in fact, one of the few realists in the Netherlands.

When disaster came, however, she was appalled by its swiftness. As a schoolgirl she had begun "to dream of mighty deeds", by no means excluding military ones, and when on the third day of the war the Grebbe Line began to crumble she was restrained with difficulty from going there "to die as the last man in the last trench", as she put it in the words of her ancestor William the Third, Prince of Orange. In the night of 12 May she called King George of England out of his bed to stress the urgency of the help the British had promised, but could not possibly supply. When on the next day the Netherlands commander-in-chief informed her that she had to leave the country or risk falling into Nazi hands, Queen Wilhelmina – almost sixty years old – burst into tears. But she never hesitated. She ordered the British destroyer which came to fetch her to take her to Breskens in the Dutch province of Zeeland. Only when this proved impossible and the German trap closed rapidly on all sides did she consent to cross to England. She arrived despondent, but the very next day she breathed fire over the B.B.C., and some of the names she called Hitler and his henchmen made me blink when I remembered the little, round figure bouncing benignly back and forth in a golden coach, not so long ago.

Clearly she had just begun to fight. Well then, so had we. Holland had lost a battle, like Britain. The army had capitulated, but the Queen and the legitimate government of the Netherlands were free, and in contrast with most of the occupied nations of Europe the

Dutch had no need for compromise. That Germany would lose the war I never doubted for a single second. My only worry was that she would lose too soon, and thereby deprive us of the chance to add some laurels to our country's battered image. But how was this to be done?

I had just resurfaced from the dunes when an incredible rumour swept Minerva: three Leydeners had cracked the passage to England in a dinghy! It was hard to believe. To outwit the Germans and actually set sail seemed improbable enough, but crossing the murderous North Sea in a little twelve-foot open hull? We went wild; it was just like the day when two fighters flew along the beach at Scheveningen, their R.A.F. markings clearly visible. Within minutes the town stood on its ear. The Occupation had descended on us with such crushing finality that in these few weeks England, like Freedom, had become a mere concept. To believe in it as a reality, a chunk of land where free people rode the Nazi tide in freedom, required an occasional sign, a concrete manifestation which was regarded in much the same way as a sign from God: England exists! Now three Leydeners, who only last week moved amongst us here in Minerva, were part of that hallowed scene? I had to get at the facts. I buttonholed Erik Michielsen, a Senior whose brother Karel was rumoured to be amongst the escapees. He pretended to know nothing, but winked. Even in Minerva you had to be careful these days. We made a date for the following midnight, in my safe little room in Wassenaar.

As all private means of transportation, including my motor-bike, had been impounded by the German Army – at remarkably fair prices, cash on the nail – I had to take the bus to Wassenaar, and for the second time that week I lost my way between the bus stop and our home, a distance of under three hundred yards. The black-out was complete, the darkness all but tangible. Where had the street gone? I looked up – sometimes you could tell by the trees outlined against the sky. I might have had my eyes closed. I stumbled about, suffocating. Then I heard footsteps, strong and sure, and a little blue light approached, disembodied, reflecting in the wet road. Voices spoke German. Suddenly the darkness seemed friendly. I froze, and three soldiers passed me less than six feet away. I felt superior, an unseen threat, at one with the Dutch night around these hostile voices. I followed the blue glimmer, stealthily, until I got home. I stepped into my room; the memory of the enemy outside made it seem like a fragment of the life which five days of war had shattered, inviolate, permanent, embalmed in night against the rot of the times. And there, smoking one of my precious cigars, feet up on my table, small, dark and obviously Indies, sat Erik Michielsen. "Make yourself at home," he grinned, with an expansive wave to my own chair.

The rumour proved true. In a dinghy called the *Bèbèk* – Indonesian for "duck" – Karel Michielsen and his friends had crossed the North Sea and shattered Holland's isolation. Erik, in on the plan, had watched the entire escape from the terrace of the Huis ter Duin hotel, overlooking the beach at Noordwijk, twelve miles north of The Hague and Scheveningen. The *Bèbèk* lay right below him on the sand half-way to the waterline, a speck against the vast sea. Visitors admiring the sunset jammed the board-walk, but the beach itself was almost deserted. Erik saw his brother and the other two Leydeners shuttle back and forth between the hotel and the dinghy with suitcases, crates of provisions, cans of water, all the trappings for a journey, as if no Occupation existed. "Boy, oh boy!" he laughed, dropping his cigar from excitement. "There I sat, drinking a double brandy, watching history being made. So did a bunch of German officers at a table next to me, guzzling jenever peacefully."

"But Christ, man, how is it possible?" I interrupted, full of admiration. "Don't you get shot for that sort of thing? How about those officers?"

"Oh hell, you know the Moffen," Erik answered, almost knocking over his glass. "You've got to bluff them! Anything crazy enough will bluff them." He suddenly cut loose in French. *"De l'audace! Toujours de l'audace!"*

"Oui, oui," I responded hastily, not to be outdone and afraid he would wake up my parents. *De l'audace*: audacity, derring-do, the unexpectedly bold – it sounded great, especially in French. But you still had to have it.

The party had begun in earnest when the three Leydeners rolled up their pants, picked up the *Bèbèk* and waded out into the surf. Dusk was falling, there could be no mistaking their intentions. In no time a crowd collected near the spot where they had put to sea. Karel, a former stroke of the Junior eights, manned the oars and heaved against the surf. The weather was calm and they got through without mishap, but suddenly the police appeared, waving and yelling authoritatively. The German officers jumped up from their jenevers and shouted across the beach: *"Zurück! Zurück!"*

"It just didn't look serious, the whole thing," Erik said. "Sort of unreal and ludicrous, even when the soldiers came and started shooting. You could see the white streaks in the water where the bullets hit, all around the dinghy, and suddenly I said to myself: 'Christ, my brother is getting killed.'"

"Well, what happened? What happened?"

"Nothing happened." Erik began to laugh; he could hardly continue. "Man, Karel never did too well in the Varsity, but now I know why: lack of motivation. That bloody boat fairly flew away."

They must have presented a difficult target in the failing light, for nobody appeared to get hit. Then they hoisted a little sail, stained blue-grey. It got smaller and smaller and finally disappeared in the dusk, due west to England. According to a guarded report from Radio Free Netherlands in London, they made it in three days and four nights. Miraculously, the weather held.

I walked Erik to the front door. The night outside was solid darkness, but it smelt of earth and rain and a million living things. "I reckon you're going after them pretty soon, aren't you?" I ventured. Here we were talking about escaping to England as an actual reality – what a tremendous thing had happened! In our minds the Nazi prison had cracked.

"I have my finals coming up," Erik answered. He studied Law. I understood him perfectly. War or no war, the idea of going through life without a degree did not appeal to any of us. "I only have a couple more weeks to go."

"And then?"

"It's getting late," he said smoothly, looking at his watch. Curfew, from midnight to four a.m., was over. "I'd better get home."

I peered at him suspiciously in the faint, blue glow of the hall-light – a slight, round-shouldered figure, hands deep in his pockets, hat on his ears, clever eyes positively twinkling with mischief and mystery. Two steps, and the night had swallowed him.

*　　*　　*

Shortly after the successful crossing of the *Bèbèk* the first moustaches and dark glasses appeared along the Rapenburg. Minerva began to hum with rumours about secret transmitters in various attics,

34

British torpedo-boats off the Scheveningen Beach Club and R.A.F. planes touching down at night in the meadows behind the soccer field. Leydeners were seen to enter unfamiliar cafés in dubious company and sometimes you ran into an old acquaintance who, winking desperately, got introduced to you by a brand-new name. A few *cognoscenti* maintained contact with "chappies", vague characters cloaked in secrecy, who had always "just talked to London", could get you to England for money and mostly turned you over to the Gestapo for a pittance. Leyden, grappling with reality, began the Occupation in a wave of restless romanticism.

The question of the hour was: to go or not to go. The *Bébèk* had not only awoken us to the material existence of England and the feasibility of reaching it, she unfortunately had also made it look easy. Throughout the early years of the Occupation, before the establishment of overland escape-routes, Hollanders in boats set out to follow in her legendary wake; less than a dozen made it. Some the Germans caught. Most of those who reached the open sea were never heard of again.

In spite of all the excitement the vast majority of Leydeners decided not to go. Considering the odds against arriving, it was a reasonable decision. Furthermore, the B.B.C. itself admitted the terrible slaughter which the Luftwaffe was inflicting night after night on the British, and warned of an imminent invasion. Winston Churchill sounded even less reassuring. "We shall fight on the beaches . . . we shall fight in the streets . . ." – obviously even if you got there, all England had to offer was danger and a lonely death. In Holland the spectre of death had passed, the fighting was over. You lived with your family and friends, your girl, in your home and amongst your people. Later, when the terror and counter-terror of Occupation and Resistance convulsed the Netherlands, Britain looked like a haven. But from 1940 through 1942 the opposite was true – he who would cross over must sacrifice all he loved, including probably his life, for this one privilege: to fight the Nazis in freedom. Only a handful considered this privilege worth the sacrifice. I decided to go.

Chris Krediet and Paul Renardel wanted to come with me, but both felt that first they had to finish their studies. As a result we drifted apart and soon lived in different spheres, not disconnected, but each unreal when seen from the other. My world was peopled

35

by those who, like me, had taken the plunge into defiance. Some were unknown to me and therefore automatically suspect, others old friends whom I discovered with delight. A long-awaited meeting with a man called "Bruno" produced my oldest friend from school, Jean Mesritz, a Jewish fellow-Leydener of great charm and brilliance. "The Hussar" turned out to be another old class-mate, Carel Kranenburg, now a lanky cavalry officer. From behind the name "Count B" popped Van Brero, whose ambition was to challenge Hitler to a duel "and settle this war like gentlemen". "Erik" was simply Erik Michielsen.

In the secrecy and confusion of plans, contacts and conveyances, nobody ever knew for any length of time where he stood. Alliances were formed, dissolved, changed and re-formed; one day you were "in", the next "out". Although Erik and I considered ourselves unattached, we spent much time together, mostly in his room under the Pieter's Church where three centuries before some of the Pilgrim Fathers had lived, prior to crossing the Atlantic. Here we studied all the possible roads to England. South, through France, Spain and Portugal? East and north, via Germany, Denmark and Sweden? To Petsamo through Finland? Up the Rhine to Switzerland? The Germans were everywhere, and each time we pulled out the map our eyes fell on that tantalizing little stretch, a mere hundred miles due west, the direct route. Across the impossible North Sea. . . . But remember the *Bèbèk*? We decided on the direct route.

"What are you going to do when we get there?" Erik asked. He himself was a reserve lieutenant in the artillery, he had his job cut out for him. But he knew that I had been classified 4F, and couldn't even drive a car without glasses.

"Pilot," I answered. "Royal Air Force, of course."

Erik laughed. He didn't think I was serious.

IV

NEVER HAVING ESCAPED FROM AN ENEMY OCCUPATION, I FRANKLY
didn't know where to begin except at the very beginning. My goal
was England; between Holland and England lay the North Sea; a
sea is crossed by boat. Where could I find a boat? Scheveningen, the
seaside resort and fishing village adjacent to The Hague. I put on an
old sweater, and after spending a week in the harbour-area talking
to fishermen, herring-peddlers, German soldiers, police officers and
loafers, I knew a number of useful facts.

The trawlers put to sea each morning under orders to be back in
harbour before dark. Their registration numbers were taken down
on departure and checked on return. They carried their own crew,
no Germans. They were restricted to a three-mile zone along the
coast, which was patrolled from Zandvoort in the north to Hook of
Holland in the south by a converted tug-boat, manned by Wehrmacht personnel and armed with machine-guns and anti-aircraft
cannon. At night it lay moored amongst the fishermen and served
as operations base for the harbour guards.

On the basis of this intelligence I conceived a plan. I would hide
aboard a trawler one night in the harbour of Scheveningen, preferably with a companion. We would bring with us an outboard
engine, petrol, provisions and pistols. The next day we would
suddenly pop up on deck, close to sundown and ideally on the edge
of the fishing zone. With drawn pistols we would force the captain
to put us out in the lifeboat, and then cross to England. The scheme

would be much strengthened if one of the crew could be in on it, to help us hide and signal us when to come out. Without this, we just had to trust our luck here and there. I went down to the quayside to pick a ship.

I had an immediate surprise. To my dismay I discovered that the lifeboats had been removed from the trawlers. I could guess the reason: shortly after the escape of the *Bèbèk* all small craft had been ordered out of the coastal areas. That this would affect even fishermen I had not foreseen. Just as I turned to go home, thoroughly disgusted, I noticed a ship in the back row, the *SCH.107*. There, on its aft deck, lay a lifeboat. Its being the only one so equipped greatly simplified my choice.

"They hit a break-water last week," the herring-man at the auction hall told me, helpfully. The proud inhabitants of Holland's fishing towns had little time for the Moffen. "It's fixed up sort of temporary, that's why they have permission to carry a boat."

"Who's the skipper?"

"Fellow by name of Van der Zwan."

"Is he O.K.?"

"Like so!" He made a smelly thumbs-up sign right under my nose.

Half an hour later I was sitting in Van der Zwan's living-room. Being considered 'like so!', perhaps he would consent to give us a hand from the inside. If we pulled our guns on him, he could protest his helpless innocence should any questions arise. The rest was play-acting. A gamble, but it could make my plan foolproof.

Van der Zwan's home turned out to be one of the little green houses at the foot of the sea-wall, behind the South Boulevard. I knocked on his door in darkness, unannounced, but he let me in without questions. With traditional hospitality we first sat down around the table in the centre of the room, where his wife served us coffee. The place felt snug and cosy and I complimented them. Only then did he ask me the reason for my visit. I gave it to him straight, in detail, without frills except for a false name and the vague intimation that Her Majesty the Queen would be pleased to see me arrive in London. I also offered double its value for the lifeboat.

"Come with two, three people. All point your guns at me, but please don't shoot by mistake. Then there's not much I could do, is

38

there?" The fisherman opened his eyes wide, looking innocent like a crusty old baby. At first he wouldn't hear of getting paid for the boat, but his wife thought double the value would be just fine. We settled some details, and that was that.

"You'd better hurry, though," Van der Zwan whispered, when we shook hands at the open door. "One of these days we'll get Germans on board, sure as sin."

"When?"

"Who knows? Next month? Next week? You never know with the Moffen." To be on the safe side we advanced the enterprise to the very next evening, 13 August.

Now I needed a crew. So much remained to be arranged in twenty-four hours, that I got on to my bicycle and pedalled straight to Leyden. With Chris and Paul out of the running, Erik Michielsen was my obvious choice. I decided to get him out of bed.

"You may come to Britain with me," I announced magnanimously, when he opened his door under the Pieters Church.

"Awfully kind of you," he mumbled, rubbing the sleep from his eyes, "but I'm already going. See you in Piccadilly." I put my foot in the door just as he tried to close it, and stepped inside.

His revelation did not really surprise me. He had been hard to reach recently and for days now I had suspected him of planning something with "Bruno", my friend Jean Mesritz; with the summer weather holding, the jockeying for position in escape schemes was terrific just now. I was right; over a beer I pulled it out of him, little by little. Jean and Erik had nailed two canoes together, with cross-links, and this contraption lay ready in a barn near Noordwijk, complete with provisions, cans of petrol and a tiny outboard motor. They were going to cross the North Sea in it, as soon as the wind turned east. Carel Kranenburg would go with them.

"Preposterous," I grumbled. I had to act fast. Not only did I need a crew for my own scheme, but I seemed about to lose my best contacts to a plan in which there was no room for me. "Child's play. You're going to make asses of yourselves, paddling around in that silly thing. Besides, you're all going to drown. Why don't you come with me instead, all of you? Lots of room, comfortable and safe."

When I had explained my set-up, Erik's objections revolved mainly around the smell of raw fish on a trawler. Once reassured on this point he agreed to join me, all of us together. We drank to it. We

39

got along famously. We were both so obsessed with Holland, that recently we had worked out a blue-print for swiping Singapore from our British allies, once the the war was won.

I stayed with Erik that night. The next evening at ten o'clock the two of us, dressed as fishermen, turned off the south end of the Boulevard in Scheveningen. In order to be less conspicuous, Jean and Carel were to join us later. They had made the switch from canoe to lifeboat with a minimum of fuss. They were also bringing their service pistols. Kobus, a friendly black-marketeer who supported any anti-Nazi cause, had found us an engine and a dozen gallons of petrol, and promised to deposit them in a shed close to the quayside. For provisions we carried four large, round Edam cheeses and canteens filled with water. At the last moment Chris had volunteered to help us out and deliver the money for the boat to the little green house at the foot of the dike, as promised. All seemed in order.

As we walked down the slope of the sea-wall the harbour lay before us, silent and dismal. A razor-sharp moon glinted through the masts; around the trawlers the water shone like a black mirror. In spite of our disguise we felt utterly out of place. It was easy enough to find the *SCH.107*, too easy – she lay practically alongside the patrol-boat. Two sentries with carbines paced back and forth, their steps echoing over the cobbles on the quay. Two more German soldiers stood on deck, smoking and talking. A few fishermen busied themselves around their ships with nets and other gear.

We found the engine hidden in the shed, as arranged. Kobus evidently wanted to ensure a fast crossing, the thing weighed a ton. To carry it, we had to leave everything else behind. It gleamed and sparkled in the moonlight. The way to the *SCH. 107* led directly by the patrol-boat.

"*De l'audace!*" Erik whispered, smiling nervously. Now I knew what he meant.

I didn't like the situation, because it lacked an emergency exit. If anyone stopped us we were finished, plain and simple. Nothing could explain a powerful outboard motor in the fishing-harbour at night, especially in conjunction with twelve gallons of black-market petrol and provisions for three days. We couldn't even drop everything, take our chances with the carbines and run; Jean and Carel would walk straight into a hornet's nest. All we could do was trust our luck.

We bundled the motor in our rain-coats and staggered towards the trawler. Never had the quayside looked emptier. The sentries had their backs turned, but when we approached the patrol-boat the soldiers on deck stopped talking and watched us. Just keep going, I thought to myself; just keep going. We passed them in total silence, then they were behind us. We safely reached the *SCH 107* and minutes later the engine lay stored below. It took two more trips to get the rest on board. Then we sat down on a hatch and smoked a cigarette.

It was a mistake. My thoughts wandered back to home, to my parents. Our parting had been difficult, we did not expect ever to see each other again. I loved them, it wrenched my heart, and yet there was no doubt in my mind — I must go. A deep, vibrating drone began to fill the sky. I looked up. The mast cut black across the moon; around it the night hummed and throbbed with planes, wave after wave thundering westwards to England. I felt lonely and scared. Erik nudged me and with a movement of his head indicated the sea-wall. Two figures were approaching — Jean and Carel. We got up to meet them.

The escape plan based on the *SCH. 107* was essentially sound. It had simplicity, speed of execution, as well as inside assistance, reducing the risk to a minimum. It aimed at freedom via the shortest route, over sea, in the safest conveyance for the purpose, a lifeboat. Proof of its feasibility came later in the war, when it was faultlessly carried out by a secret agent named Ab Homburg. It had everything necessary for success, except a little luck. The two figures were not Jean and Carel, they were Chris and Van der Zwan. I could tell by their faces that the deal was off.

"Gentlemen," the fisherman whispered, shaking with nerves. "Here's your money back. Tomorrow we get German soldiers on board, with rifles. Every day from now on, they told us this morning. I want no trouble. My sincere regrets to Her Majesty the Queen, but please go away."

"You're just in time to help unload," I said to Jean and Carel who arrived at this moment, wearing ludicrous sailor's bonnets and looking like something out of *H.M.S. Pinafore*.

When everything had been lugged back into the shed I got on my bicycle and set out for Wassenaar, alone. It was a long, gloomy trip. At the edge of Park de Kieviet I straightened up and sniffed — from here you could always smell the flowers in the gardens. The house was dark, my parents were asleep. I felt my way to the kitchen, grabbed a beer and a piece of cheese, and tiptoed to my room. I switched on the light, closed the door tightly, poured the beer, turned on the radio and put my feet on the table.

It was great to be home.

V

ALL NEXT DAY I STAYED IN BED, BUT AT ELEVEN O'CLOCK THE following morning I was back in Michielsen's room under the Pieters Church. They were sitting around the sherry bottle – Erik, Jean, Carel, "Count B" Van Brero and Anton Muller, who turned out to be the fourth man in the canoe scheme. "Look who's here," Carel said, with marked lack of enthusiasm. "The herringman. Nothing today, thank you."

"Count B", unaware of our recent adventure, nevertheless smelled action and intrigue. He jumped up, grabbed a cane and pointed it skywards like Lord Raglan on the ramparts of Balaclava. "Charge!" he yelled.

"For Christ's sake, Van Brero, shut up," I said irritably. Then I turned to Carel and the others. "Your plan is still no good," I began again. "You can't cross the North Sea in a canoe." In fact, I was wrong. The following summer a pair of students from Delft set out for England in a kayak. Almost two weeks later they were picked up off the coast of Suffolk, more dead than alive. But right or wrong, I had to fight the canoe plan, because it would leave me stranded. I threw the Van der Zwan money on the table.

"Look. All you have is a base of operations near the sea. Important, but that's all. Forget about that canoe stuff. I have a big engine, lots of petrol and this money here. Let's buy a good boat, and we'll go together. Like tonight."

"Tonight?!"

"Tonight." It was my trump card. The weather had been reasonable enough, but not for canoes. For weeks now they had been staring at the weather-vane on the Pieters Church, hoping for an east wind which would flatten the North Sea. It seemed stuck in the west, and I judged that they must be getting fed up. I also counted on Erik's sense of the dramatic; to decide at lunch-time and leave the same evening should prove irresistible to him. (*De l'audace!*) I was right. Anton Muller quickly fell in line. Jean and Carel, somewhat cagey after the *SCH. 107*, took a little longer.

"How about me?" Count B asked. He had just executed a perfect sabre-thrust and remained poised in its final position. He looked at us pleadingly over his shoulder.

"No room for you," Erik stated flatly. "But you can help. Put that bloody thing away and do another recce of the dunes. You know the path, meet us at the bottom near the road. Wait for us there." Van Brero saluted and made his exit stage right.

We borrowed a carrier-tricycle on which Carel left for Scheveningen, under protest, to pick up the engine and the other gear and bring them to our base of operations near Noordwijk. Jean Mesritz and Anton Muller set out for De Kaag, a near-by yachting centre, to buy a boat. Erik and I stayed with the sherry bottle. At four o'clock the telephone rang; Jean reported that matters had been arranged and the goods could be collected at the basin in Warmond. "It's a little heavy," he added.

"How heavy?"

"A good-size truck and a dozen blokes."

A dozen blokes, they must have picked a boat to fit the engine! At such short notice the only solution was to contact 11 Morssingel, a rooming-house full of Indies students, keen and reliable. For the truck I once again fell back on Kobus. After half an hour on the telephone I went home to Wassenaar.

At about ten o'clock that night Park de Kieviet trembled to a thunderous roar, like that usually made by military transports. Everybody in our street peered from between black-out curtains. In the half-light I saw an enormous pantechnicon, consisting of truck and trailer, pull up smack in front of our gate with a blast of air-brakes. Kobus and his megalomania! I shot out of the house and off we rumbled on our secret mission.

That evening nobody had thought in terms of half-measures – the group which greeted us in Warmond could have been a fraternity reunion. In no time the boat, a lapstrake dinghy as strong as a battleship and about as heavy, was tucked away inside the trailer, escorted by a special detail of Leydeners sportily dressed for the occasion. We set course for Noordwijk to the cheers of our well-wishers and immediately made a wrong turn into a stone courtyard. Our subsequent manoeuvring must have woken up Gestapo officers all the way to Haarlem. At our base we picked up Erik and Carel and all our gear. Then we thundered along sleepy country lanes, until we blasted to a stop at the foot of the dunes. Finally the van pulled away empty, and as the roar died in the night the silence behind it bore in on us from all directions.

The moment we entered the dunes we found ourselves in a "shoot on sight" area, indicated by signs showing death's heads. The skulls grinned at us all along the way. Van Brero had reported several bunkers in the neighbourhood, manned and armed with machine-guns. We couldn't help making some noise, struggling in the dark for more than an hour with the ponderous dinghy on our shoulders, uphill and down through the soft sand. Suddenly a figure stood darkly outlined on a dune. Some of the carriers ran and the boat crashed to the ground. The rest of us froze with fear. But it was only Count B, shielding his eyes against an imaginary sun in the classic pose of an Indian scout.

At last we crossed the outer dunes and before us stretched the sea, black and baleful under a sliver of moon. We let the boat slip from our aching shoulders and collapsed in the sand. A German patrol would have heard us puff and pant a mile away. We sprawled as we had fallen, motionless, like figures on a frieze: "Leydeners – 1940".

"Come on, gentlemen. Let's get it over with," Erik Michielsen whispered. As the only Senior present he had logically taken the lead. Van Brero waved us on frantically. The entire coastline was patrolled, so we scurried across the beach in one haul. The last hundred yards we dragged the dinghy through the sand, until it lay half in the water. At close quarters the sea looked unexpectedly rough. Carel Kranenburg climbed into the bow, facing back; Erik and Anton, both former rowing stars, took the oars; Jean Mesritz installed himself on the rear seat. Everyone was careful to keep his shoes dry. There was a rush to push us off. I waded in to steer the boat head-on into the surf. When I was out of my depth I hoisted

myself aboard, next to Jean. It struck me that the spume was sloshing by uncomfortably close. From the little band on the beach rose
a muted cheer, barely audible above the roar of the sea, then they
quickly dispersed. The bow shot up in the first wave and crashed
into the trough. Every one of us was immediately soaked through.
Erik and Anton pulled as if it were Varsity Day.

"She performs elegantly," Jean grinned, wiping the brine from
his eyes. We had ten inches of freeboard and the water came up to
our ankles, but we were on our way to England and freedom, one
hundred miles due west across the North Sea.

Jean and I were almost immediately seasick. The surf proved
wider than we had expected and the wind seemed to be rising. Erik
and Anton rowed silently, carefully keeping the nose into the waves.
Carel sat huddled in the bow, taking most of the spray. Every so
often the dinghy was shoved sideways by a treacherous lateral
movement and took some water over the gunnels. Then we swore and
muttered, pumped and bailed, while for a few moments she would
lie dangerously low in the waves. From time to time Jean and I
threw up.

Now the surf lay far behind us, but the sea was getting no more
tractable. We dared not stop rowing for fear of the cross-movement,
yet we had to attach the engine sometime. Slowly the Dutch coast
receded, but I never felt as if we were coming closer to England. At
last the moon shone through the shreds of cloud on nothing but
water – we were in open sea. We decided to hook on the motor.

It happened exactly the way we had dreaded, only worse. While
the engine was being handed to me from amidships, the rowers were
temporarily out of action. At this exact moment a lateral wave
hit us; with the heavy machine in my arms I almost fell overboard.
Our balance was totally upset and water rushed in. We flung ourselves in the opposite direction and succeeded in righting the boat,
but the water sloshed after us and pushed the other gunnel below the
waves. In seconds it reached up to our knees. As a last resort I threw
the engine into the sea, but it was too late. Bubbling gently both
gunnels sank below the waterline. Suddenly we were sitting just as
before the disaster, Jean and I neatly side by side, Anton and Erik
at the oars, Carel in the bow, facing back; but the boat was nowhere
in sight.

"Bail, everybody!" Jean shouted.

"Where?" Carel shot back. A round Dutch cheese bobbed disconsolately past his chest.

When at last we crawled back on to the beach, half dead but all together, we had spent more than five hours on and in the water.

* * *

After this experience we were all somewhat disenchanted with the North Sea. The other four finally attempted their canoe scheme, in which there was no room for me, escaping death by the narrowest of margins. They chose the same route through the dunes at Noordwijk, but the Germans, possibly alerted by our thunderous approach the previous time, had meanwhile positioned two machine-guns in the path, pointing landwards. The little expedition had advanced to within three hundred yards of the ambush, when by sheer coincidence it ran into Count B on one of his scouting trips. He had discovered the trap and, recognising the Leydeners in the dark "by their foul language", warned them just in time. Before they had organised a new route to the sea, the autumn storms forced them to abandon their plan.

Of necessity I went it alone. In the bathing section of the Scheveningen Beach Club lay a rowing-boat belonging to the life-guard. Apparently the Germans didn't consider it seaworthy; at night it was merely pulled up on the beach, half-way to the Boulevard. It looked pretty good to me. I set the date at 19 August, three days after the Noordwijk débâcle.

It didn't require much organisation. Kobus, disappointed at the lack of result in spite of his mighty contributions, let me have a greasy little outboard motor and four cans of petrol on credit. Jean and Carel declared themselves willing to help push the boat into the water. On the morning of the nineteenth I put the petrol cans in two suitcases and hid them in our private cabin at the Beach Club. There, nothing had changed. The sun beamed warmly and in due course everybody came drifting in.

"Well, hullo there, Jacques!" When I saw Jacques Maasland I automatically looked around for Alexander Rowerth. Only they of my friends had failed to turn up in Leyden after the capitulation. Jacques had undoubtedly spent his days buried in books at the judge's house, but for gregarious, fun-loving Alexander it struck me as most odd. True, I had been less than encouraging on the phone

47

when he invited me to stay at his home, but that was months ago. None of us, least of all Alexander, would hold a grudge that long. In fact, every time when I was about to meet another would-be escapee I half expected to see Alexander's dashing figure step from behind some fancy nickname. He seemed cut out for the R.A.F. and I couldn't hope to find a better companion for my own plans in that direction. It was high time we dug him up.

Jacques had come with Mia, an old flame of mine. She looked great, as always. They bumped into me just as I was pushing the compass deeper into the sand with my toes; I didn't dare leave it lying about in the cabin. "How come you're so tanned?" I chatted on, trying to act naturally. "Aren't you working?"

"Certainly am," Jacques answered importantly. "Got to keep in shape, though." He patted his flat belly with obvious satisfaction. He exuded health and prosperity. I gave the compass an irritated shove with my big toe and sauntered off towards the sea to take another look at the dinghy. Along the way I flopped down for a minute under a gaily striped beach-umbrella, where I had spotted some Leydeners. They lay dozing in the sun with their sleek, brown girls like a school of otters. Now and then someone told a joke, some heads would perk up, a few bodies shake with laughter and then doze on. I felt like a visitor from Mars. Jacques came over with Mia and stretched out on his back with a placid smile on his face. Beyond him I saw a well-built man stroll by, swastika on his shorts, S.S. forage-cap on his blond head. He looked at Mia, leisurely, and didn't miss a thing. I peered past him and eagerly watched my little boat dance on the waves.

"By the way," I asked around. "Anybody here seen Alexander Rowerth?"

Nobody had —

Once again it was ten in the evening when I said good-bye at home. Nobody cried this time, we were getting used to it. With the motor under one arm and the usual cheese under the other I arrived on the beach. Jean and Carel were waiting for me; could I please hurry up a little, they were going to a party. I went to our cabin, turned the key in the lock – the cans of gasoline were gone!

Later I learnt that in the heat of afternoon the lids had popped off. The entire solarium had smelled of petrol and a number of patrons complained to Gijs, the attendant. Possession of petrol was

Leyden 1937. Could it ever change?

Our heads bald as eggs, as tradition required.

Minerva, Leyden's hallowed students' club.

Paul Renardel, betrayed for a handful of guilders.

Jean Mesritz missed the plane to England.

KONINKRIJK DER NEDERLANDEN.

BEWIJS VAN ONTSLAG

uit den dienst als **gewoon dienstplichtige** van de landmacht

met ingang van *7 April* 193*7*, wegens *gebreken*

uitgereikt aan *Hazelhoff Roelfzema Siebren, Erik,*

geboren *3 April* 191*7*, die op *23 Maart* 193*7* bij *het Regiment Jager* werd ingelijfd als *dienstplichtige* der lichting *1937*

uit de gemeente *'s-Gravenhage*,

provincie *Zuid-Holland*, onder nr. *971*, en laatstelijk diende als *gewoon dienstplichtige.*

's-Gravenhage, *7 April* 193*7*

DE COMMANDANT VAN *het Regiment Jager,*
De Luitenant-Kolonel,

10863-'35

162

I myself had been rejected for
military service.

Count B's ambition
was to challenge
Hitler to a duel.

They all turned up, including Mia *(right)*

In this contraption they were going to cross the North Sea.

Students poured from the university building and voted to strike.

The Occupation suited
Frits van der Schrieck.

Lodo van Hamel,
Holland's first secret agent.

The 'Orange Hotel', one step away from the firing-squad.

The St. Cergue, A grubby hunk of mystery.

illegal and could get you into serious trouble. Being my friend, Gijs had taken it home for safe-keeping.

Jean and Carel rushed off to their party. Suddenly I felt utterly, endlessly weary. Little motor in hand I wandered aimlessly across the sand, then north along the water's edge. The tide was out. I walked to the end of a stone breakwater and turned around. A tepid breeze brought the scents of summer from far over the land. Above Rotterdam, as usual, spattered the delicate lacework of anti-aircraft fire, soundless and eerie. Scheveningen lay in the moonlight like a grey cardboard model – the row of hotels on the Boulevard stretching south, the beach alongside cluttered with summer structures, spanned far into the water by the gingerbread mass of the pier. Just visible at the southern tip of the Boulevard rose the darkened lighthouse above the outer jetties of the fishing-harbour. A single strand of surf whispered rhythmically – curve, hiss, silence, curve, hiss, silence. Somewhere a train whistled. The impatient sound died, the surf sang on.

I lifted the motor high above my head. "O.K. then, to hell with it. They'll have to do without me in England," I growled. "To-morrow I'm going to lie in the sun, like everybody else."

It was the second engine I had hurled into the North Sea that week. With a splash it disappeared in the black water. Specks of phosphor whirled like fireflies in the deep. I watched them die, then walked back along "the little stone pier by the North Boulevard" – as it came to be known in the reports of the British Secret Service.

VI

IN THE YEAR 1574, WHEN THE BESIEGING SPANIARDS HAD ALMOST starved Leyden into submission, burgomaster Adriaan van der Werf addressed his desperate citizens. "Here is my sword," he said. "Take my body to appease your hunger, but expect no surrender as long as I am alive." Relief was near. The Dutch had pierced their sea-walls in seventeen places and ships from Zeeland attacked the enemy "in a fierce naval battle amongst the branches of quiet orchards and the chimney-stacks of half-submerged farm-houses". On 3 October, after routing the Spaniards, they sailed into the city. Leyden was free! In recognition of its heroism, William the Silent granted the town a university. It was built forthwith on the Rapenburg, where it stands today.

From my little balcony on the opposite side of the Rapenburg I peered intently at the sombre old hulk. Even before the autumn storms brought the beautiful, endless, deadly summer of 1940 to a close, I had returned to Leyden. England had been a dream. Had I really presumed to imagine myself part of it, a free man, a pilot in the R.A.F.? My academic career was falling apart, I hadn't opened a book since May. I had shunted my life on to a dead track, I must get it rolling again. I hung a sign on the door, "Do Not Disturb", and dejectedly rummaged my law tracts together.

It was agony. With methodical thoroughness the Germans imposed their authority and every day the Dutch had to bow a little lower. Each humiliation increased my depression. For hours on end

I sat bent over my texts with unseeing eyes, nursing my resentment until it consumed me, finally returning to work for no other reason than to escape the unbearable reality.

But now something was up. I stood in my dressing-gown in the grey, chilly morning, a glass of sherry in hand, and watched the university. There was something going on in there. Since early in the day I had heard canes tapping through the Kloksteeg, more than usual. Now everything was quiet, but from behind those silent walls seeped tension, which touched me across the water. I listened – all I heard was the sharp click-clack of a tradesman's horse gathering speed to cross one of the hump-backed bridges. And then, through the passive stillness of the German-occupied town, unbelievably, sounded the first notes of the "Wilhelmus", Holland's national anthem.

A shiver ran down my spine. The singing came from hundreds of voices, unevenly, but spontaneous and strong. I had felt it all morning: the presence of drama, whatever it was, a happening full of passion and violence worthy of Leyden's noble history. The defiant song, long since forbidden by the authorities, penetrated the massive stone as if from far away, and Wilhelmus and university, both born from the same Dutch agony of four centuries ago, fused to a symbol of permanence. Poor, silly Nazis and their vapid dreams!

I quickly put my glass on the table behind me. I couldn't help myself – in my blue dressing-gown on the ludicrous little balcony I proudly pulled myself up to my full height. Through two interminable stanzas I stood rigidly to attention, glued against the house-front in the deserted street.

The occasion turned out to be Leyden's protest, which I had somehow missed, against the first act of persecution of the Jews in Holland. Our professor Meijers, an authority on International Law, had been dismissed on grounds of race. His colleague Cleveringa, a raw-boned Frisian Protestant, who had addressed the meeting with a defiant attack on the Nazis, was arrested the very same day. To the students this came as a shock, but the professor had packed his suit-case in advance, knowing full well that such words would land him in the "Orange Hotel" – the S.S. prison in Scheveningen. Unanimously we students voted to strike; in reply the Germans closed the university. At last we had locked horns. The romantic phase of the Occupation, in Leyden, was over —

Shortly afterwards Chris Krediet dropped in on me, in the middle of the night. Since my return to the fold of legitimate students I had gravitated back to my old circle of friends, yet we had seen little of each other recently. Like me, Chris had been trying to concentrate on his studies. He stood in the door of my bedroom.

"Good-bye," he said simply. "I'm on my way."

"On your way where?" I got out of bed, checked the blackout curtains in the living-room, turned on the light and offered him a smoke.

"Portugal, Switzerland, Sweden — does it matter a damn? Any convenient stepping-stone to England."

"Why? Why now?"

"Why not now? Leyden is closed, this seems as good a time for a trip as any, wouldn't you say? In fact, we're going to Petsamo."

Obviously he wasn't giving me the real reason. Of all of us he had been the most determined to finish his studies, come what may. Nobody expected the university to stay shut for long; it was felt that the Germans would surely prefer to keep the students busy. I watched him closely. He was always difficult to read. His blue eyes looked ingenuously into mine, but still more deceptive were his healthy Dutch cheeks. I suspected that he was suffocating, cooped up in little Holland, unable to get out when the spirit moved him to build dams in Brazil. The closing of Leyden had given him the excuse his conscience required. He would never admit it. I understood him perfectly. Who would be next? Paul Renardel? I myself?

"To Petsamo? And who is we?"

"Count B and I."

"You must be kidding," I sighed. Chris grinned and shrugged his shoulders. I knew that his assurance sprang largely from his view that there wasn't much in life which didn't totter on the edge of absurdity.

"Do you have any kind of a plan?" I asked.

"Too true we have," he bantered. "Listen. We're signing on as crew on a coaster. Out of Delfzijl. Count B says they're having trouble finding cooks." The thought of Van Brero exchanging his duel with Hitler for the job of cook on a coaster broke me up, but Chris went on. "Then we're going to jump ship in Scandinavia and make our way through Finland to Petsamo which, I'm reliably informed, lies somewhere near the North Pole. Anyway, it's the one place the Germans haven't got to yet. American ships still come in there, and we'll stow away or something. Do you want to come?"

"No, thank you." He couldn't be serious. "You know, you can get killed doing this sort of thing."

"You can get killed doing all sorts of things," Chris answered evenly. He smoked his cigarette to the very end, then abruptly got up. "O.K. then. Good-bye! Farewell! Adieu! See you on Piccadilly!" He opened the door. "Petsamo or bust!"

"Why don't you come and have a drink next Sunday," I called after him. "Bring the Count. Maybe you'll both feel better."

But on Sunday Chris had disappeared. So had Van Brero, as cook on a coaster. Three days later the German army occupied Petsamo, shutting off that tiny loop-hole in the far north. Poor Chris! Poor Count B! . . . But they sent me a postcard from Helsinki. Then one arrived from, of all places, Moscow. A month or so later a letter came from Vladivostok, on Siberia's east coast. Then another postcard, from Tokyo. Then one from San Francisco. The last card, five days later from New York, showed the Empire State building. It read: "We're off to see the *Bèbèk*." Chris Krediet and Van Brero, the strangest team with the lousiest plan, had reached England, one hundred miles due west, by going east, all the way round the world.

In Leyden dusk was falling. The rain whispered against my windows, interrupted now and then by the rattle of hail. The university, deserted, huddled across the water. Chris' postcard lay in front of me on my desk. I burst out laughing. I laughed till my guts hurt. Then I grabbed a book and hurled it across the room with all my might.

*   *   *

To everyone's surprise Leyden remained closed. I locked myself in my study and ploughed through volume after volume. The outside world penetrated my cocoon by rumour only. Now the authorities shut down Minerva as well; students hung around their rooming-houses. The mood changed. Gone were the show-offs, the moustaches, the wild stories, the laughs. Everybody, everything seemed normal again. Life became very quiet, very drab. . . . But under the surface things grew silently, in the dark, in deadly earnest. One

53

night my door-bell rang. A round-shouldered figure stood in the rain, hat on his ears, water dripping from the brim. "They got Jean," Erik Michielsen said. "It looks pretty bad."

Jean Mesritz was my oldest friend. On our first day of school, in The Hague, we shared a bench, and for six years we plodded through the grades together. He was taller and smarter than most of us, quite handsome, and not afraid of girls. For all these reasons we looked up to him; he was set apart and his friends were few. I was proud to be one of them. When we came to Leyden we both took Law, and nothing astounded me more than to learn one day that he might leave the Netherlands before he had finished. Then he told me that he was Jewish. I had never known; one usually didn't in Holland.

"Come in," I told Erik.

"Not here, if you don't mind."

"O.K. Shall we go to the Pieters Church?"

"I don't live there any more."

"Then where do you live these days?" I thought he had merely moved.

"Nowhere, really," Erik smiled. "I sort of float around. Let's meet tomorrow in Wassenaar, at your place, all right?"

The next night I got the story.

At just about the time when our dinghy sank off the coast at Noordwijk, the R.A.F. parachuted Holland's first official secret agent into the bulb-fields behind the dunes, a few miles to the south of us. He was Lodo van Hamel, a Netherlands Navy lieutenant who had sailed for England one jump ahead of the Germans. We all knew Lodo from school in The Hague — Jean, Erik, Carel Kranenburg and I. Perhaps for that reason he had contacted some-one outside our group.

Lodo's mission was to prepare the groundwork for a Dutch intelligence service, after which he was to return to London in order to become its head. Capture would mean death, so he stayed out of sight; but with the help of some Leydeners he accomplished his task in less than two months. Then he set out to contact England with his secret transmitter. Since the Gestapo employed a fleet of sophisticated radio-receiving cars to intercept any unauthorised message and plot its point of origin while driving there at top speed, Lodo never dared transmit more than three minutes at a time, and never twice from the same location. With some difficulty he persuaded his superiors to send an aircraft to pick him up and bring him back to England. They consented to try a landing on the Tjeuke Lake, in the province of Friesland, as close as possible to midnight on 13 October or, in case of bad weather, on either of the following two nights.

By sheer coincidence Lodo and Jean, both under cover names, had meanwhile run into each other. Jean joined the team and suggested that, if the plane had room to spare, it should take some other useful people along to England, where anyone with first-hand knowledge of the Occupation should be highly valuable. Lodo agreed and Jean put himself at the top of the list, naturally, with Erik Michielsen and "the Hussar", Carel Kranenburg, next in line. I was passed over as lacking any military qualifications.

On the agreed night the little group sat in a rowing-boat on the Tjeuke Lake, except Erik and Carel who were standing on the dike. At the last moment they had been bounced in favour of two other candidates.

"There I stood again, blast it, watching other people escape," Erik grinned, pouring himself another beer.

The first night — nothing. Nothing but silence and cold, and the occasional slap of a fish's tail over the misty lake. The next midnight they heard the plane approach, but they themselves sat wrapped in a heavy ground-fog, surrounded by a luminous world of water and vapour with no way to tell where one ended and the other began. The aeroplane circled for twenty minutes in the moonlight above the mist-bank, then they listened to the drone disappearing in the west.

On the third night, 15 October, the weather was perfect. A bright moon poured its tricky light over the water and almost on the dot of midnight the sound of engines neared from across the Zuider Zee.

"We knew it was going to be a Fokker T8, and a Dutch pilot. Can you imagine, landing a plane on water by moonlight? Anyway, you could hear it, but you couldn't see it. I didn't see a thing, until they started flashing lights from the boat. I knew those signals were phoney; there were German soldiers in the boat, but there wasn't a thing I could do. Jesus, it was awful."

"What the hell do you mean?" I gasped, totally confused.

"Lodo and Jean and everybody had been locked up that morning in the Orange Hotel. They were betrayed. By the wife of a farmer."

"Why? Why would the wife of a farmer . . .?"

"Eels," Erik said, shaking his head. "We had this heavy suitcase with us, full of papers and secret documents, you know. This bitch thought it was dynamite, to blow up her lousy eel-traps with. Poaching, would you believe it? So she calls the police. One thing leads to another, and in the end they're all grabbed by the Gestapo, handcuffed, guns on them, everything. Except for Carel and me — we hid on the embankment. I came back that night when the weather was so great, to see what would happen."

"Well, what happened?" My head hurt and my throat felt dry. Eels!

"I heard the plane taxiing right up to those lights — nothing I could do. Next somebody calls across the water, quite far from where I'm standing, mind you, and suddenly there's terrific shooting, back and forth, machine-guns, not very loud but lots of it. At the same time this pilot opens up, engines roaring, I suppose he got off, I sort of lost track of him. Because there was that scream, just one scream across the lake, quite far away, soft and long and really terrible." Michielsen lit a cigarette and puffed a couple of times. "Anyway, next day everybody tells the story that a boat with four Germans in it has been blasted out of the water by a plane. Carel and I beat it back to Leyden."

"What'll happen to Jean?"

"I don't know about Jean." Erik shrugged his shoulders dubiously. "But anyone can tell you what's going to happen to Lodo."

Lodo van Hamel was interrogated for more than a year. He never divulged a single name or fact. Then one morning they marched him out into the dunes at Scheveningen and shot him.

*   *   *

Still I studied. I hadn't returned to Leyden for nothing. Besides, as the months went by I began to get somewhere; if ever the university re-opened, I would be ready. Yet I knew that I was fooling myself. Sometimes the sheer immobility of the building outside my window overwhelmed me, all three hundred and fifty years of it, and I felt as if we two stood still while life rushed by. Now Hollanders were suffering for their convictions, taking risks. The jails were filling up, the ragged blasts of firing-squads began to be heard from stone court-yards and secluded dells. Sooner or later my moment of truth would come.

When the Germans indicated their intention of re-opening Leyden, it immediately became clear why they had not done so before – they had been waiting for a *quid pro quo*. Now they issued an ordinance, the *"numerus clausus"*, under which all Jewish students were required to register as such. At the same time they hinted broadly that if the student body accepted the order "in a spirit of cooperation", the authorities would relent and permit the academy to resume its functions. By this time all the professors with any guts had been fired or jailed, and many of the worthwhile students were immersed in Underground activities. The rest held the power, and they seemed inclined to go along with the German terms. I was beside myself. A spirit of cooperation?! Burgomaster Van der Werf had offered his life rather than surrender Leyden to the Spaniards. Now we, in whose hands this torch was placed, were going to offer up our Jewish colleagues to the Nazis "in a spirit of cooperation"? Not I – nor anybody else if I could prevent it, by fair means or foul.

The moment the curfew ended at 4 a.m. on the night of 14 February 1941, six teams of two men each, all Indies students from the faithful rooming-house at 11 Morssingel, led by Paul Renardel, took to the icy streets. Every team carried a bucket of glue, a brush and a stack of papers, and apart from scaring each other half to death every time they ran into one another in the dark, they brought off a pretty smooth operation. The next morning every wall in town, including the door of the Gestapo H.Q., displayed its copy of the "Leyden Manifesto" – under which name it was preserved.

The Manifesto, printed on heavy paper, was addressed to the Occupation authorities and began with the sentence: "The Leyden students, true to their traditions, after mutual consultation, herewith announce the conditions under which they can support the re-opening of their university." Then followed a list of demands, including a ban on all racial discrimination, which would not have shamed an activist thirty years later. Contrary to its opening sentence I had not bothered to show it to anyone in advance and had signed it flatly: "The Leyden Students."

57

The German authorities, including Hitler's top henchmen in the Netherlands, received their copies through the mail. As expected, they exploded with rage at this impertinence and promptly declared that the academy would remain closed until the end of the war. Only the student leaders matched their fury, especially those who were hauled off to jail, vainly protesting their innocence. As far as I was concerned, it served the cowards right; Leyden's disgrace had been narrowly averted.

One immediate result of the upheaval was a sign of life from my old friend Jacques Maasland, in The Hague. "What the hell is going on?" His voice boomed down the telephone. "Have you all gone mad up there? All this time I sit here waiting to do my exams, and now this! Do you know what this means to me? Do you know what it means to have Leyden closed for the duration? Eh? Do you realise what it . . ." I hung up on him.

As for me, I knew very well what it meant. It meant that my only valid reason for staying in Holland had evaporated. Back to the war! Off to England! After Chris! Back to my defiant, illegal Resistance pals!

I took the phone off the hook and dialled a number, from memory, where Erik Michielsen — two times a day, carefully, handkerchief folded around the mouthpiece, never more than once from the same location — checked for calls.

VII

Five days later the Gestapo arrested the printer of the Manifesto, Van Beelen from Katwijk. He told me himself. I saw him sitting in a café in Leyden with two men, but before I could greet him he got up and went to the toilet. Brushing right by me without a sign of recognition he hissed: "Beat it!" Instead I followed him into the empty lavatory. We each stood on a toilet-bowl with the doors closed and talked over the partition.

"A Mof came with a gun, and they locked me up in the Orange Hotel," he whispered. "At night I'm in jail, in the daytime I walk around Leyden with those two Moffen. They're Gestapo, they've got guns. They're waiting for me to point you out."

"Jesus!"

"After I point you out, I can go home." For a while he didn't say anything. Neither did I. It seemed awfully quiet in that lavatory.

Suddenly Van Beelen laughed. He was a simple sort of man, blue eyes, blond hair, very Dutch. "Don't worry," he said, "I won't give you away."

"Why not?"

"Look," he explained, speaking with some difficulty. His chin reached just above the partition and apparently he had trouble keeping a foothold on the slippery ring of the bowl. "I told them I'm just a printer. I don't read what I print, I just make a living. Me, they'll let me go pretty soon. You, they'll hang on to."

59

"Are you quite sure?" I said, trying to hide my relief. I had an overwhelming desire to get out of the w.c. and start running.

"Quite sure. Besides — "At this moment he slipped and disappeared. Then he popped up again. " — not everybody gets the chance to do something for Holland. Well, this is my contribution. They want you badly. To hell with the Moffen. Beat it."

He left ahead of me. On his way out he pushed a piece of paper under my door. It had a bank address and account number on it. "Just make sure that my wife doesn't starve while I'm gone," he whispered.

I didn't dare go home any more, not in Leyden, not in Wassenaar, not even to pick up some clothes. They were after me; sooner or later they'd find out my name. Then they would come. I called my father at his office and asked him to arrange temporary shelter for me with one of his friends. They lived in big houses with plenty of room, but they all turned him down. Too risky.

"You know," one of them said. "It's all fine and dandy, all these heroics, but after all, these boys have nothing to lose."

"Nothing but their lives," my father answered.

I went to stay in Amsterdam, where everybody hated the Moffen. While the heat was on I needed a cut-out, a reliable person to maintain my contact with the outside world while I remained "underground" — a location so generally recognised that people began spelling it with a capital U. The choice was easy. I called Frits van der Schrieck, a pale, thin Leydener whom before the war we had often shockingly neglected. Partly he had himself to blame — he was so self-effacing and colourless that we usually forgot about him, in good faith, and he always behaved so modestly that after a party nobody could recall with certainty whether Frits had been present or not. He was aware of it, but never resentful, and smart enough to realise its potential under an enemy occupation. Immediately after the surrender, when most of us were still mindlessly staggering about, he began to do brave and useful things. Once, reconnoitring escape routes to the south, he bicycled all the way to Bordeaux, close to neutral Spain, before returning to Leyden.

"When you got that far, why didn't you keep going?" I asked, when he reported on his experiences.

"Oh well," he answered, in his gentle, diffident way. "I don't really want to go to England. I've only got one kidney worth a damn, you know. In England they'd just stick me behind a desk, and that's not for me. You wait and see, there'll be plenty of excitement right here in Holland pretty soon."

The very first time Frits acted as my cut-out, he saved my life. In the ever-shifting alliances of the Underground — with Jean Mesritz in jail and Erik Michielsen reduced to a nervous shadow — Carel Kranenburg and I had suddenly jelled into a team. Nobody was more determined to reach England than the Hussar. After three failures to get there by sea his hopes were now based on a "chappie" we referred to as "Blubber", one of the many descriptive aliases in a society where real names were death. Blubber knew me by sight, as I had participated in a few meetings regarding an overland route to Switzerland which he declared himself willing to divulge to us, for a consideration. Our next meeting was to be in a tiny bar on the edge of Wassenaar. Frits van der Schrieck went as my cut-out.

The Hussar never appeared. Blubber arrived late and brought with him a German security officer who burst into the bar, pistol drawn. "*Hände hoch!*" (Hands up!) he shouted, in the curiously antiquated jargon of the Gestapo.

Frits happened to be the only customer in the place. He put up his hands and looked surprised, as undoubtedly he was. Blubber, not knowing him and expecting me, had to admit that they had stuck up the wrong man. This so infuriated the officer that, while courteously apologising to Frits, he pistol-whipped Blubber to the floor. The three of them ended up drinking beer together, which my cut-out did not dare refuse. Carel meanwhile, sold by Blubber for a few guilders, spent his first night in the Orange Hotel. I never saw him again.

"I also brought you this," Frits said, when he had reported back from the meeting. "I picked it up in the café." He threw an illustrated magazine on my lap. The cover showed a marching group of S.S. officers. Right up front, towering above the others, dashing and debonair in the cruel black uniform, a tiny smile around the charming eyes, strode my friend and colleague, Leydener Alexander Rowerth. The picture came from Munich and the uniform belonged to the Dutch S.S. Brigade "Standarte Westland". I stared at him a long time without experiencing the slightest emotion — no regret, no sadness, no hate, not even curiosity. He was not only dead to me, he

61

was dead retroactively from the moment of his birth, more dead than Carel is today. He had never existed —

With the Gestapo looking for me on two counts, I hardly showed my face in daylight any more. Only when Paul Renardel left for England did I make an exception. Erik Michielsen told me about it, but he did not come with me when I went to say good-bye, around cocktail time on 2 April. I hadn't set foot in 11 Morssingel since the night of the Leyden Manifesto. Paul gave me a big hug. His dark eyes sparkled with excitement, he even had some colour in his cheeks. Another Indies boy was going with him, I didn't ask how or along what route. I felt lonely — with Paul also gone, who would be left? At the last moment he hesitated, went into the kitchen and came back with a precious crock of jenever. He poured three shots, then broke into a broad smile. We lifted our glasses in a silent toast, the door-bell rang, two men pushed their way past the landlady and stepped into the room with guns in their hands, and off we went to the Orange Hotel. It was that simple.

We sat side by side on the back seat of a grey police-car. One Gestapo officer kept his gun on us all the way to Scheveningen. "Tell me," he asked suddenly. "How much did you pay this traitor, this fellow who was going to take you to England and came to us instead?"

"A hundred guilders," Paul answered glumly — some ten pounds.

"The bastard," the officer said, shaking his head.

We stopped at a small wooden door beside the main gate of the Orange Hotel. The blind wall stretched the length of the block and around both corners. Through a second entrance we stepped into the building and now the view hit me like a blow — the long, deserted corridors, the shiny, tiled walls, rows of green cell-doors in absolute silence. My heart cramped in my chest; were there really people behind those doors? Then suddenly, like a clarion call, the realisation: Jean is in here! And Lodo! and Carel! And Van Beelen! And Jan and Piet and Dirk and Gerard and Robert, friends, some Leydeners, all Hollanders, those who had dared to fight and risk, the best! When I walked into my solitary cell I listened proudly for the crunch of the door behind me.

It wasn't long, however, before most of my thoughts revolved around the problem of getting out as fast as possible. Two points emerged: my arrest had been a mistake, incidental to a situation in which I was truly innocent; and those of the Gestapo who were looking for me with valid reason searched for me by sight, not by name. My single chance lay in convincing certain Germans of my innocence before I was identified by others. It was a race against time, because sooner or later someone would recognise me, in the corridors, during interrogation or in the court-yard during our daily fifteen minutes of fresh air. Occasionally the thought of Van Beelen and Blubber and their diligent Gestapo escorts combing the streets of Leyden for me, while I sat hidden in their own jail, cheered me up. However, with the passing of each day my spirits sank. It couldn't last. I became desperate. Every guard who stuck his head into my cell I belaboured about my unjust arrest. Finally I wrote a letter to the prison commandant on a three-foot strip of toilet paper. The guard who delivered it for me brought back word that the commandant would have me shot if I did it again. Still, it must have impressed him — together with the fact that they were running out of room in places like the Orange Hotel — because the next day a sergeant unlocked my door, handed me my personal effects including every penny of my money, and barked: *"Raus!"*

"What was it like?" Frits van der Schrieck asked, when once again we sat safely in my lair in Amsterdam, back in hiding from those who had just released me.

I told him. It's been told many times since. Once you know one S.S. establishment from the inside, you know them all. At the very last, however, one moment made up for everything. I had already left my cell and was scurrying through the cross-corridor to the main exit. Suddenly someone called my name. There, at the far end of hall C, broom and bucket in hand, stood Jean Mesritz. Not another soul was in sight. He put his bucket on the floor, leaned the broom against the wall and stretched both arms into the air as wide as he could, hands open, fingers spread. So he stood motionless between the blind cell-doors, a warm smile on his face, in a silent, unbelievably exuberant greeting. I waved hurriedly and rushed on, terrified that someone might still recognise me before the prison walls lay behind me. It was the last time I ever saw Jean. He died in Dachau in the spring of 1945, a few weeks before VE-day.

*   *   *

In June 1941 the German authorities opened Leyden university for ten days. Nobody knew why. As it came without warning after eight months of inactivity, nobody was prepared to take advantage of it. Except I. Submerged in my hide-out in Amsterdam, too scared to venture into the streets, waiting for Frits van der Schrieck to get me out of the country, I had continued my studies out of sheer boredom. When Leyden opened I knew more about the Law than would ever have been the case under normal circumstances. I applied for immediate examination, which was promptly granted. On 10 June, in accordance with hallowed tradition, I emerged from my underground hole in tails, white tie and silk top hat, and solemnly strode into the ancient building opposite my abandoned rooms.

Frits, meanwhile, was sitting in a harbour café in Schiedam, talking to a sailor. He was as pale and thin as ever, yet he had changed. His soft voice carried authority and there was an ease to his bearing, a spring to his movements. In less than a year he had grown from a colourless boy into a purposeful man, as happened to some people for whom the Occupation seemed to fill a need. After a while he got up, jumped on his bike and pedalled to Leyden, where he arrived early in the afternoon.

I closed the door of the examination room behind me and stood in the hallway. Now the professors inside would deliberate for fifteen minutes before announcing the result of my performance. The building was empty and hushed, few outside sounds penetrated the heavy walls. The high central hall, which once rang with voices and laughter and cheers for the graduated, oozed silence like a mausoleum. When in the gloom I saw the outlines of a figure I immediately recoiled behind a pillar. But it was Frits.

"Well?" I asked, tensely.

"A strange business," he answered. "It's a Swiss ship sailing under Panamese flag. A Swiss captain, for Christ's sake! The official line is that it will go to the U.S.A., in charter for the Spanish government, to load grain. But you wouldn't believe the rumours which are floating around: munitions, Russia, North Cape, supply ship for U-boats – take your pick. They're having a tough time getting a crew together."

"What do you think? Yes or no?"

"Yes."

"O.K. How? When?"

Frits looked pleased. He talked softly and hardly moved his lips. "I thought you'd say that. It's all fixed. I got you on as cabin-boy. She sails in about two weeks, destination unknown. I'll let you know when. Plan to be on board forty-eight hours before. Report to the bo'sun. The ship is called —"

The door of the examination room opened, the beadle motioned me in. He rapped the floor three times with his staff before closing the door behind me. A few minutes later I was back in the hall, a fully-fledged Doctor of Law. Frits was no longer alone. Jacques Maasland came towards me, positively beaming. "My dear fellow, congratulations! A great occasion!" He shook my hand endlessly. He appeared genuinely delighted.

"My God, Jacques," I said, with a vivid recollection of our short telephone conversation after the Leyden Manifesto. "Don't tell me you bicycled here all the way from The Hague for this?"

"Of course I did, old boy. First Doctor of Law, class of '37! A great occasion, greatest day of your life. I'd come from anywhere for that." He patted me on the back. I looked at him, fascinated — the earnest, decent face, the fine features, his immaculate suit. In spite of everything I found myself admiring his stubborn refusal to change. He had set his course through life, no inconveniences like wars, surrenders or enemy occupations would budge Jacques Maasland from his chosen path. In the empty hall he stood like a remnant of the old Leyden, lost, yet somehow indestructible.

"*St. Cergue*," Frits whispered, while Jacques went to fetch my hat from the window-sill. "She's called the *St. Cergue* and she lies moored in Schiedam. You'll hear from me."

"Well, doctor," Jacques called. "Where's the champagne? I trust it's on ice?"

The stone of the spiral staircase was hollowed by centuries of students' feet. I pushed the top hat to the back of my head, put one arm around Frits' shoulder and the other around Jacques. Together we walked down the steps, out the gate and into the slow curve of the Rapenburg.

VIII

NOBODY KNEW WHERE SHE CAME FROM, NOBODY KNEW WHERE SHE
was headed. Like a grubby hunk of mystery she lay moored at the
quayside in Schiedam. She didn't look quite serious. From the
middle of an 18,000-ton hull rose a single funnel, tall and thin.
Below it, from deck to water-line, the centre section of her sides had
been painted bright red with an enormous white cross – the flag of
yodelling mountaineers in land-locked Switzerland. From her stern
flapped the bizarre banner of a Central American republic; two
stars, one red, one blue. On the bow, in dirty white letters, stood the
name: *ST. CERGUE*. On the day of her departure, the only realistic
note was the slate-grey policevan on the pier and the German
soldiers guarding the gangway.

Jean de Kuyper, of the jenever and cordials family, had given me a
tip weeks before that somewhere in the river near Schiedam a
freighter lay anchored which was scheduled to sail abroad. Its
captain was supposedly signing on crew. The whole thing sounded
like a jenever-inspired tale to me. Besides, Leyden had just been re-
opened and in a few days I would be taking my final examinations.
I couldn't be bothered to investigate, but I did mention the rumour
to Frits.

"Why don't I nose around a bit?" he suggested. "By the way, just
in case, are you a registered seaman?"

I nodded, I had worked on ships before. Then we started laughing. The Seaman's Registration Book, while essential for employ-

66

ment in the merchant marine, was an official document showing not only my real name but also a picture. It struck us as funny that I might come out of hiding from the Gestapo to apply legally for a one-way journey to freedom. Even if I were hired it would be a miracle if I passed the inevitable identity check without landing in the Orange Hotel. But nosing around could do no harm.

To our surprise the tip had proved correct. On the very day that Frits arrived in Schiedam, the *St. Cergue* pulled into harbour in preparation for a late June sailing. But her destination remained a mystery. The rumours which filled the local cafés agreed on only one point: the ship and every man aboard were doomed. Germany had just assaulted Russia, and in most quayside bars they saw us disappearing around the North Cape in a white arctic night, generally laden with explosives for the German forces advancing on Leningrad. No Dutch sailor wanted any part of this. Now the Nazis were clearly trying to crimp a crew under false pretences, hence the fancy flags and markings. Even so it wasn't easy, as shown by the fact that Frits had managed to sign me on with a minimum of embarrassing questions, as second cook and cabin-boy.

The final weeks before departure, if departure there was to be, I spent trying to inveigle someone to join me in the venture, but even Erik Michielsen laughed in my face. I had to admit that the whole scheme smelled of trickery and disaster. But if the Gestapo were after you, they got you in the end. I decided to take my chances here and now and finally stepped aboard alone.

When the Security Police came up the gang-plank we were sitting on hold 3, between bridge and galley — two sailors, a cook's mate named Toon and I. From their reactions to the green uniforms I gathered that only Toon really belonged on a ship. There was good reason for their concern: the police detail consisted of an officer and two sergeants, customary in cases of arrest with possible physical violence. Looking over the railing I saw a car and a large prison van standing on the pier. All the indications pointed to a full-scale identity check.

I might have known. The *St. Cergue*, a neutral vessel caught in Rotterdam by the German invasion of May 1940, and subsequently immobilised, had finally obtained permission to continue her journey. The original crew had melted away, so Hollanders had to be hired. Who could be expected to sign on for a journey without knowing its purpose or destination? Watching the Gestapo-men make their way to the bridge, the thought even entered my mind that the old freighter was only a lure, a trap for such as I who were desperate to escape. Certainly the Germans seemed to have come prepared for anything – except, of course, for the quirks of Dutch character which so often complicated their task in Holland.

I went into the galley, filled some mugs with lukewarm coffee-substitute and followed the policemen to the bridge. Perhaps I could pick up something useful. Our captain, a handsome Swiss mariner, stood talking with two German Navy officers. The Gestapo lieutenant was studying the crew-list.

"Well then," he said, after a while. "Thirty-four men. Captain, First Officer and bosun are Swiss. The rest, Hollanders. Thirty-one. Right?"

"Right."

"Identity check. All crew members on deck, immediately. Bring all papers and documents."

The captain didn't blink an eye. "Officers and bosun are aboard. The rest – " With an expressive gesture he indicated the little group on hold 3. The Germans walked over to the railing of the bridge and stared down on the three Hollanders, who pretended not to notice.

"But . . . three men? And this one here, and four officers and the bosun . . . and you . . ." The lieutenant counted on his fingers. "Where are the other twenty-four?"

"Hey!" the captain called down. "Where are the others?"

A certain amount of discussion took place on the hold. Then Toon got up and replied: "In café Sterrebos!"

"In café Sterrebos," the captain repeated politely.

For a few moments the police-officer looked at him dumbfounded. Then he pulled himself together. He had a round, vicious little face and in talking focused his eyes on a point above the captain's head. "Didn't you get orders to sail at noon?" he snapped. It was eleven-thirty.

"Yes."

" Didn't you get orders to the effect that, beginning twenty-four hours before sailing-time, nobody was to be allowed on or off the ship?"

"Yes."

"Didn't you communicate these orders to the crew?"

"Yes." It was perfectly true. Forty-eight hours ago I had stepped aboard and in the course of the afternoon the rest of the men had come trickling in. At noon the next day, twenty-four hours before departure, we had been called together amidships. They looked a tough bunch, mostly over thirty, except for a few younger ones like me who were clearly ill at ease. The captain had addressed us from the bridge, first reading the police order restricting us to the ship, then promising damnation to anyone who failed to comply. He roared and threatened. We listened and smoked, trying to decipher his Swiss dialect.

"What is the old man saying, except damn and blast?" asked Sjakie, a wiry little Rotterdammer with greying hair.

"Mostly damn and blast, and that we have to stay on board," Toon translated. "Compliments of the Moffen."

"The Moffen can keep their compliments," Sjakie snorted. "And their orders, too. What do you say, Cockeye?"

"I say to hell with 'em," answered the cook, who amply deserved his nickname. When at ten the next morning I served the second round of coffee – apparently my principal duty aboard the *St. Cergue* – I found the ship all but deserted. Led by Sjakie and Cockeye the entire crew had sneaked away to café Sterrebos, doubtlessly to toast an uncertain future. Now, half an hour before sailing-time, they still hadn't returned.

The captain shrugged his shoulders at the German officers. Hollanders and orders. . . . He dug a loose cigarette from his breast-pocket, lit it and watched a gull cutting sharply by the mast. This brought his eyes on me, standing quietly in a corner. "Beat it," he said, not unkindly.

The Gestapo lieutenant had given up. This was a situation for which his brain had not been programmed. Aware of his sinister presence, he obviously felt he had a right to find everyone aboard the *St. Cergue* in a state of acute anxiety. Instead, half an hour before departure the crew was absent drinking jenever in a local café. Against all orders. He paced up and down, shaking his head. The two navy officers consulted with each other, then called down some instructions to the soldiers on the pier. We heard them start the engines and drive off. I left the bridge reluctantly and positioned myself shore-side at the railing near hold 3. Ten, fifteen minutes went by. No one spoke. The bridge radiated tension. The harbour looked dismal and dead, only the gulls wheeled against the grey sky. Then I heard singing, softly in the distance, suddenly loud and rowdy as I saw the prison van come round the warehouse. It had barely stopped when the doors flung open and out spilled the crew of the *St. Cergue.* I could almost smell the jenever. The police-lieutenant jumped to the railing and shouted at the soldiers, who quickly blocked the way to the gang-plank. In the resulting confusion Sjakie stepped forward to argue the case, waving his arms about, to no avail. The Gestapo officer observed the scene with unconcealed satisfaction. He'd show these disrespectful Dutchmen!

After a few minutes Sjakie realised the ineffectiveness of his approach. Turning away he walked to a crane which towered between the ship and the warehouse and started to climb the iron ladder. Some sixty feet above the pier a platform protruded towards the *St. Cergue,* a few paces long. On the extreme end of it Sjakie took up his position. Now he stood on the same level as the Swiss and the five Germans, in line with the bridge, on the edge of a dizzying void.

"Good morning, captain," he said with dignity across the precipice. He politely tipped his hat. And then pleasantly to Toon, whom he perceived sitting on the hold: "Good morning, Toon."

"*Sie sind besoffen!*" the lieutenant shouted, visibly reddening. "*Ganz besoffen!*"

"What does the gentleman say?" Sjakie asked Toon, down on the hold.

Toon beamed. "He says you're plastered."

"The statement is accurate," Sjakie confirmed, not without satisfaction. He swayed slowly back and forth, I expected to see him plummet to his death at any moment. Apparently the rest of the crew had come to the same conclusion; some of the more sober ones had pulled a canvas cover from a stack of crates and spread it like a fireman's net over the spot where he could reasonably be expected to land. The idea was received with enthusiasm; everybody wanted to hold a corner of the net to help catch Sjakie and every time he swayed the noisy crowd at the bottom of the abyss moved faithfully with him.

"Captain," he asked, disregarding the German. "When do we sail?"

"*Schweig!*" the lieutenant yelled. To be ignored was the ultimate insult.

"The gentleman says: shut up!" Toon translated without waiting to be asked.

Sjakie looked into the void and tottered. Expectant shouts greeted him from below. "Shut up!" he called down. "The gentleman says: shut up!"

"Shut up yourself, or we won't catch you," a voice came back. Sjakie raised himself indignantly and looked past the Gestapo officer to the captain.

"You have wilfully disobeyed the orders of the German authorities," the captain said. He tried to speak sternly, but didn't do too well.

Sjakie understood the predicament. He shrugged his shoulders. "Aw captain, those Moffen. . . ."

The icy silence which descended on the bridge was broken by the police-lieutenant. He banged the railing with his fist. He was puce with fury. *"Es wird niemand von euch an Bord kommen! Niemand!"*

"Now what's on the gentleman's mind?" Sjakie asked Toon.

"He says, as far as he is concerned you can all stay in Holland," Toon grinned. He seemed to regret having missed the party in café Sterrebos.

"Aren't we allowed on board, then? Really not?" For the first time Sjakie sounded taken aback.

"Nein!" the lieutenant barked. "No!" his little round eyes glittered. At last he had them where he wanted them. He would show them. He would have to be persuaded. He raised himself to his full length. He strutted up and down on the bridge. He waited.

Sjakie digested this news in silence, wobbling gently to and fro on the tip of the platform, sixty feet above the ground. Then, with a heart-stopping stagger, he turned around. He pointed imperiously in the direction of Schiedam. "Men!" he proclaimed. "Back to the Sterrebos!"

A roar of approval rose from the quay, where the Hollanders shoved and pushed to get back into the German prison van. For such eventualities Gestapo training had failed to provide. The two Navy officers, who had kept in the background, now took over. They came to the railing and shoved the lieutenant aside. "Halt!" one of them called down. "Everybody board the ship immediately." Then he turned to the captain. "You're sailing without any further

71

delay. We stay on board, orders of German Naval Headquarters. There's a convoy waiting for us, three miles outside Hook of Holland. Not a moment to lose. Let's go!"

The lieutenant did not interfere. With his two sergeants he retired from the scene. If any identity check ever took place, I never noticed it. It wasn't always easy to be a Mof, especially in Holland.

The captain clapped his hands and motioned me up to the bridge. He pulled me into the chart-room and shut the door. "Get the hell down to the stoke-hold," he whispered. "Two of the three fires are out. If the last one goes, we're stuck. The stokers are so drunk, they can't stand up straight. Keep that last fire going or we won't get away. Shovel in the coal as if your life depended on it!"

It so happened that it did. I rushed below decks. I never saw the police again. One of the sailors from hold 3 ran down with me, a dark, handsome, Indies boy called Peter. Around his neck he wore a thin, gold chain. He seemed just as eager to get away as I, and when we stood side by side shovelling coal into the fire, half naked, black and sweating in the flickering heat, he burst out laughing. I had to join in. We leaned on our shovels and our laughter bounced around the hot iron plates in the bowels of the old freighter.

The *St. Cergue* limped down the river to the sea.

*   *   *

As soon as the stokers relieved us, looking bleary-eyed and morose, Peter threw his shovel down and motioned me to follow him. A narrow passage led us from the stoke-hold to the engine-room. Through hissing and thumping pipes, shafts like tree-trunks, wheels and rods golden with grease, he took me to the farthest corner. We stepped off the floor-plates on to the bare hull of the ship, from which they were separated by a space of two feet. "Well," a cheerful voice said, somewhere knee-high. "Another phoney, if I ever saw one."

I bent down and looked into the black void, straight at Bob van der Stok, another former classmate from my school in The Hague which had produced, amongst others, Jean, Carel, Erik and Lodo. One of Holland's foremost fighter-pilots, he had shot down two Messerschmitts in the five-day war, before the Luftwaffe over-whelmed the Netherlands Air Force. The last serviceable Dutch plane had taken off alone; predictably it never returned. Its pilot had left a debt of honour which rankled. I did not have to ask our passenger his destination or, once there, his intentions.

From the moment we left Holland the sun came out, and day after day it beamed from a cloudless sky. The officers stuck to the bridge, apparently disinclined to mingle with the shifty Netherlanders. In the confused and generally friendly surroundings it didn't take us long to improve Bob's circumstances. Sometimes I saw him sitting in a quiet corner on deck, sunning himself like a tourist on a summer cruise. As a special guest I served him his coffee — still my main occupation — before the German Navy officers got theirs. Then Peter and I would join him in his leisure.

We steamed north, up the Dutch coast, close in for protection against the R.A.F. — look! Scheveningen, the Beach Club, the Boulevard and behind it, the Orange Hotel . . . Noordwijk, the hotel Huis ter Duin from where the *Bèbèk* had preceded us all, a lifetime ago . . . and there the dunes we struggled through, and the beach on which we had washed ashore. . . . Where we were headed we still didn't know, but it certainly beat hanging around Holland.

We turned east into the Kiel Canal and lay in the blue bay of the German naval base, tucked in snugly next to the pocket-battleship *Admiral Scheer*, for four days with nothing to do but swim, fish and laze in the sun. Then we sailed north again, to Oslo. There the full moon brought out girls in rowing-boats who circled the ship, at anchor in the fjord, but the captain called us together and threatened to flog the first man who succumbed to temptation. We listened patiently — from the poop the ropes hung ready. Minutes after he dismissed us he was practically alone on board. In the middle of the fjord I met my boss, the cook, a woman in each arm, a bottle on his lap and twice as cockeyed as usual. Next we steamed south for a while, hugging the coast of Norway around the bend at Kristiansand until the compass showed north again, always north.

Of course we weren't really getting anywhere at all. We followed the German-occupied shores closely and remained as firmly in the Nazi grip as if we'd stayed at home. The nights of twilight reminded us of the dire predictions in the cafés of Schiedam, and every mile brought us nearer to the North Cape. But the sea beyond the coastal waters was British, and one evening I suggested half-seriously to Peter that we overpower the officers, turn the ship due west and make a run for it. He agreed without a moment's hesitation. By now I

73

knew his strength, or weakness: the plan was romantic, it was dangerous, what more could a man wish?

Midshipman cadet Peter Tazelaar, formerly of the Royal Netherlands Naval Academy in Den Helder, now deckhand and fugitive aboard the *St. Cergue*, was born in Fort de Kock, in the heart of Sumatra. As soon as I saw his brooding black eyes under the high forehead, the sudden exuberance of his smile flashing across his chiselled features, I wondered what wild blood stirred his soul. Probing, I asked him the story behind the little chain around his neck. He didn't answer. A princess' reward for saving her life? The glorified memento of a dull love? A Sunday morning bargain at the flea market? He glowered – take your pick. Who wants the truth if it's commonplace? Who wants reality if it's boring? The truth has a thousand faces. Behind reality loom larger things, vague, tremendous, mightier than fact. Only they are worth the effort of living. I understood him like a brother. I felt as if I'd known him all my life.

We decided to check Sjakie on the attitude of the crew. To my surprise he turned us down flat. "You can't do that," he said. "That's called mutiny."

"So? Who cares what it's called?"

"You can't do that," he repeated. "Not if you're a sailor."

"Not even with German officers on the bridge? In war?"

"Not when you've signed on as a seaman," Sjakie stated definitively. Peter and I shrugged our shoulders. What was so special about mutiny?

Anyway, it wasn't necessary. Fate had picked on the *St. Cergue* to make amends for the violence all around us. On one side, the dark horror of enemy occupation stifling the Continent; on the other, destruction and death in the streets, fire and battle on sea and in the air. In between, at peace, carrying its own untroubled little world with it, the ugly old freighter with its Panamese colours, Swiss markings, Swiss captain, German officers, Dutch crew, lawyer for cabinboy, naval cadet for deckhand, fighter-pilot as stowaway, all together in harmony on gentle seas under the clear, blue sky. Through the silence and serenity of the fjords we finally entered the toy town of Alesund. The next morning, while serving breakfast on the bridge – the smell of coffee in the early breeze, specks of sunlight on the sea – it seemed only fitting that I found the German officers gone, peacefully, and the coast of occupied Europe a fading shadow astern. In spite of all rumours the *St. Cergue* had been released to continue her original journey to New York.

Just then light-signals flashed on the western horizon. A smudge grew with stunning speed into a warship. It looked huge. The British cruiser, H.M.S. *Devonshire*, cut across our bow. We both hove to. A sloop was lowered, manned by sailors with flat, round hats, and minutes later an English midshipman stepped on to the deck of the *St. Cergue*. He couldn't have been more than sixteen years old. He wore a white cap with a little crown, and suddenly I knew that I was free.

I went below to pick up my gear – a toothbrush, two pairs of underpants, five socks, a gold cigarette-case and a favourite book, *Kai Lung's Golden Hours* – and reported to the English boy for service in the Allied fighting forces. This clearly presented him with a problem, but he requested me to take a seat in the boat. Here and there I said good-bye, without much feeling; already these people belonged to my past.

"Couldn't you wait till New York?" the Swiss captain asked, crossly. "The war won't go away, you know."

I wasn't so sure of that. I was in a tremendous hurry. "Sorry," I said. I meant it.

Bob van der Stok, Peter Tazelaar, a boy called Volkers, Toon the cook's mate and I walked down the gangplank and sat down in the sloop. "Do you have a cold or are you bawling?" Toon asked. He felt embarrassed by the tears in my eyes in front of the British sailors.

Above all else it was a moment of sadness, this step into freedom – an awareness of all I was leaving behind in the dark, a farewell to much that would be gone for ever, an end. "I'm bawling," I informed Toon.

Of course, it was also a beginning.

IX

IT BORE DOWN ON US, FIERY RED. WE HELD OUR GROUND. STEADILY the roar increased, the earth trembled. We judged our chances. At the very last moment we made our move, deftly, decisively, death-defying, and hopped on the moving bus to Piccadilly. It was the greatest excitement we'd had all day. We climbed to the upper deck, Peter and I, and took a front seat. Here you still had a view – the other windows had been covered with glue against bomb-blast. A notice pleaded with passengers not to remove the opaque substance:

> "I hope you'll pardon my correction,
> This stuff is here for your protection."

Underneath was written in pencil:

> "I thank you for the information,
> But I can't see the bloody station."

Above Green Park a barrage balloon, naked and helpless, sluggishly nuzzled the breeze.

On the corner of Piccadilly and Regent Street we jumped off again. The pavements were jammed with people, all of them wearing uniforms, clean, fresh and pressed. Except Peter and I. We still walked around in the clothes, now baggy, dirty and smelly, in which we had stepped off the *St. Cergue*. For a few minutes we admired the men's fashions in the windows of Austin Reed. Then we went inside and each bought a suit, shirt, tie, the works.

76

"Cash?" the salesman asked.

"I'll sign for it." I showed my identification and wrote my full name across the bill, clearly and legibly. I had them send it to Professor Pieter S. Gerbrandy, Stratton House, Stratton Street. Then we crossed over to Oddenino's for a morning sherry.

Stratton House was the seat of the Netherlands Government in exile. Professor Gerbrandy was the Dutch Prime Minister. The bill would undoubtedly shake him up. We devoutly hoped so. What did we care? Ten days ago we had arrived in London, and now there was little doubt in our minds: it would have been better had we stayed in Holland —

Every now and then under the Occupation Chris Krediet and I would walk by a house in Wassenaar for a special reason. It was the home of Jan Willemse, a military pilot who, after the May days of 1940, had been evacuated to England with remnants of the army. Everybody in our neighbourhood knew about him, and whenever a plane flew overhead at night, a little lower than usual, Wassenaarders in their blacked-out living-rooms would put down their books and sewing for a moment and look at each other with grim satisfaction: "That's Jan Willemse, on the way to bomb Germany. He's flying over his house."

Parents pointed out the neglected garden to their children, the shuttered windows which held the emptiness of the house like a treasure, a shrine of self-respect in the midst of humiliation. And if we saw Germans in the street where Jan lived, we smiled at each other with secret triumph.

Jan Willemse was the first familiar figure I ran into in London, in Sackville Street. Freedom is a miracle which shows in unaccustomed eyes for a while, involuntarily, and I had just arrived. I jumped at him and grabbed his hand. He looked into my face with embarrassment, as if what he saw there were naturally distasteful to a normal person.

"Jan! Good God, Jan, how are you? Where are you stationed, what are you flying? Do you often come over Wassenaar? When are you going next . . .?"

"I'm fine," he answered coolly, pulling back his hand which I had been shaking like a maniac. "I'm stationed in London. I work here."

"In London . . .?"

77

"That's right. Liaison officer at the Ministry of War. And you? Did you get out of Holland?"

I nodded weakly. "I've come from Wassenaar."

"Well, that's great!" His eyes wandered off to follow a girl in a summer dress, getting on a bus. He looked sharp in his uniform, captain's stars and all. Then he tapped me airily on my shoulder. "Drop in one of these days. We'll have a chat. No time now. Drop in for coffee, or tea as it is here. Around eleven. Ministry of War. Stratton House."

Off he went with a wave of his swagger stick, across the street and into a tailor's. I stared after him, speechless, a little ridiculous. Somewhere deep inside me something trembled.

Jan Willemse, the pride of Wassenaar, sat in an office in London. Major X, whom half Holland believed to be fighting heroically in the desert, sat in an office in London. Admiral Y, whom the entire Netherlands knew to be chasing Germans at the head of an Allied fleet, sat in an office in London. Hans Z, who was said to have been seen in disguise in a café in Amsterdam, sat in an office in London. And Chris Krediet, my own friend who had arrived here more than six months ago? After an hour on the telephone I finally managed to contact him, in an army camp near Wolverhampton. Wasn't Wolverhampton somewhere in the centre of England, far from any fighting front?

"Chris," I asked him, after the first excitement of our long-distance reunion, "what the hell is happening here?"

There was a pause. "What do you mean, happening? You mean with us?"

"Sure. With you, with all of us. With all those Hollanders here."

"Very simple," Chris answered. "Not a damn thing."

In the course of a few days my worry grew to bewilderment. All those Dutch squadrons that we'd seen over Holland? True, they were specks against the sky, but people with binoculars swore that they could distinguish the orange in the markings; we had hugged each other with emotion. Now I learned that since the capitulation not a single Dutch plane had ever flown over the Netherlands (except for the ill-fated landing on the Tjeuke Lake). How proud we had been, jogging along in the old Leyden tram, when someone whispered to have heard on the B.B.C. that Dutch troops fought with General Wavell in the desert! Now it appeared that the entire

78

Netherlands army lay encamped somewhere in the Midlands and had not fired a single shot in the fifteen months since May 1940. Only at sea did we seem to be at war here and there, anonymously tucked away in British formations.

But the hardest blow had come right after our arrival in England. The *Devonshire* had landed us on the Faeroe Islands, half-way to Iceland, whence a British freighter took us south. Again we sailed in small convoy under a bright blue sky, just like two weeks before, but now in the opposite direction. I stared for hours at the red ensign fluttering from the stern, but couldn't grasp reality.

The big moment when we first set foot in Britain came in Edinburgh. Scotland Yard agents met the ship and promptly put us in a Black Maria. "Security," they said. "Hope you don't mind."

"Not at all," I answered. "I suppose you're only trying to make us feel at home." The last car we'd seen in Holland had also been a prison van. Would we ever belong again, anywhere?

Under guard we boarded a train to London. It was packed with troops. The compartment, almost as dark as the endless night outside, smelled of gun-oil, bodies and Players tobacco. Amongst greatcoats and duffelbags white-faced British soldiers sat silently, erect and self-controlled even in sleep. Only by the orange tip of a cigarette glowing in the blueish dark one could tell who was awake. As I stared at the little lights, reality slowly penetrated my consciousness. I had to control myself, just as on that first day in the Orange Hotel. Transitions of freedom create changes of pressure in your soul. You must accustom yourself, carefully, otherwise you explode like a diver who rises too fast from the deep. When we reached our destination — the "Patriotic School", an intelligence and security camp near London — I had fully adjusted, except that occasionally I burst out laughing from sheer happiness. I didn't laugh for long.

The principal purpose of the camp was to obtain from the escapees useful information about the countries they had just left. At my first interrogation I thought they were pulling my leg. The questions had to do with facts so universally known in Holland, such old chestnuts, that I couldn't help smiling. It seemed ridiculous to me that Allied Intelligence should fool around with this childish nonsense. A British major watched me irritably from the fireplace.

After a while I began to squirm. With apparently genuine

interest my interrogators jumped on every crumb I gave them. I could hardly clear my throat without them taking notes. Could they really be serious? The next day I was called in for another session, the following afternoon for a third. Now the major himself took an active part, but I still refused to believe that I was telling them anything new. If so, then they knew nothing here in England about occupied Holland, absolutely nothing!

Finally someone put a question to me which made me jump up in disgust. It related to a subject on which Erik Michielsen and I, in my illegal period, had reported to England via an underground organisation in Delft. "Let's stop this nonsense," I snapped. "We're wasting each other's time. You know all about this business."

The major looked at me keenly. "What are you talking about?"

"I'm talking about the report we sent you on this matter. It so happens I wrote it myself. It gives the whole story in detail, and I personally delivered it for transmission to England."

He shook his head. "We've never received any reports from Holland here."

"That's a damn lie!" I burst out. A slow chill was spreading inside my chest. What about the Group Rudolf, who had collected military intelligence and sent it to London in weekly reports, week after week, until they were caught and locked up in Scheveningen? What about Han and Wim in Delft, who had built their own secret transmitters and sat up night after night tapping out their deadly messages? What about the Geuzen, twelve of whom had just been shot for sending information to England? Brave bastards, how dare this punk deny them all recognition!

"I'm sorry, but we've never received their signals here."

"What do you mean? Their messages are always acknowledged. They always get an answer."

"Not from us." The Intelligence Officer fired off the three words like bullets and they hit. I flopped back on my chair. I felt ice-cold inside. Could it really be true that in all that time we in Holland had contributed nothing to the Allied cause? That all those chaps at home were sticking out their necks for nothing? That all that suicidal underground work was pointless, because the Gestapo intercepted and answered every message, a game of cat and mouse with the firing-squad as its only possible conclusion? Or would perhaps the contact with occupied Holland be considered a purely Dutch affair, from which even the British were excluded? I didn't know, but I was damn well going to find out, on behalf of those Hollanders who this very minute were risking their lives under the Nazis. And if I found that the fault lay here in London, where jerks like Willemse pranced about while his very house was venerated by the people at home, then I would consider myself their outpost in this enemy camp.

"Now I'd like to get out of here," I finally said. "I don't have a moment to lose." The circumstances gave my words meaning.

The major nodded. "I'll get you released tomorrow," he promised. At ten the next morning I was let loose on the Netherlands colony in London.

*   *   *

"Unbalanced adventurers" — that was how the Netherlands Minister of War, Van Boeyen, referred to us. Many of his colleagues openly or silently agreed with him. "Fossilised fuddy-duddies" was one of our more restrained allusions to His Excellency and his associates, and to the vast majority of the Dutch authorities in London.

Both appellations were unfair, but both contained a grain of truth. Conducive to a smooth relationship between the escapees and the power structure in London, however, they were not. Both categories consisted of Hollanders who believed themselves to be serving their country to the best of their abilities. This was their only point of similarity. Beyond this we thought differently and acted differently, felt different and were different. We talked, and listened to each other's words in blank amazement. We acted, and regarded each other's actions with indignation and disgust. Sometimes it was difficult to realise that we were both mammals, let alone countrymen.

The most important function of the government, which had left Holland just ahead of the German army in May 1940, not without some arm-twisting by Queen Wilhelmina, was the maintenance of a principle: the uninterrupted legitimacy of the Dutch state. This required no activity of any kind. Those who had escaped from the Occupation — about fifty men between 1940 and 1942, and many more later, to whom the Queen gave the name of "Englandfarers" — were totally indifferent to such subtle points. They saw the Netherlands' mystique safeguarded in the person of the Queen; from the government they expected action. This expectation proved as vain as it was unreasonable.

The characteristic feature of a government in exile is that it has nothing to govern, except itself. Certainly, Professor Gerbrandy as Minister-President spoke for Holland on the rare occasions that its opinion was asked; Navy Minister Furstner had some ships and planes, and consequently did exactly as he pleased; Minister of Foreign Affairs Van Kleffens undoubtedly had to keep a few things going; there was a Minister of Colonies who read the reports of the Governor General of the Dutch East Indies; Radio Orange broadcast to occupied territory, and the handful of soldiers in Wolverhampton and Canada had to be looked after. But apart from this it was difficult to imagine, in the summer of 1941, what kept the Netherlands' rulers in London busy, except to make sure that everybody got his pay on time.

This forced inactivity was being administered by hundreds upon hundreds of Hollanders in Stratton House, Arlington House and other government buildings. They didn't seem ashamed of this at all. They lived in a world of jobs, salaries, promotions and raises, which to us was as illusory as were to them the cell and the firing-squad. Because they were all in the same boat they didn't notice that reality had left them behind, that there no longer was an audience on the other side for their tired old act. But to those who had just whirled in from there, the faces of their suffering countrymen before their eyes and the names of their executed friends on their lips – to them the situation in London in 1941 seemed a bad, bitter joke.

The early Englandfarers, on the other hand, were unfit for any society based on pre-war concepts of authority and discipline, respect for rank, title or position. They judged by one yardstick only: what is his record in the fight against the Nazis? They set their own, tough standards, and whoever in their often superficial opinion fell short, even had she been the Queen herself, they dismissed contemptuously.

Like supercharged particles flung from the cauldron of the Occupation we spattered around the arid Netherlands colony, and wherever we made contact, sparks flew. Genuinely bewildered, the authorities tried to screen us off from the community by sticking us in uniform and tucking us away as far as possible from London.

Most of us arrived penniless and had to fall back on the government in order to eat, so this ploy usually succeeded. Then another keen Hollander would sit disillusioned in some camp, slowly going to pieces or, if he was lucky, would see action with the British and hope never to hear another word of Dutch.

After a week I still didn't know whether or not contact with our occupied country existed. "Not a moment to lose," I had urged the British major, but for all the progress I'd made I might just as well have stayed inside the Patriotic School. From building to building, from waiting-room to waiting-room, from excuse to excuse I was shunted around and slowly I felt myself suffocate in the porridge of bureaucracy. Whether it was I or my dirty clothes, the subjects I raised or the intensity of my arguments, I made everybody nervous. If I touched on money or clean clothes they got rid of me politely, but if I used words like "Occupation" or "secret contacts" they recoiled as if I showed signs of leprosy. Finally, after hours of waiting, I managed to attain the presence of the Minister of War. His Excellency opened with the statement that he was really too busy to see me, whereupon I flew into such a rage that he, greatly alarmed, quickly terminated the audience by calling in the M.P.s and having me thrown out of his office and Stratton House.

Peter Tazelaar stood at the entrance waiting for me. After coming to identical conclusions in the Patriotic School, we had decided to team up. When he saw me being escorted into the street, he burst out laughing. Bizarre situations always delighted him. "Come on," I fumed. "I'm through with these bastards. Let's buy clothes, lots of them. Austin Reed's is just down the road. We'll send the bill to Stratton House. Let'em bleed. To hell with the bastards." An hour later we were sitting around the sherry bottle at Oddenino's, in Regent Street. The pockets of our smart new suits contained our total wealth: two pounds four shillings.

At the bar of Oddenino's, in 1941, Dutchmen of a very different stripe got together. Living outside Holland at the time of the invasion, they had volunteered for service from every corner of the world. Jan Plesman just walked in, followed by Taro Bosch. They wore R.A.F. uniforms with wings on their chests. They were operational on Spitfires. Taro still had a few months to live before being shot down, Jan would last a year or so longer, but right now I was green with envy. In a corner sat a crew from 320, the Netherlands Navy

Squadron engaged in U-boat patrols; Oddenino's kept a few crocks of jenever under the counter for its Dutch customers. These men exuded a quiet dignity which soothed my raw temper after the petty pomposity of Stratton House. They knew their jobs, they risked their lives; what more could a man give, what more could a man wish? Between us lay the Occupation, an awkwardness, a careful groping in areas where we couldn't follow each other. But it didn't matter – from either side of this void we recognised each other as equals: life itself was no longer our paramount concern.

Peter and I ordered another round. We got along splendidly. I felt protective towards him; not only was I a few years older, he also seemed curiously helpless sometimes, as if he needed guidance through reality. He spoke very softly, mainly from laziness. "You couldn't be bothered to talk a little louder, perhaps?" I once prodded him.

"Sure I could," Peter grinned. "If I could be bothered to open my mouth a little wider."

We ordered another round. Then another, and another. Then it was finished; the drinks were finished, the money was finished. "I guess we're finished," Peter said, with a flash of his smile. That was exactly how I felt: finished.

"You guys ever had a chat with Van 't Sant?" Jan Plesman suggested, after ordering us another round. He had overheard some of our remarks. "He's with the Queen. Mysterious chap. They hate his guts. Boy! They spit fire when they hear his name. They say he's a traitor, working for the Moffen. They . . ."

"Hold it a minute. Who is 'they'?"

"Well, those chaps over at Stratton House. You know, the government . . ."

That was all we needed to hear. For us no finer recommendation existed.

X

Françoise van 't Sant, titular major-general, head of the
Central Intelligence Service, Private Secretary and confidential
adviser to Her Majesty Queen Wilhelmina of the Netherlands,
stood before an open window in his study at 77 Chester Square,
London S.W.1, and gazed at a bluetit. It sat on the rim of a freshly
filled stone bird-bath, at the foot of a lime tree. It turned its head
to left and right, dipped it in the water and shook itself with a whirr
of feathers, spattering droplets like pearls in the sun.

Van 't Sant watched, motionless, every muscle in his face relaxed,
his light blue eyes without expression. Clearly he had forgotten
about us – he was watching a bird and giving it his full attention.
Without turning he pressed an ivory bell on the desk behind him.
There was a knock on the door and in came a corporal of the
military police, in khaki battledress.

"Oh Tepper, bring me a piece of bread or something?" The
order was put in the form of a request, as if Van 't Sant regretted the
necessity that for Tepper – and undoubtedly for many others – his
word was law. He had a surprisingly gentle voice for a robust six-
footer.

Corporal Tepper appeared entirely at ease. He moved over to the
window and looked at the bluetit drying itself in the sun. "Sparrows
don't go for bread in the summer," he stated.

"This one does," the general answered drily, without taking his
eyes off the tiny creature. That left the corporal with little to say. He

85

departed and shortly returned with a breadcrust. Van 't Sant opened the glass doors to a balcony, which protruded low above the square, walled garden. He stepped outside and scattered some crumbs around his feet. The issue was never in doubt; the bird flew up to an overhanging branch of the lime, from there to the wrought-iron fence of the balcony and was presently hopping about unconcernedly between the general's shoes.

"Rascal," Van 't Sant muttered approvingly. "Bold as the hangman." Tepper grinned appreciatively and without further formalities retired to his post in the hall. The bird made off with an oversize bit and disappeared into the tree. General Van 't Sant pulled the doors shut behind him, put his arms around our shoulders and walked us away from the window.

It was an ample room, furnished with taste to the verge of luxury. Books covered an entire wall to the ceiling, sofas and armchairs surrounded a wide fireplace and in one corner stood a grand piano. Yet, for all its brightness and comfort, something lacked. Not a cushion was dented, not a volume out of place. All the ashtrays were empty and on the shiny black piano the gladioli creaked with freshness. Something which could have been warm and alive had come under an icy influence which had frozen it into orderliness. Van 't Sant, passing his desk, automatically shifted a letter-opener and a ruler an inch or two, arranging them symmetrically on each side of the spotless blotter. Then he picked up the telephone, rotated it one half turn and placed it back in the cradle, so that the cord hung straight.

The Chief of the C.I.D. – "Centrale Inlichtingen Dienst", the Netherlands Secret Service in London – might have been anything from forty-five to sixty years old, but whatever his age, General Van 't Sant in 1941 was clearly at the peak of his powers. Trim in his dark suit, a pearl under the knot of his grey tie, his face smooth and sun-lamp-tanned, the thin strands of steel-grey hair carefully brushed back over the spacious cranium, he moved through the room like an integral part of it, decorative, impeccable. He hummed the *Andante* from the *Symphonie Pathétique*. Van 't Sant was thinking.

Suddenly he stopped at the couch where Peter Tazelaar and I sat waiting for an opening. He bent down very close to us. "This is where we do some *real* talking," he said with his soft voice, as if he

86

had arrived at some conclusion which escaped us. He smiled, all charm.

We came straight to the point. In an instant his face tensed around watchful eyes. Every feature seemed focused on a distant spot, like the motionless head of a tiger who out of a thousand indeterminate jungle-sounds has picked up the one meaningful rustle.

*　　*　　*

We had met General Van 't Sant once before, when as yet he meant nothing to us. On 31 July, shortly after our release from the Patriotic School, he had accompanied us to Stubbings House, near Maidenhead, where Queen Wilhelmina expected us for tea.

Throughout the war Wilhelmina received everyone, irrespective of position or social status, who arrived in England after escaping from her occupied country. At first we assumed this to be a reward for dangers faced in the process, but while driving through one scarred suburb after another Van 't Sant put us straight. The five of us from the *St. Cergue*, still looking like tramps, were sitting squeezed in the back of an army-green Buick; the general sat up front, next to the driver.

"These meetings are most important to her," he said. For reasons of security he never referred to the Queen by name or title. "More than any other meetings, even with ministers and people like that. It's very exciting for her."

"Why?"

"It's all she's really interested in; the people in Holland. England-farers like you are the people, the only ones she has a chance to meet. Only from you can she find out what is really happening over there. It's all she lives for."

"What's she like?" I asked. In common with almost everyone in the Netherlands I knew little about our Queen, as one knows little about the moon: there it is, always has been, always will be. Very familiar, very unknown. It's difficult to recall how it got there and in what way it affects our lives, but it obviously belongs where it is and fulfils its purpose, whatever that may be. And is somehow comforting to have around.

On 3 May 1895, old Queen Victoria of England wrote in her diary, on the occasion of her meeting with Queen Wilhelmina: "The young Queen, who will be fifteen in August, has her hair still hanging

87

down. She is very slight and graceful, has fine features, and seems to be very intelligent and a charming child. She speaks English extremely well, and has very pretty manners." Wilhelmina had obviously been on her best behaviour and displayed none of the temper and impatience which she had inherited from her father, King William III. Almost half a century later, however, Winston Churchill was moved to confess to a friend: "I really fear no man in the world – except Queen Wilhelmina of Holland." If this story is true, then she was one up on him; for she feared no one, not even Winston.

When I first saw her ride through The Hague in her Golden Carriage, bouncing back and forth in the seat, she had already reigned twice as long as I had lived. I had cheered myself hoarse, but the idea that in spite of being Queen she was also a human being never crossed my mind. Had she known this, she would have approved. She had never heard of public relations and detested publicity. She glowered into cameras as if they were deadly weapons and had never held a press conference. She communicated with her people through the appropriate channels and considered her private life to be nobody's business but her own.

In the absence of knowledge, I worried about the rumours which surrounded her: you must never say "no" to the Queen, resulting in weird replies such as: "Yes, Your Majesty, I don't have a cold"; you must walk backwards out of her presence, until you're out of sight; you must never offer her any physical assistance, even if she falls right in front of you; smoking was not allowed within a hundred yards of her; and, faced by his displeasure, generals were known to have wet their pants. If these stories were true – and at some point most of them were – they seemed hardly conducive to a relaxed afternoon tea.

"Just be yourself," Van 't Sant answered, accurately sensing the real purpose behind my question. "Address her as 'Your Majesty' and behave as you would around any distinguished old lady."

We were ushered into a study full of portraits and pictures, many overlaid with snapshots of family groups centring around the Queen's only daughter, Princess Juliana, her son-in-law Prince Bernhard and her two little grand-daughters, the Princesses Beatrix and Irene. Dogs were much in evidence. There was one framed picture of a horse. Within minutes the door opened wide and on the threshold stood Wilhelmina of Orange-Nassau, aged sixty-one, in the forty-fourth year of her reign as Queen of the Netherlands. She was small and pear-shaped, but held herself so straight that the impression conveyed was one of height. Her grey eyes, set close together, regarded us in silence, while a shy half-smile appeared on her lips. Then she did a curious thing. She made an awkward bow in our direction. In doing so she looked slightly over our heads, creating the impression that her solemn greeting concerned not so much ourselves as our nation behind us, lost in the darkness from which we had miraculously emerged as its anointed ambassadors.

We must have disappointed the Queen that afternoon. All my life I had seen her image, on coins, stamps, posters, in books, magazines, newsreels, even for a magic moment as a puppet in a gold coach – suddenly face to face I needed time to get down to earth. Instead of talking intelligently I had trouble suppressing an urge to pinch her arm, to see if she was real. Furthermore, we simply couldn't bring ourselves to destroy the fairy-tale by hitting the fairy with negative news. One doesn't emerge from the galley of the *St. Cergue* and inform the Queen of the Netherlands of one's opinion that her government is a bunch of fossilised fuddy-duddies – how was I to know that she would heartily have agreed? We were guests of Royalty, it was a lovely day, and every disagreeable subject that somehow raised its head we killed off on the spot. Wilhelmina, with neither inclination nor talent for small talk, tried unsuccessfully to bring the conversation to a meaningful level.

"Once the Moffen are gone, what are we to do with those unspeakable quislings?" she brought up. We had gone out into the mellow afternoon and were sitting along a tea-table on the lawn, in the shade of a chestnut tree: the Queen, her lady-in-waiting, General Van 't Sant and we five strangely attired crew-members of the *St. Cergue*. Toon the cook's mate fielded this one. He spoke gently, soothingly, and at any moment I expected to see him reach across the table and pat his royal hostess reassuringly on the arm. "Her Majesty," he began – it sounded more familiar to his ears than "Your", which lay outside his experience – "Her Majesty, don't you worry your head about those bastards. We shall personally tear out their guts for you."

Wilhelmina, whose impatience had been about to flash into the open, gave in and smiled. The conversation, which had been faltering, died down altogether. For a full minute there was silence. The lady-in-waiting imperturbably poured tea. Between the two elderly noblewomen Peter Tazelaar darkled like a stray buccaneer. Involuntarily I glanced down the table for the Dormouse and the Mad Hatter.

"It's not easy to meet new people," Queen Wilhelmina once confided to me. "I must never forget that for them it's a memorable occasion. Therefore I must always be at my best so that I don't disappoint them." However kind her consideration, it contributed to the aura of unreality which surrounded first meetings with the sovereign. The long table looked cheerful, homey and Dutch. The silver shot out sparks in the sun. Peter had started a conversation with the lady-in-waiting – who shared the fate of all women, irrespective of age, and gazed captivated into his dark, restless eyes. Her Majesty was still involved with Toon, darting sidelong glances at him from time to time like a skittish thoroughbred, a fixed smile on her lips in nervous anticipation of the cook's mate's next broadside. Bob van der Stok, both hands in flowing motion, demonstrated the course of an aerial dogfight to Volkers. General Van 't Sant stared unseeing into the distance, humming softly. Shadows of clouds flitted across the grass towards a mighty cedar at the end of the lawn. It was a charming scene, full of sun and ripe colours and the sad evanescence of an English summer afternoon, around lonely people far from home who touched each other shyly. But with reality it had no connection.

Then Van 't Sant leaned over to Tazelaar and asked: "You're a midshipman, aren't you? Did you ever know a young navy lieutenant . . . Van Hamel? Lodo van Hamel?"

The words were "did you", not "do you". Apparently Lodo, after the betrayal at the Tjeuke Lake and his many months in the Orange Hotel, had now been shot by the Germans. *This* was reality, and it struck me that the general knew about it. That he was head of the Secret Service we did not discover until our visit to 77 Chester Square —

While we finished our drinks at Oddenino's, Jan Plesman had telephoned general Van 't Sant. Jan's father was the founder of the world's first airline, K.L.M., and Jan's connections were superb.

"Can you make it this afternoon?" he shouted across the room, to our astonishment.

"Tell him we're on our way," I called back.

After so much sherry a little fresh air seemed a good idea. We walked through Green Park, past Buckingham Palace. London sparkled in another day of sunshine. There had been no bombing for weeks and the town seemed to be catching its breath. Something trembled in the air, a wish, a hope that perhaps the struggle had entered a new phase. New names covered the front pages – Kiev, Smolensk, Sidi Barrani, North Atlantic – no less critical or deadly, but farther away! People still jammed the subways at night and yet, in August 1941, London breathed the summer air more deeply and the lovers in the parks heard the birds bustling in the bushes once again.

Chester Square, behind Buckingham Palace, had been one of the best addresses in London. Now most of the houses stood empty. Windows were covered with cardboard or stared darkly out into the street. Here and there shrapnel had pitted a graceful façade, as if a giant had hurled a handful of pebbles. In two places a direct hit had punched a gap in the row of houses, exposing dingy back-alleys. The rubble had been cleared, and the foundations showed the lay-out of the vanished homes – rooms, a lavatory, steps to the cellar. In the middle of the debris a chunk of wall still stood, its paper intact: little bears and monkeys. From the bare stone grew grass and moss and a splash of loosestrife.

No. 77, Queen Wilhelmina's residence in London, stood in a corner. On 16 April 1941, it had been hit by a bomb. The damage was repaired, but the front looked shabby and badly needed a coat of paint. However, painting required a special permit not available to ordinary citizens, and Wilhelmina would not hear of it.

We had just sat down in the general's office when a tall young man in R.A.F. uniform opened the door, without knocking. "I'm Bernhard," he said simply, shaking hands all around. "My mother-in-law told me about your visit in Maidenhead. I just wanted to say hello. If there's anything I can do for you, just let me know." He smiled and left.

"Christ," Peter muttered, staring after the Prince. "That sure beats getting thrown out of Stratton House."

"Things are different here," Van 't Sant explained. "All they care about here is the people in Holland. Especially the old lady. If she thinks it's for the good of the people at home, she'll walk all over the government-in-exile any time."

Peter and I looked at each other, obviously thinking along the same lines: Stratton House was not the only source of authority – there was the Queen, and the Prince, and General Van 't Sant, and maybe others for whom we were not "unbalanced adventurers" but representatives of the Netherlands people under enemy occupation. Queen and People, Orange and the Netherlands, it was a true and tried combination. What did we need this lousy government for? The bitter disappointment which almost undid us in London came to a turning-point in the study of General Van 't Sant at 77 Chester Square.

Finally we broached the subject of our visit. "We would like to know if there is contact with occupied Holland," I said. "The British told us that there is not. Surely that's not true?"

Van 't Sant looked at me unblinkingly. The head of the C.I.D. was an old hand at the game. In World War I, as chief of the river police in neutral Rotterdam, he had operated a counter-espionage network on which both German and British secret services leaned heavily. His personal sympathies were with the Allies, and when an enemy spy called Mata Hari – Indonesian for "Eye of Day", the sun – became too successful, Van 't Sant was sent to Paris to arrange for her arrest.

"What was she like?" I once asked him.

"Ordinary Dutch girl," he answered. "Greetje Zelle was her name. A bit Indies, of course."

"Was she attractive?"

"Not very, really. Good figure, though."

"Did you and she ever . . . well, you know . . . did you ever really get together, sort of . . .?"

Then, just as now, Van 't Sant gave me his most typical answer: silence. Disinclined to impart confidential information he just looked straight ahead, not moving a muscle, apparently entirely comfortable in his cloak of secrecy. He considered this one of the legitimate gambits of conversation. After vainly repeating the question, you were forced to draw your own conclusions; this had the effect of strengthening the original leanings of your mind. With regard to Mata Hari it merely titillated my curiosity; in the case of occupied Holland it reinforced our terrible doubts.

I went to the window and stared out over the garden. The bluetit, back on the rim of the bird-bath, cocked its head at me expectantly. When after a while I turned around, the general, to whom time meant nothing, sat quietly waiting next to Peter. "We have a plan," I began. "By sea. At night. To the beach at Scheveningen. . . ."

An hour later we took our leave. As we walked out of the door Van 't Sant was already patting the creases out of cushions and emptying ashtrays. He hummed a passage from "Dance of the Hours". He had approved our plan in principle, now he must find someone in the cabinet willing to cover it with ministerial responsibility. The choice was simple. Only one minister possessed the fighting spirit to stand behind such an audacious scheme: the Prime Minister himself, Professor Pieter S. Gerbrandy, the little Friesian with the big whiskers.

He went to the desk and picked up the phone. "Oh Miss," he said to the operator, as if asking her a favour. "Would you please connect me with the Walrus?"

XI

"Contact holland" — that was to be the name for the opera- tion; choosing it was the first thing we did. Our plan was simple: last summer's escape attempt at Noordwijk in reverse, with a war- ship—a submarine or torpedo boat—to ferry us back and forth across the North Sea. We set the date for the first action at 12 Oct- ober. We still needed an official green light from somewhere, but that didn't concern us a great deal. Contact with occupied Holland was essential; we knew that we could achieve it, the details would just have to take care of themselves. Peter and I bulldozed ahead.

The choice of date revolved around the curfew in the Nether- lands, which the Germans enforced from midnight to four a.m. Anyone out of doors between those times aroused suspicion, espec- ially near the beach. Consequently our landings would have to be executed either before midnight or after four in the morning. For this we needed long nights, which also had to be dark. The moon- calendar showed 12 October to be the first date to satisfy both requirements; this was a full two months away, but I foresaw that we would need every minute of it.

We now cut ourselves off completely from all normal government agencies. The bill for our new suits constituted my farewell blast at Stratton House; from now on I fought the war out of Chester Square—77 Chester Square and 4 Chester Square Mews, an adja- cent flat above Queen Wilhelmina's garage which General Van 't

94

Sant had put at our disposal as combined office and living quarters. Any Dutch areas outside these I regarded as enemy territory. I never set foot in Stratton House again.

When we had moved into our Mews – a courtyard where in former times the servants lived above the stables – I called Chris Krediet in his army camp near Wolverhampton. "Come to London immediately. Don't ask any questions, I'll explain everything later. Bring all your stuff. No kidding, we need you here."

This was quite true. Our basic concept called for one of us, Peter, to return to Holland in order to establish one pole of our contact. The other pole would be organised by me in London. Its tasks would be to maintain radio communication with Peter and his successors, execute further actions into occupied territory for the purpose of landing secret agents and wireless sets and collecting intelligence reports, photographs and possibly people, as well as the daily running of the office and liaison with our British counterparts. This division of labour had been agreed between us. Neither of us would have it any other way – romanticists we both were, but on the ship of our dreams Peter saw himself before the mast, I myself on the bridge. In that position I needed assistance, an absolutely reliable right-hand man. Who could be more perfect for this than my friend and fellow Leydener, Chris Krediet?

There was a moment of silence before he answered, and then he sounded just a little taken aback. "But Jesus man, I'm a soldier. I'm in the army. You can't just up and do as you please in the army."

"Come off it. What the hell are you *doing* up there in the Midlands, anyway?"

"Not a bloody thing, to tell you the truth."

"Well, then. Think of the war, man! You can be useful. You don't want to sit on your arse all your life, do you? What's the matter, have you no pride? O.K. then, come on down. We need you here. Number four Chester Square Mews, S.W.1."

"But who is going to cover all this? How am I going to get paid? Who will keep me out of jail?"

"We'll fix all that. Don't worry," I answered vaguely. We had Van 't Sant on our team, didn't we?

Chris burst out laughing. He bellowed for half a minute. "Oh Jesus," he finally gasped. "Don't worry, he says. You really don't understand much about the military, do you? But I'm game, I'm with you. No more peace. Up and at 'em. I don't know where we're going, but let's go. Where is this crappy Mews of yours?"

Suddenly I was tremendously excited by the prospect of Chris' arrival. I had worried that our long separation might have pushed us apart, but now I could hear it, the brash, cheerful voice, the touch of an Indies accent, nothing had changed. Dams in Brazil, mayhem in Minerva, Kant and *Yachting Magazine*, Moscow, Petsamo, here we come, baby face and all, watch out! Fair, slick, cool Chris and dark, sloppy, supercharged Peter, two Sumatrans and a Javanese, how could we miss?

"By the way, what's your rank?" I asked, as a parting shot.

"Private," he snapped back. "*Mister* private, if it's all the same to you."

We were faced with one more problem before we could concentrate wholeheartedly on the establishment of secret communications with our occupied fatherland: we had nothing to eat. For several days now we had sponged shamelessly on others, but the word had got around. Towards dinner-time our popularity waned abruptly. Since we hadn't reported to the government, there was no one to pay us, and for some reason General Van 't Sant refused to advance us money. "If I do, they'll accuse me of having bought you," he stated cryptically. Who were "they"?

I found a pawn shop on Charing Cross Road and hocked my gold cigarette case for fifty pounds. That kept us going for a week. Meanwhile Chris arrived in London, ostensibly on leave; but he had brought along everything he owned. Just as the money ran out I received a commission as second lieutenant in the Netherlands Army, with corresponding pay – about the fact that I had failed to pass my "physical" in Holland I tactfully kept my mouth shut. At the same time midshipman Corporal Tazelaar and Private Krediet were actually assigned to me. They also got paid. I felt a twinge of conscience when I learned that all this had been brought about by the personal intercession of Professor Gerbrandy.

Now we were ready to roll. Officially we did not exist and everybody referred to us simply as "the boys of the Mews". Where we belonged and to whom I was supposed to report were matters on which we wasted no time. We didn't know, and we didn't care. All we asked for was the backing of a person with enough authority to

Tucked away in the back, our little H.Q.

General van't Sant, private secretary and confidential advisor to
H.M. Queen Wilhelmina.

From now on we fought our war out of 77 Chester Square

Peter

The 'Mews'.

Erik

Stratton House – enemy territory.

Chris

This enemy shore – Yet it was home!

M.G.B. 320 cheerfully whisked around the North Sea.

By Case I.

ROYAL NETHERLAND FORCES

Chief Liaison Officer

LONDON, W. 1
Stratton House,
Stratton Street.

August 31st 1941

Dear Sir —

        We herewith beg to inform you that we
have charged
        Lt. S.E.Hazelhoff Roelfzema
with the establishing and keeping up of all contacts
with our occupied country. Lt.Hazelhoff Roelfzema,
who has just recently left Holland,will be exclusively
responsable in this respect and has full authorisation
to act as he deems advisable.

        As we put our Intelligence Service at his
aid,we feel confident that you will grant him your
highly valued collaboration that has always marked
our relation.

The Head of the

Netherlands Intelligence
Service

The Chief Liaison Officer

Bernhard
Prince of the Netherlands

Seen by :

I typed up my own letter of appointment.

Colonel Euan Rabagliatti M.C., A.F.C.,
Head of Secret Intelligence Service
Section Holland.

Dutch Prime Minister Gerbrandy;
Churchill called him Cherry Brandy.

Bob Goodfellow, first British
knight M.W.O. since
Wellington at Waterloo.

Gerard Dogger hid in the
ice-covered sea.

Frans Goedhart was
condemned to the
firing-squad.

Louis Baron d'Aulnis de
Bourrouill, a very gifted
secret agent.

enable us to build "Contact Holland" with as little interference as possible. In General Van 't Sant we had just such a person.

We cheerfully set out to organise our new headquarters and went to work in earnest. At last we found ourselves on solid ground. But not for long. On 14 August 1941, two weeks after our first meeting, François van 't Sant, titular major-general, resigned as head of the Central Intelligence Service.

It was the culmination of a campaign of slander against Van 't Sant on both sides of the North Sea. By combining the widely disparate functions of Private Secretary to the Queen and Head of the Central Intelligence Service, the general had concentrated an unusual amount of power in his own person. This gave his enemies an opening. Eventually the government made known its view that this combination might one day seriously embarrass the Queen. Aware of his passion for the Secret Service they expected that this would lead to his resignation as Private Secretary, after which, as an ordinary civil servant, he would be at their mercy. Van 't Sant, however, forced to an agonising choice, opted to frustrate them and resigned from the C.I.D. instead. (After the war a parliamentary inquiry established the general's unquestionable loyalty and traced the roots of the smear campaign to personal antagonisms in the distant past.)

The Mews was on the rocks. In the plans of the general's successor, who transferred the C.I.D. from Chester Square to offices in Eaton Square, there appeared to be no room for us. Every day for two weeks I called him in an effort to establish a working relationship, but always found him busy or about to go on leave. Finally I felt I had no more time to lose – the words of the British major in the Patriotic School had lost none of their urgency. I borrowed a typewriter and wrote a letter to the Head of the British Secret Service, section Holland, who in the final instance would have to supply the ships for our crossings anyway, as follows:

"We have the honour to inform you that we have charged Lt. (*my name*) with the establishing and maintaining of all contacts with our occupied country. Lt. (*my name*), who only recently left Holland, will be exclusively responsible in this respect and is fully authorised to act as he deems advisable.

As we are putting our intelligence service at his disposal we are

97

confident that you will accord him your highly valued cooperation, which has always marked your relationship."

Underneath this I typed "Head of the Netherlands Intelligence
Service (C.I.D.)", with a neat little line for his signature. With it I
barged into his office in Eaton Square, unannounced. He was sitting
behind his desk. I put the letter in front of his nose for signature,
without a word. He signed. Ultimately Prince Bernhard, as Chief
Liaison Officer, countersigned.

With the authorisation of the C.I.D. in my pocket I could deal
directly with the British. Now at least things would begin to move.
Van 't Sant watched these developments not without glee. Knowing
that the Queen put contact with her occupied country above all
else, he placed himself squarely behind the Mews. It was all we
needed. Now we worked directly for the House of Orange, with in
the government one solitary point of support: the Prime Minister.
Never having met him I decided to pay him a visit.

Professor Gerbrandy, alone of the Dutch cabinet ministers, had
remained in the heart of London in spite of the Blitz. In view of my
aversion for Stratton House I preferred to pay him my respects at
home. I called him from the lobby of his hotel and asked if I could
come upstairs — my experience with ministers had taught me that in
order to gain their presence you had to press them hard.

"Come up in ten minutes or so," was the answer. "Room six."
He didn't seem a bit surprised.

I went into the bar and ordered a whisky. I found myself looking
forward to meeting the little Friesian who headed the Netherlands
government-in-exile. He was part of Stratton House, of course, but
Van 't Sant considered him a friend, and he intrigued me. In his
early sixties, leader of the dour Dutch Reformed party, Gerbrandy
had a reputation for uncompromising hatred of the Germans. But
it was his outsize moustache which fascinated everybody, drooping
incongruously from his small round face like the whiskers of a
walrus. Winston Churchill, who called him Cherry Brandy, professed to be fond of him, and the story of their first meeting still
circulated in London. After crossing a vast lobby on his short legs
the Dutch Prime Minister, who had rarely been abroad and hardly
spoke English, put out his hand to greet his British counterpart and
said cordially: "Good-bye."

"Sir," Churchill reputedly answered. "I wish that all political meetings were as short and to the point."

When fifteen minutes later I stepped into his room, Gerbrandy was invisible. Two gentlemen, sitting around in easy chairs, motioned me to make myself comfortable. The door to the bathroom stood ajar and judging by the sound the Prime Minister lay in the tub. From there he was conducting a political discussion along uniquely pre-war Dutch lines.

Suddenly the door of the bathroom opened wide and before me stood His Excellency Professor Pieter S. Gerbrandy, Prime Minister of the Netherlands. Around his waist a towel fitted tightly over his tiny pot-belly. From between slight shoulders his little head, held high, rose round and bald as a cannon-ball. Above the massive moustache his eyes looked out fearlessly into the world. This entire apparition stood less than five feet high. He was a fire-eater in miniature. He looked angelic.

"Gerbrandy," he introduced himself, with a rasping of g's and r's. He shook my hand, entirely at ease. Then laughter closed his eyes to slits and he added: "The clothes make the man."

When the others had left, our conversation lasted into the small hours of the night. On so many subjects did we find ourselves in agreement that I felt vaguely embarrassed about my blanket condemnation of Stratton House. Finally I came to the point of my visit and obtained his full support for our landings in Holland.

He walked me to the door and I took my leave. Then, just as I was about to step outside, he took my lapel between thumb and forefinger and rubbed them together, testing the material. Even before he said anything I blushed — it was indeed the suit for which I had stuck him with the bill.

"I say!" he exclaimed in his flat Friesian accent. His little eyes glittered. "That's a hell of a fine suit you're wearing."

XII

ON 3 SEPTEMBER 1941, A SLIGHT, BEAUTIFULLY DRESSED ENGLISHMAN strode into Chester Square Mews and rang the bell of No. 4. Hearing the buzzer I watched him from the kitchen window as he crossed the court-yard and entered the garage. We heard him stomping up the stairs, then he stood in our little hall. He came towards us and took off his hat. He had thin, reddish hair shot through with grey and in the top of his head was a dent the size of a florin.

"Awfully nice to meet you," he said in impeccable accents, stroking his tiny moustache. I stood in front of the stove, wearing an apron, a pan of slightly smoking eggs in my hand. Chris and Peter lay draped across the couch in pyjamas, feet on the table, reading the morning papers. Our guest turned out to be Colonel Euan Rabagliatti M.C., A.F.C., Head of the British Secret Service, section Holland.

England's secret services in World War II – not counting the security organisations – consisted in essence of two distinct and separate branches: the Secret Intelligence Service (S.I.S.), which applied itself exclusively to espionage, and the Special Operations Executive (S.O.E.), which concentrated on sabotage and the co-ordination and support of resistance in occupied countries. The S.I.S., section Holland, had as its counterpart the Dutch C.I.D. and its successor. The S.O.E., section Holland, worked with a Dutch military bureau known as M.V.T. Between the two groupings existed no operational contact, and, at least on the Dutch side, co-operation was minimal and reluctant. Many years later it was established that, while the S.I.S./C.I.D. combination contributed materially to the Allied war-effort, the S.O.E./M.V.T. had suffered one of the worst defeats in the secret service area of any war, as a result of the capture by German counter-espionage of a code by means of which they were able to lure many Allied agents to their deaths ("Operation Nordpol").

It has been suggested, however, that from a nationalistic stand-point the Mews leaned too heavily on the British. In practice we had little choice. The British were determined to remain the bosses in their own country and, until the Americans arrived, kept a tight and exclusive control of all military action emanating from Britain. There was another factor, too, which was well illustrated when I asked the English for a flight of fighter-planes for the protection of an operation, while at about the same time requesting from the Dutch a little steel cabinet for locking away secret documents. The former was granted in half a day's time. On the latter we gave up after three months of persistent effort, and the documents remained in a hole behind the mirror in our bathroom. If you had to have results, the British weren't the worst ones to lean on.

The appearance on the scene of the Rabbi – to which we inevitably shortened the name Rabagliatti – heralded a period of feverish activity for the Mews. We worked directly with the S.I.S., for whom nothing proved impossible. Yet, in some mysterious way, General Van 't Sant remained at the core of the enterprise. From the living-room of our flat, where day after day we laboured on the operational plans for the landings, we saw him pacing around his study, endlessly, back and forth, back and forth. Occasionally he stepped out on to the balcony, facing us a bare twenty yards away, sometimes in the company of Prince Bernhard who always gave us a big wave. On clear days he walked with the Queen along the geometric paths in the walled garden, below our bedroom windows, down to the end and right and back and left and down again, over and over, always half a step behind her. Apart from them we saw nobody, except the Rabbi. It seemed as if we were involved in an important family project which the general, discreetly in the background, directed by force of his unmistakable competence.

In broad outlines our plan seemed simple enough; worked out in detail it covered almost eighty pages. During the full moon period around 1 October a wireless-operator would be dropped into Holland; during the new moon period around 15 October we would cross to Scheveningen in a motor gun-boat; one mile offshore Peter, Chris and I, together with an experienced rower, would transfer to a dinghy; a hundred yards outside the surf Peter and I would go overboard and swim ashore; on the beach I would give Peter moral and practical support – such as the removal of his waterproof over-alls – and guide him to the Boulevard; after waiting five minutes to cover a possible emergency retreat I would regain the dinghy and the M.G.B., while Peter proceeded to an agreed address where he would meet the wireless-operator; after providing the latter with a safe hideaway, Peter would begin to organise an intelligence collection operation; as soon as feasible they would come on the air during a prearranged period when we would be listening daily in London, thereby initiating "Contact Holland".

We picked Scheveningen as our landing place for a number of reasons. For one thing, the profile of the hotels and the pier was familiar, alleviating the effects the black-out might have on successful orientation. Our familiarity with the town and the knowledge that we had contacts there in case of an emergency would also help us to feel at ease. In addition, the presence of the German naval H.Q. at Scheveningen made it less likely that that part of the coast would be mined, and most unlikely that they would be on the watch for secret landings in the area – de l'audace! Lastly, the night-life at Scheveningen was pretty gay; even in winter it would not seem unreasonable for a party-goer to be taking the air on the Boulevard or even on the beach. Peter would be put ashore in evening dress and smelling of alcohol for this reason, and we felt that his presence in the danger zone between the surf and the first houses would be less conspicuous in such a seaside resort than in a deserted area of dunes.

In the final weeks before our departure three unexpected problems materialised: first, it was decided that we were to bring people out from under the Occupation on our very first trips; second, the wireless-operator, dropped on schedule by the R.A.F., failed to come on the air to confirm his arrival; third, Peter Tazelaar fell in love.

The first problem was brought to my knowledge during a luncheon in Brown's Hotel, on 22 September, in the presence of Prince Bernhard, Prime Minister Gerbrandy, General Van 't Sant and Colonel Rabagliatti. In my second lieutenant's uniform I was immediately suspicious of this illustrious gathering and wondered about its purpose. Not without reason – the assignment turned out to be a political one, and I had always viewed "Contact Holland" as primarily a project of military importance. Instead of picking up civilians I considered it far more important to concentrate initially on slipping agents with wireless-sets into the country. Besides, we were simply not ready for so complicated an effort. I must have put up a stubborn resistance, for finally they informed me that Queen Wilhelmina herself considered the mission urgent and wished to see me at 77 Chester Square.

Much had changed since the tea-party. In the past few weeks the Queen had called me to her several times to discuss conditions in Holland, and we had begun to get used to each other. This did not always prove to be a blessing, because once we got down to business Her Majesty could bore into a subject with unbelievable tenacity, particularly if she sensed that I was not too sure of my facts. Before long, in sheer self-defence, I always told her the truth, good or bad, in straight language, and found out in the process that this was all she wished to hear. It must have played havoc with the traditions and niceties of the old court, but she never seemed to mind. On the contrary, I got the impression that she enjoyed our distant yet democratic relationship, as between people rather than Queen and subject, and that this new experience gave her ideas. One morning she suddenly said, almost shyly: "Would you like to smoke?" and produced a most incongruous pack of cheap Woodbine cigarettes.

Knowing of her fierce antagonism towards smoking in the past, I was sufficiently confused to take the pack from her hand and offer her a cigarette first. "No, thank you," she said primly, looking pleased. "I don't smoke."

At the base of Wilhelmina's wish to have us bring people out from her occupied country lay the conviction that there, and only there, lived and grew the Holland of the future. The few reports which reached her, something in the attitude and tales of the England-farers, her instinct as Queen of a dynasty which had led the Dutch nation since its inception half a millennium before, alerted her to the mood of her people and the stirrings of something new, something important and tremendously exciting, born out of suffering. With the bearers of that spark she wanted to plan the future of the country, not with a tired old government of which she once remarked, bitterly: "When the chips are down, they all hide behind my skirts."

I assured Her Majesty of our best efforts. On a sheet of paper she wrote in longhand: "We deem your coming to London desirable. Wilhelmina." I took it to Gerbrandy for signature by a responsible minister, after which the S.I.S. reduced it to the size of a fingernail. Then we placed it inside the double bottom of Peter's watch.

The wireless-operator, Johannes Terlaak, had been dropped into Holland on 29 September. The R.A.F. pilot had seen the parachute open, but beyond that we had no assurance of his safe arrival, which he should have reported by now. There proved to be no other suitable wireless-agent available on short notice, but we decided not to miss the moon-period and to put Peter ashore in Scheveningen in any case. Then, if he was unable to find Terlaak and contact us through him, we would bring him another operator on our next trip.

But the most immediate problem was Peter's romantic involvement. In the last few weeks our personal lives had become fairly chaotic anyway. Since our plans had been approved and we faced the certainty of our hazardous enterprise – and since the Rabbi supplied us with pocket-money – we felt an irresistible urge to live it up. We weren't exactly worried about the future, in fact we could hardly wait to get cracking, but our horizon had suddenly contracted to the moment of our departure and that short time we simply had to cram full of life.

We didn't get much chance, really, because we had much to learn and the Rabbi proved to be a tough and thorough taskmaster. One moment we found ourselves thrashing about in the pitch black sea off Appledore, on England's west coast, hanging on for dear life to the capsized dinghy in the fierce Atlantic surf. Another night we barely rescued Peter, who was bobbing upside down in the icy waves off Barnstaple, because the air had collected in the boots of his waterproof suit. One evening we unexpectedly dined as guests of honour in H.M.S. *Dolphin* at Portsmouth, Headquarters of Britain's Submarine Command – midshipman Tazelaar beaming between two English admirals – where candlelight glowed on polished mahogany and port in a crystal decanter solemnly circulated. Or we rolled on the floor of the secret pistol-range under Baker Street Station, where the rumble of the trains swallowed the noise of shots fired at cardboard Hitlers. Or we studied in a school with several exits, so that you never met the other pupils, and learned that in escaping from a moving train you should always jump from the right-hand side, thereby forcing your captors, presumably speeding along in helpless frustration, to shoot at you left handed.

But around nine in the evening, whenever we were free, we emerged from the Mews resplendent in our new uniforms, washed, shaven and polished for the girls. Almost by instinct we made our way through the blind night of London to our favourite haunts of the moment, bursting miraculously from the darkness into the blast of light and noise and humanity at Oddenino's or the Gay Nineties or the Cracker Club, for drinks and a first tentative glance at the "talent" in town. Then off to Hattchett's, La Speranza or the Chinaman for dinner with friends in continually shifting patterns of the same faces, and finally to the Suivi, the Embassy Club or the Coconut Grove, or one after the other – bodies pressed together on tiny dance-floors, a whirl of khaki and colour and music and laughter, everybody high on booze and war and youth and love and life. Why not? We felt we deserved it.

For Peter it wasn't enough. Every man – or woman – who volunteered to take the lonely plunge into enemy territory during the war was a special case. He elected, in fact, to spend what would in all probability be the rest of his short life in solitary, unremitting terror, knowing that barring extraordinary luck* his end would come violently, desolately and without the balm of public recognition. To sustain him he had the human tendency to disbelieve in one's own death; but he also had courage of the highest order and a sense of private glory. Beyond the humdrum, fearful fate of the spy, beyond all reality, he was attuned to vague, tremendous concepts which in turn made him unfit to be measured by ordinary yardsticks.

More and more we had to take Peter in our stride, those last weeks. He did as he pleased, slept whenever he was tired, ate whatever he could find and spent every cent he could lay his hands on.

* Between 10 May 1940 and September 1944, when the Netherlands south of the Rhine were liberated, 144 Dutch secret agents were dropped and landed in occupied Holland, of whom 28 survived the war.

He became ever more uncommunicative and when he started staying out nights we knew there was trouble — other people had romances, Peter Fell in Love. After two weeks in London we had barely managed to stop him from marrying the cloakroom girl at the Coconut Grove, now we feared similar problems. Three days before our scheduled departure to Holland he disappeared altogether. Two days later there was still no sign of him. Rabagliatti, suspecting a collapse of Peter's morale, became desperate. We knew better; somewhere in London a Great Love flourished.

"What if he doesn't come back?" the Rabbi asked.

"He'll come back."

"When?"

"In time."

The night before our departure for Felixstowe, where we were to embark for Holland, Peter returned. It was four in the morning, he had forgotten his key and didn't want to wake us up. But I was going over some final details and saw him climb over the wall of the Mews. "Well?" I asked, the moment he stepped into the room.

"Let's go!" Peter said, grinning broadly. "What are we waiting for?"

We roused Chris and opened a bottle of champagne. We drank and toasted, we laughed and slapped each other on the back. Now things would start to hum!

But under all the exuberance something vaguely disturbing stirred, although at first I failed to recognize it, something which I had driven from my consciousness, a bad dream exorcized forever, I thought, but which now seeped into our friendly, free little room: the quiet streets, the set faces, the grey cars, the stone wall, the empty corridor, and way in the back, alone amongst the green doors – Jean Mesritz, arms spread, fingers wide apart.

XIII

REPORT

on the establishment of the

CONTACT HOLLAND

operations

As per enclosures 4 and 5 (not enclosed), the first part of the operations had as its objectives:

1. the parachuting into the Netherlands of wireless-operator agent *Johannes*;
2. the putting ashore in Scheveningen of agent *Peter*.

ad 1 On September 29th 1941 agent Johannes was dropped by parachute over Holland. He failed to come on the air with his transmissions and was followed by agent *Willem*, who arrived in occupied territory on December 9th.

ad 2 The putting ashore of agent Peter constitutes the subject matter of the first part of this report. The material concerning the actions is taken from the "Operations Reports" submitted by me to Colonel C.E.C. Rabagliatti M.C., A.F.C., Head of the (British) Secret Intelligence Service, section Holland – Etcetera.

On 20 October Peter, Chris and I, accompanied by Colonel Rabagliatti, departed for Felixstowe. Two days later we returned to London because of deteriorating weather-conditions.

On 25 October Chris, Peter and I, accompanied by Colonel

Rabagliatti, again left for Felixstowe. Three days later we returned to London because of bad weather.

On 30 November we once more set out for Felixstowe, this time accompanied by the Rabbi's assistant, Lt. Charles Seymour. On 2 November we once again returned to London because of the weather. Herewith the favourable moon period had come to an end and no actions could be scheduled until 12 November.

We were bitterly disappointed; Peter, however, managed to get through the ordeal in pretty good shape, so Chris and I had something to live up to. It wasn't so bad in Felixstowe – the officers of the M.T.B.s and M.G.B.s, mostly peacetime yachtsmen, were a happy crowd who cheerfully whisked around the North Sea in search of action. At night, when they weren't prowling for "jerries", they kept the near-by Felix Hotel jumping. But the Rabbi was afraid that our presence there would attract attention, and when Peter's pistol – an awe-inspiring instrument of German make – clattered to the dance-floor during one of his torrid tangos we had to concede the point.

So we returned to London, time and again. Nothing depressed us more than to step back into the Mews, where the signs of our high-spirited departure for Holland lay all around. And every time, after a few days in London, the next start seemed a little more difficult.

In the days before the beginning of the second favourable moon period, we hardly saw Peter at all. God knows what he was up to. He rarely came home at night and he never told us where he slept. Not that we ever asked – by his sullen secretiveness Peter indicated that it was all entirely too tremendous for discussion. We found ourselves humouring him, and even Rabagliatti treated him gently, as someone whose time is running out. Peter promptly took advantage of this by requesting, and getting, exorbitant advances on his pay and allowances. No one cared to deny him anything, but neither did anyone ever worry that he might not turn up in time for the next departure.

Chris and I spent the days strolling about the West End, dressed to kill, buttons gleaming, Sam Browne belts buffed and shiny. We dawdled for hours over subtle lunches, pecking at black-market delicacies and arguing the relative excellence of various vintages. Then we walked up Bond Street and ordered suits and other unnecessary luxuries we could not afford, suitcases, smoking-jackets and silver lighters. After dark we ran wild. Meanwhile we kept an eye on the waning moon, projecting its brightness on to the wet sand of Scheveningen beach. When finally we locked our front door behind us, we swore never to set foot in the Mews again unless we had set foot in Holland first.

On 13 November we set out again. This time Great Yarmouth was to be our point of departure. Again the weather was bad and the crossing had to be postponed. The next day, however, we finally put to sea aboard the M.G.B. 320, captain Lt. Loasby.

M.G.B. 320 turned out to be a sleek little warship, not much larger than a tugboat. Three Rolls-Royce–Packard engines drove her to a top speed of about fifty miles per hour. The centre motor could also push her along in complete silence at eight knots. Behind the narrow bridge stood two multiple machine-gun towers, on the tiny front deck an Oerlikon rapid-firing all-purpose cannon. The entire cabin downstairs measured six by ten feet.

The operation of 14 November all but convinced me that the execution of our plan exceeded our powers. The bewildering violence of the sea on the fast, slender vessel, the murderous blows of the waves, the blind darkness, the gushing water everywhere, the inescapable cold, the stuffy, bouncing, tumbling cabin where we blundered about, dreadfully sick, retching and shivering, trying to prepare for a delicate landing-action – did we have to cope with all this on top of the danger of mines, enemy aircraft, E-Boats and R-boats, to achieve a point where we had to board a dinghy, jump into the freezing water and swim through the surf, cross a beach likely to be strewn with land-mines, outwit the Moffen, and finally go through all this once more in the opposite direction? I frankly didn't consider it humanly possible, and could hardly hide my irritation at the casual manner of the bearded navy boys.

Five hours out, at an estimated twenty miles west of the Dutch coast, the front wall of the chart room was smashed in by a wave. Accurate navigation was now impossible and the operation had to be abandoned. We returned to London.

"Sorry," captain Loasby had said cheerfully, as I took my leave thanking God for having created solid earth. "Better luck next time." Next time? I really couldn't see it. But after a couple of jenevers at Oddenino's and half a bottle of Bardolino in La Speranza I remembered the trip somewhat differently, and by the time we arrived at Le Suivi I was ready for the next one. Four days later we were back on the 320, in relatively good spirits.

We left Great Yarmouth at 2.30 p.m. in a calm sea. At about four o'clock, estimated position forty miles west of Scheveningen, the port motor developed a defect and simultaneously the ship took in water through the engine room. Efforts to repair the motor and/or find the leak failed, and bailing with all hands barely managed to keep us afloat. After about an hour it was decided to return to Great Yarmouth, where M.G.B. 320 arrived shortly after midnight.

The next day we tried again. About twenty miles outside Yarmouth the port motor developed a defect. No leakage occurred, and it was decided to proceed on two engines. Next, the centre motor developed a defect, simultaneously incapacitating the "silent" engine. Distance from the Dutch coast was estimated at thirty miles, and enemy searchlights were visible. Efforts at repair remaining unsuccessful, the ship proceeded on one motor. Two hours later the hydraulic steering system developed a defect. It was decided to steer by means of the hand-rudder on the stern. Contact between the bridge and the sailor at the rudder was maintained by means of two ropes attached to his wrists, by which instructions were transmitted. A few minutes later the ship's telephone system ceased to function. When in addition the weather began to deteriorate, it was decided to return to base. At 10 a.m. on 21 November, after twenty hours at sea, M.G.B. 320 put in at Great Yarmouth.

We returned to London. That evening we went to the Embassy Club. We were sorry we had ever started the whole damn business. On paper our plan looked fine, but obviously we had misjudged the practical problems. Too much could go wrong, and we hadn't even come near the difficult part of the operation – the landing. Never had Holland seemed farther away than it did that night while we sat in our usual corner, pouring whisky from our own bottle, listening to the music of Harry Roy and Marjorie Kingsley, cosy in the warm, noisy, familiar cocoon of wartime London. But the following midnight we lay at anchor off Scheveningen, in dark and deadly silence, a stone's throw from the pier.

*   *   *

At eight in the morning Rabagliatti had called us out of bed with the news that the weather had suddenly changed and Lt. Seymour was on his way to fetch us. We shrugged our shoulders and got our things together. In Great Yarmouth we drove directly to the harbour. When we went aboard it struck me how much we had begun to feel at home on the 320 – the cheerful greetings, the bearded smiles, the sound of our footsteps on deck, the indeterminate nautical smells, even the miserable little cabin where we had by now learned to organise ourselves. Shortly after two we rumbled past the outer jetties.

The weather was so calm that Chris and Peter didn't need to worry about seasickness, but I immediately went below to dress for the landing. I took off my clothes and covered myself with a thick layer of sheep's fat, cold and smelly. Then I struggled for ten minutes to fit my sticky limbs into long woollen underwear. Over it all I put on battle-dress. By now it was high time to hurry on deck, into the fresh air.

It was a still, dreamy afternoon, drained of all colour. The sea, shiny like mother-of-pearl, lost itself in the distance where, somewhere, it became sky. The 320 streaked easily along, leaning into a slow swell now and then, due east into evening. We seemed suspended in greyness, and all around was pale and peaceful – until suddenly fifteen feet away a mine stood on the swell, its horns higher than our deck, jet black in the dusk.

When night had fallen it became unthinkable that we were not alone in its blind emptiness, until a light appeared over starboard. A buzzer hummed through the M.G.B., ordering the crew to "action stations", but in view of our mission we preferred to avoid all contact with the enemy. The light turned out to be a buoy. Never having been this close under the hostile coast, Loasby switched to the silent engine. At eight knots we stole towards Holland.

Peter and I decided to turn in. We still had an hour to go and fell asleep in seconds. I was dreaming vividly of a football game when Chris shook me awake. It was 9.30 p.m. Dutch time. "We're there," he whispered. "Scheveningen."

We went on deck. Lying stationary in the water, the M.G.B. flopped unpredictably from side to side. Rather than go all the way up I stayed on the upper steps of the stairs, holding the hand-rails. Chris and Peter stood in front of me, huddled together against the cold. We peered into the dark. The outline of Scheveningen loomed against the sky, blacker even than the night. Our distance from the shore, though difficult to estimate, couldn't be more than a few hundred yards. Everybody whispered and the sailors wore socks over their shoes to avoid the slightest noise. At this moment the 320 took an unexpected swerve and I was thrown against the ledge above the stairs, where with typical English logic the button of the ship's siren was located. A wail built up which ripped through the silence. We looked at each other, stunned, unable to grasp the meaning of the deafening racket which continued unabated. Finally someone pulled me away from the ledge and the howl died down plaintively. It was the captain, Peter Loasby. In the hush he put a finger across his lips and said, amiably: "Shsh!"

An hour later Peter, Chris and I boarded the dinghy, together with First Officer Lt. Bob Goodfellow, who was to handle the oars. Prior to this I had helped Peter into his evening clothes; now, if he were spotted on the beach or the Boulevard he could pretend to be a partygoer catching a breath of fresh air, German naval life in Scheveningen being much the same as the British in Felixstowe, and its participants by no means all Moffen. I knotted his tie for him – even for this occasion the Mews scornfully rejected the use of a clip-on bow – and surveyed the end result: in the dim cabin Peter looked like a teenager all keyed up for his first formal dance. He grinned at me, but his dark eyes glittered unnaturally. I quickly hoisted him into his watertight overalls.

Seconds after pushing off we lost sight of the 320. From the black mass ahead of us came not a sound, not a single pinprick of light. And yet, surely, that hump there was the dome of the Kurhaus, and that long straight line the roof of the Palace Hotel, with to the left the summerhouses where we used to have all those parties? No doubt about it, this had to be Scheveningen. But the nearer we came, the stranger the outlines behaved, and when we reached the edge of the surf the big seaside resort had vanished like a mirage – nothing but rugged dunes rose up before us.

We got back to the M.G.B. with the help of a single flash of light. Now we had until 4 a.m. to find Scheveningen, provided we were prepared to execute the landing after the curfew. There would be a moon, but nothing could be worse than to return to England with another failure, after having come this far. We all agreed to accept the added risk. Bob Goodfellow ventured the opinion that we might be too far south, so we decided to start out in a northerly direction. Loasby kept the 320 close in, prowling along the coast on the silent motor. After two miles we saw some lights. We crept even closer inshore, where they turned out to mark the entrance to a harbour. We stopped to get our bearings.

"This is the fishing-harbour of Scheveningen," Chris finally stated. He had the sharpest eyes of us all.

"In that case, let's get the hell out of here," I suggested. We were lying smack in the channel between the jetties, and I vividly remembered the rows of E-boats jamming the outer harbour all last year. We heard a church bell chime, which surprisingly brought a lump to my throat. Then the slits of blacked-out headlamps came towards us from the left and Chris announced that he could distinguish the Boulevard. We pulled back and continued north just off the beach, to make sure, and minutes later almost crashed into the pier.

Well, that was that. Now all we had to do was wait until four o'clock. Loasby took his ship a few hundred yards out and noiselessly dropped anchor. Peter, Chris and I made ourselves comfortable in the cabin and slept till Bob woke us at three-thirty. Falling asleep was never a problem; nor was my seasickness which, I discovered, invariably disappeared in sight of the Dutch coast. When we came on deck a half-moon hung low above the horizon.

Once again we lugged Peter in his clumsy watertight suit aboard the dinghy and shoved off. I tied one end of a long line to my belt as a means of communication with Chris, who would stay in the boat with Goodfellow outside the surf. From there within his range of vision he would give us cover with a tommy-gun. Glancing back at the 320 I realised for the first time how miserably light it actually was. She stood out as though sketched in Indian ink on the pearly sheen of the sea and took forever to fade from sight, although Bob rowed strongly and steadily. With every stroke a green pool of phosphor whirled around the oar-blades.

Coming in from the south-west we had to detour around the pier in order to reach our predetermined landing place, at the foot of the German Navy Headquarters in the Palace Hotel. Against the dark land we saw it too late, and before Bob managed to pull out to sea again it towered high above us for a moment. From the tip of its curved promenade we were challenged in German —

"*Wer geht da!*"

"Keep going, pay no attention, just keep going," I whispered to the Englishman, who had reacted rather strongly. It was probably the first "live" enemy voice he had heard all war, producing a psychological impact to which we Hollanders were long since immune. Goodfellow had a further surprise coming, however, for Chris turned around and shouted back in a gruff voice: "*Maul halten!*" ("Shut up!")

After my first consternation I had to admit that it was a smart move. Obviously the sentry had noticed something which normally he would report, endangering our future operations, unless something persuaded him against it. After all, Scheveningen being the headquarters for the entire German coastguard system from Denmark to France, who could tell what all that brass was up to? It might be impolitic for a simple sentry to get involved. Maybe he'd better keep his nose clean. Besides, there was a familiar, comforting ring to the order: "*Maul halten!*" Not a sound came back from the pier.

As an extra safety measure we rowed a little further north before turning inland. An offshore breeze kept the waves down and with the temperature around freezing-point I cherished a momentary illusion that we might make it all the way by boat. However, when we approached the surf we decided not to take any unnecessary risks. Bob stopped the dinghy, Chris cocked his tommy-gun and while Peter shook hands with them I slipped into the sea to catch him coming over the side.

I could just stand on my toes. When the water streamed into my clothes I gasped for breath, but pretty soon the cold became bearable. Peter landed almost on top of me, the air in his suit keeping him buoyant like a giant inflatable toy. This time I kept him upright. I pulled him through the surf until he could stand. Then we waded ashore, hand in hand. Puddles of light clung to our legs and around the communication-line a glowing green band led to where the dinghy stood black against the sea, so sharply drawn that I could see the barrel of Chris' tommy-gun.

While wading I started to undo the top of Peter's overalls. Suddenly he stopped. Something was standing on the water's edge, barely visible against the dark land. Did it move? I drew my Mauser, but Peter walked on. It turned out to be a sign on a pole, possibly a warning against land-mines. From very close up we could read it: "Ladies only." We had landed in the women's bathing section of the Scheveningen Beach Club. It was 23 November 1941, 4.35 a.m. Dutch time.

A stuck zipper at this moment had formed the recurrent theme of my nightmares, but everything about the waterproof clothing functioned properly. In less than thirty seconds Peter stood before me in evening dress, dry, immaculate. I sprinkled a few drops of brandy over him to strengthen the party-goer's image, Hennessey XO, at his special request. We crossed the beach to a point from where I could show him the ramp to the Boulevard, still hand in hand. Here we both took a swig from the brandy-flask and said good-bye. In fact, we didn't say much at all. We just sort of patted each other on the back and abruptly Peter turned and walked away towards the black buildings. He disappeared into the night.

I stood quite still for a moment, very much alone. I felt a great desire to get back to the dinghy, to Chris and Bob. I jerked the line a few times to let them know that Peter had left, then I re-crossed the beach to the water's edge, faced the land and cocked my pistol. These were Peter's most dangerous minutes, but if he got into trouble now we could still make a dash for it and, covered by Chris' tommy-gun, perhaps reach the dinghy. Nothing but silence. I waited.

Suddenly I realised that near by my parents lay asleep. And Frits and Jacques and Mia. And Jean and Carel and Paul and all the fellows and girls in the "Orange Hotel", a few hundred yards away. This deadly stretch of land which we were stealthily assaulting was not only enemy territory, it was Holland. The grim Palace Hotel like a lump of rock, the Kurhaus there, dark and dismal, this cold, deserted beach—yet it was Scheveningen. I heard a church clock chime the quarter hour, then the whistle of a train. A dog barked, an unbelievably normal sound. Under this black crust something lived, and it wrenched my heart. Last year from the tip of the little stone pier to my left I had hurled a motor into the sea, despairing of deliverance. Now, returned from freedom, I stood like a ghost among everything I loved, invisible, cut off as if by a curse.

I was about to wade out to the dinghy when on the roof of the Navy Headquarters a light came on. Moments later it had gone. It worried me and I decided to keep Peter's retreat open a little longer. Again a light appeared, then another one on the opposite side of the roof. What was going on? Not a sound. The lights went out. The

115

communication-line jerked urgently—our operation was meticulously timed, we had to go back to the M.G.B. Everything seemed quiet. Gingerly I stepped into the ice-cold surf and a few minutes later Goodfellow rowed us seawards. The current had carried us north and Chris had to wave his flashlight a couple of times before the 320 came to pick us up. The landing action had taken one hour and ten minutes.

We set course for home. When after a while I looked back Scheveningen had dissolved into the coastline, but for a few seconds a speck of light flickered through the dark. I was exhausted; even so, this time sleep wouldn't come. All the way over I worried about the mysterious signals. Only when we neared the English coast was I affected by the general mood of jubilation on board—after all, we had just achieved the first secret landing across the North Sea, if not on Fortress Europe then certainly on occupied Holland.

The morning mist lay in patches on the water off Great Yarmouth. Slowly we approached a jetty which reached out into the sea, deserted. On the very tip stood a small, solitary figure, motionless, immaculate in British Army uniform, rising straight and tough from the wisps of fog around his feet. Colonel Euan Rabagliatti M.C., A.F.C., Head of the Secret Intelligence Service, section Holland, was paying his respects to the boys of the Mews.

XIV

"In the secret service," general van 't sant liked to preach, "you must discount all your unhatched chickens in advance." His words shot through my mind when, two weeks later in Scheveningen, the surf suddenly grabbed us. As the first breakers hurled us landwards Bob Goodfellow and I immediately jumped overboard. We hung on to the dinghy fore and aft and tried to keep it from capsizing. We were within our depth and for a moment it looked as if we might succeed. But all of a sudden the nose went straight up, Bob was yanked out of the water and dangled in mid-air like a bearded catfish, the new agent wireless-operator Fat Willem tumbled from the bow with a pained expression on his face and landed smack on top of Chris, who squealed as the wind was knocked out of him. The entire boat overturned and all three disappeared into the waves. In spite of everything I couldn't help laughing. The next moment I went down myself.

When I came up again I saw only Goodfellow, still hanging on to the dinghy. A strong undertow pulled us seawards, but when Chris and Willem popped up we managed to get the waterlogged hull on to the beach. Chris apparently had first gone after the oars and wireless-set – packed to stay dry and afloat – but these had rapidly drifted out of reach to sea. The tommy-gun and pistols had also been lost.

I took in the sad, wet scene. Hadn't I lived through all this once before, off Noordwijk, two summers ago? But that was child's play compared to now — now it was midnight, the beginning of the curfew, we were standing barely fifty yards from the Boulevard, directly in front of the German Navy Headquarters, in Dutch uniforms, with a secret agent and a British officer in tow, huddled around a water-filled dinghy without oars. And somewhere out there in the dark, unreachable on the far side of the surf, lay our only link with freedom. Already I was trying to figure whether my mother had enough beds in the house for this unexpected invasion —

When two weeks earlier Peter Tazelaar and I had waded ashore at virtually this same spot, the first part of "Contact Holland" had been accomplished: 1. the parachuting into the Netherlands of wireless-operator agent Johannes; 2. the putting ashore in Scheveningen of agent Peter. After this, Tazelaar's primary mission consisted of the creation of espionage groups, which would be supplied by us with a steadily increasing number of wireless-operators with secret transmitters. However, having had no word from Johannes we had to assume the worst, so that the contact remained in fact non-existent until we had supplied Peter with a new operator. For this purpose Rabagliatti's men had trained Willem van der Reijden, a highly qualified W/T-man out of the Dutch merchant marine.

Before Peter's departure we had amongst other matters arranged that if he failed to contact us via Johannes, we would meet him three days later, on 26 November at 4.30 a.m., on the little stone pier by the North Boulevard — weather permitting. This would give him time to contact and persuade the two people we were instructed to bring out with us to London, an assignment we still considered of little relevance to our dream of a military "Contact Holland". We also felt that we weren't quite ready for this kind of complicated manoeuvre. But it had to be tried and at least we could combine it with the delivery of Peter's new wireless man. When three days had passed without word from the other side, we prepared to execute the alternative plan.

In view of the secondary assignment the 320 was accompanied on this occasion by another M.G.B., while for the return journey an R.A.F. Spitfire escort was standing by. The first part of the crossing was effected at half speed, in order to reach Scheveningen at the scheduled time. Then, at about 1.15 a.m., M.G.B. 320 ran aground on the Brielles shallows, shortly followed by the other M.G.B. Many lights were observed, some at close quarters, which originated from enemy convoys. Half an hour later we managed to refloat the 320 and after standing by for some minutes proceeded north alone, keeping our distance from the shore. But by 4.30 a.m. we still hadn't located Scheveningen and so our plan had to be abandoned. Owing to sudden heavy weather off the British coast we didn't regain Great Yarmouth until 1.30 p.m. the next afternoon.

In such ideal weather conditions there could be no doubt that Peter had been expecting us in Scheveningen on the night of 25 November. Unfortunately, the sudden change in the weather precluded further efforts during that moon-period. In order to reassure Peter that our absence was due solely to operational problems, we took special steps. On 26, 27 and 28 November (through the intercession of the Prime Minister) Radio Orange transmitted the following message: "The arrangement with the Mews remains in force. All is well."

This broadcast, and Peter's proper understanding of it, established that our meeting had been moved unchanged to the next moon-period. On its first night, 9 December, we had consequently set out for Holland once again, with Willem in tow. The weather was dubious, but at all costs we wished to avoid the risk of confusing Peter by another failure to appear. For the same reason we had pressed on with the operation despite having reached Scheveningen less than half an hour before our deadline, the midnight curfew. In our haste we had misjudged the surf and now found ourselves on the beach, stranded in every respect.

"Let's go," I urged. It was fairly light, and we were probably visible from the Boulevard. "Let's get out of here, there's nothing else we can do. We can get to my house through the dunes." We had been briefed to expect land-mines in the dunes, but we didn't have much choice.

"I appreciate your hospitality," Bob Goodfellow said quietly, "but if you chaps don't mind, I'd rather stay here."

Bob was a tall, spare Englishman, taciturn and unflappable. His pale face and full, dark beard gave him a holy air, but one never knew what to expect when he opened his mouth. Of this I got an inkling during our first crossing, when I saw him searching high and low for his chocolate ration which I had just eaten. Chocolate was worth its weight in gold, even in the Navy. I decided to confess.

"Thank Christ!" was his reaction. "This spares me a long and tedious search."

To Bob, British to the core, the M.G.B. represented his link with the only world worth living for – England. For Chris and me occupied Holland still offered some possibilities, but I realised that, as long as the 320 lay out there somewhere behind the surf, Goodfellow would not budge from the beach. Obviously we couldn't leave him behind. I decided in any case that first I must take care of Fat Willem, who as a spy in civilian clothes would never survive capture, if and when it came. "I'll be right back," I said to Chris, who was trying to tilt the dinghy without much conviction or success.

I took Willem by the hand and we started across the beach. He shivered like a nervous poodle. The current had carried us north and a hundred yards or more separated us from the ramp to the street. To stay out of sight we hugged the wall along the base of the Boulevard. At one point we passed right below a guardpost on the sidewalk above us, and heard German soldiers talking. We now realised why they hadn't seen us: the sentry-post faced landwards instead of seawards.

We came to the ramp along which Peter had disappeared two weeks before, but this time I went up to the Boulevard with Willem to get him started in the direction of his hide-out. For this first night I was sending him to the house of an old friend, a resourceful girl with whom Peter had also established contact. At the very least she would bring the two together, and perhaps consent to function as a central point of information. I promised to come and see him as soon as I had tucked Goodfellow away safely somewhere. We shook hands. Even in the dark I noticed how miserable he looked. No wonder – for two solid weeks I had bolstered his morale by assuring him that he had nothing to worry about, and the next thing he knew he lay thrashing about in the freezing surf at the foot of German Navy headquarters. I wanted to say something cheery but couldn't think of anything, and the thought crossed my mind that probably I looked just as miserable as he. I slapped him on the back, and when he didn't show any sign of moving along I gave him a shove in the right direction. I watched him disappear in the darkness across the street, and at that moment the same mysterious little light on the roof of the Palace Hotel which had worried me so much on the previous trip, flickered through the night. I hurried off the Boulevard, back on to the beach.

I followed the waterline as the only sure way of finding the dinghy and almost immediately stumbled over the oars, laid neatly side by side a hundred yards *south* of the spot where the northerly current had swept them away from us. I wasted no time trying to understand this minor miracle and delivered them triumphantly to Goodfellow. Suddenly there was hope, assuming that we could get off the beach without being seen and through the surf without being swamped. Chris and Bob began to bail feverishly. Just to make sure I ran to the little stone pier where I should have met Peter, a few hundred yards north. He would have waited till midnight, the start of the curfew. It was now almost twelve-thirty, and nobody was there.

Fifteen minutes later we shoved off into the surf, two men on the oars. I dangled from the stern, as usual, to keep the bow into the waves. When I finally hoisted myself aboard we almost foundered, but breaker after breaker missed us by inches and suddenly it was calm around us. At ten past one we were back on the 320. As a matter of interest I kept a close eye on Bob Goodfellow, but true to type he didn't show a trace of emotion.

Fat Willem lost his way in the dark and was so reckless as to ask directions from a late passer-by. It being well into the curfew, this should with almost total certainty have led to his arrest. He was lucky; the passer-by happened to be Peter Tazelaar, on his way home from the pier where for the second time he had waited in vain. Peter, on the logical assumption that Willem was a Gestapo agent about to arrest him, almost gunned him down. They recognised each other the following day, at the hide-out, when my friend introduced them to each other.

*   *   *

After the operation of 9 December a confused situation existed. There had been no contact with agents Johannes and Peter for seventy-one and fourteen days respectively. Agent Willem, who should have put an end to this unsatisfactory state of affairs, had lost his transmitter at the time of his landing. Furthermore it was likely that he believed Chris, Bob and myself to have been stranded in occupied Holland and he would probably have convinced Peter of this erroneous assumption. We decided that the next operation would have to clarify the situation and improve communications through the delivery of additional radio-transmitters.

A few days later the Rabbi unexpectedly dropped in at the Mews with the information that Johannes, Peter and Willem were all three safe and sound, but unable to establish contact as Johannes' set had also been wrecked on landing. They were concerned about our fate, but Rabagliatti had informed them of our successful return to England and added that we should be expected at the same place – the little stone pier by the North Boulevard – as soon as moon and weather permitted. He had also instructed them to investigate the mysterious little lights on the Palace Hotel.

This was great news, but it hit us with the jolt of a low blow. Where did it originate? How did the Rabbi get it? Was there some means of contact with occupied Holland already in existence after all? Were we sticking out our necks night after night for nothing? Rabagliatti wouldn't talk, and we accepted the necessity for secret agents to be kept in the dark as much as possible, especially for those like us who might fall into enemy hands. We also knew enough to be sceptical of anyone connected with an intelligence operation, even our own, realising that in the final instance the end always justified the means. But surely this went too far. Not until after the war did I learn the facts.

When Peter Tazelaar stepped ashore in Scheveningen, five agents – not counting Johannes Terlaak – had preceded him into the Netherlands under the responsibility of the C.I.D. Lodo van Hamel was the first, dropped on 28 August 1940, captured later that summer with Jean Mesritz at the Tjeuke Lake and shot in June 1941. One of those who followed him had returned to London after a spell of ten months in occupied territory; another had been arrested and shot, while a third had drowned in an attempt to return to England. Consequently only one C.I.D. agent was alive and operating in the Netherlands at the time of our landings, and it was he who had transmitted Peter's message for him: Aart Alblas, dropped on 5 July 1941, arrested a year later and shot in 1944. One single agent – we need not have worried about the crucial importance of our mission. After a stormy session Rabagliatti managed to convince us of this, and at the start of the new moon-period we were ready to continue our efforts.

However, our next two attempts were abortive. On each of these nights Peter stood on the dark and deadly beach, huddled together against the ever-increasing cold with the two Resistance leaders whom Queen Wilhelmina had invited to London. Via Aart Alblas he had requested us to devise some means of warning him of our approach, so that they would not expose themselves needlessly. Once again we fell back on Radio Orange, which opened its nightly broadcast with the singing of the Dutch national anthem. We arranged that on certain evenings, when alerted to this effect by General Van 't Sant, they would have the anthem spoken instead of sung, thereby indicating to Peter that we had sailed and were on the way. On 11 January 1942, the general was having dinner with the Queen at Maidenhead. They had tuned in to Radio Orange. When the broadcast started he threw up his hands. "Now we're in the soup," he said unceremoniously to Her Majesty. The anthem was being sung as usual instead of spoken – such a simple little goof! – and Van 't Sant knew that we were well on our way to Holland.

In blissful ignorance we executed the perfect operation that night. Our new captain, Lt. Hall, pushed the 320 at full speed across the North Sea, in the process dashing smack through a cluster of four German E-boats who lost us in the dark before they realised what had happened. The navigation officer, Lt. Letty, took us faultlessly to Scheveningen. With a full hour in hand we anchored off the pier. At 3.45 a.m. we pulled away in the dinghy, nice and easy. On the dot of four we hove to above the surf from where I had to swim ashore. Pinpricks of snow punctuated the east wind, the temperature stood at minus fifteen and ice floated on the sea, rustling like cornflakes. For several days I had been fighting a bout of whooping-cough and fever, and I finally scrambled up the beach coughing and wheezing; but this night only a bullet could have stopped me.

The night was so dark that I could only follow the waterline blindly, step by step, but at 4.25 a.m., fully five minutes before the agreed time, I had taken up my position at the foot of the little stone pier by the North Boulevard. My heart pounded with excitement. We'd finally made it, here we were, the Mews, on the right spot at the right time, and in a matter of moments we would have accomplished our Queen's special mission . . . at last!

After fifteen minutes my uniform was frozen stiff as a board, and while an hour passed – minute after minute after minute – I slowly felt myself petrify down to my innermost core in the icy loneliness. Of course nobody came.

XV

In the night of 17 January the two resistance leaders were arrested on the Boulevard, on their way to meet us. Peter and his closest collaborator, midshipman Gerard Dogger, escaped the same fate by hiding for more than an hour up to their necks in the ice-covered sea. In due time the captives were sentenced to death. One of them — Frans Goedhart — managed to escape on the morning of his scheduled execution. The other — Dr. Wiardi Beckman — died in Dachau.

When we learned of this development, a week later, we did not reproach ourselves. Radio Orange, making no mistake this time, had alerted Peter to our imminent arrival and he was ready. Aboard the 320 we confidently expected to repeat our smooth action of 11 January. But meanwhile the M.G.B. had been fitted with new propellers which apparently affected Lt. Letty's calculations. In any case, at the crucial time we found ourselves twenty miles out to sea and ultimately we reached Katwijk instead of Scheveningen. Still, at one point along the way to the Resistance leaders we had missed a mine by inches; we could just as easily have been blown sky-high.

Looking at it cold-bloodedly, this failure of our secondary mission did not really affect the essence of "Contact Holland". Sometime later we'd have another crack at it, but our basic purpose was to establish regular, reliable communications between occupied Holland and the Allied war-machine in London. For this it was of far greater importance to increase the number of agents in the Netherlands and, above all, supply them with wireless-transmitters as soon as possible. In any case, as we returned from Katwijk to Felixstowe we were unaware of the arrests in Scheveningen. The crew had laboured all night in sub-zero temperatures, without sleep for anyone, but Captain Hall filled up the 320 with petrol and turned right around. The mood aboard was grim — now or never. At dusk we headed out into the North Sea once again.

We reached Scheveningen at 3.15 a.m., in bitter cold. The sea was so smooth that Bob Goodfellow rowed the dinghy right to the tip of the little stone pier. We unloaded the two transmitters and put them at readiness for Peter. But at just about this moment Peter was looking into the muzzles of two Luger pistols, aimed at his head. Earlier that evening he had heard the national anthem being spoken on Radio Orange instead of sung, and decided to try and meet us in spite of the arrests the previous night. He knew that we would be bringing him the transmitters which at that moment represented the key to the entire "Contact Holland" operation — one for Johannes, one for Fat Willem — and furthermore he wanted to warn us away from Scheveningen for a while; after all, we were totally unaware of the disastrous turn events had taken there.

For Scheveningen trembled with nervousness. The Germans sensed that something was up. The Dutch traitor Ridderhof had got wind of our activities, but at first failed to convince his Nazi bosses of the seriousness of his suspicions — after all, who would be so crazy as to attempt secret landings right in front of the Naval Head-quarters? However, the arrest of the two Resistance leaders changed their minds. They promptly doubled the regular beach patrols, which by sheer luck had always missed us so far, and increased surveillance of the Boulevard. In the dark dance which Peter and I executed around each other in the Scheveningen night that winter, he tiptoed to disaster a stone's throw from the spot where I stood waiting for him, right into the arms of a German patrol.

After the action of 11 January, when Tazelaar had failed to appear, we had devised a contingency plan for a similar occasion, should it arise. As for the moment everything revolved around the two trans-mitters, it was decided to leave them behind in Holland, buried in the sand in a spot which could be passed along to Peter via Alblas' radio. After that, I was to proceed to a public telephone and call the

125

girl who maintained contact with both Peter and Willem, in the hope of effecting through her the clarifications we so desperately needed. The nearest booth, if my memory served me right, stood on the Deynootplein, a square in the heart of Scheveningen behind the Navy Headquarters. In order to be at least somewhat less conspicuous permission had been arranged for me to wear British Navy uniform, which apart from the hat with the crown bore some vague resemblance to certain German uniforms.

When at 4.45 a.m. there was still no sign of Peter , I decided that we'd better put the contingency plan into operation; I gave the line to the dinghy a couple of jerks to indicate that we were going into action. A few moments later Chris appeared, carrying his tommy-gun and a steel shovel, reluctantly provided by navy ordnance. We each picked up a transmitter, a watertight parcel no larger than a picnic-basket but unexpectedly heavy. Then we set out across the beach towards the Boulevard, Chris in the lead with the tommy-gun. I kept a prudent twenty yards behind with an eye out for landmines, and noticed sadly that from this distance he stood out against the white ice like a charcoal sketch.

We made for the northern tip of the Boulevard. Here, at the foot of the wall, we would bury the transmitters. This spot could be clearly indicated in a wireless message. Furthermore, at this maximum distance from the sea the sand should be dry to a considerable depth. Chris positioned himself a few feet up the dunes, from where he could cover both the beach and the Boulevard with his tommy-gun. I took a firm hold of the shovel and drove it into the sand with all my might. You could have heard the crash all the way to the Kurhaus: the beach was frozen and hard as a rock.

After the disappointments of the last weeks, this final set-back drove me to the edge of frenzy. I attacked the sand with total abandon — it barely dented. The metallic clangour reverberated through the icy silence. Even Chris was beginning to get uncomfortable. "For Christ's sake!" he growled. "You're wrecking that shovel." He looked unhappy, and with reason. We later learned that two soldiers were normally stationed on the North Boulevard; their absence at this time was due solely to the happen-stance that just then they were marching Peter down to the guardpost. The dance continued its intricate pattern.

With the transmitters under our arms we glumly returned to the pier. Goodfellow, who had obviously heard the racket, received us with a broad grin. Chris stepped straight from the stones into the dinghy, without even getting his shoes wet; if only Peter and his passengers were here! Where could they be? The phone-booth on the Deynootplein might provide the answer.

This part of the operation didn't worry me too much; if anything, experience had bolstered my faith in Erik Michielsen's credo: *de l'audace, toujours de l'audace*. Seen from that viewpoint, walking into a German naval base in British uniform should provide an ample measure of safety. I fully expected that no one would look at me twice. It came as a shock to learn that I was wrong.

Shortly after five I stepped on to the Boulevard, via the ramp at the northern end. To get away in darkness we had to be back on the 320 no later than six, which left me half an hour for my sortie. I chose the pavement on the landside. The most difficult moment came in switching from our usual stealth to the normal, heavy step of a German officer. I walked the entire length of the North Boulevard without meeting a soul. When I approached the Palace Hotel, the little light on the roof flickered on and off. I had no choice but to keep going, right along the interminable length of the Navy Headquarters. Nothing happened.

At the Beach Club I turned off to the left, into the street which led to the Deynootplein. Now I met my first German soldiers, a group of four. We passed each other on the same side of the road. It proved light enough to distinguish each other's uniforms, but too dark to recognise them. I began to feel good.

I had to cross the Deynootplein diagonally. Here the town was awake. Grey figures, huddled in their coats, hurried through the bitter dawn. Nobody paid the slightest attention to the British officer in their midst. A tram came creaking by me, slowly; I touched it with my hand. Line 8. Under the blue lights sat dozens of men with livid faces, probably Dutch labourers. I looked about me round the familiar square, full of ghosts from my past. Everything was grey and sallow and sad, as if a memory had bled to death.

The telephone-booth stood in a slightly different spot from where I remembered it, a glass cubicle barely illuminated by blue light. I stepped inside, pulled the door behind me and opened the directory.

I couldn't read it. I held the book next to the bulb, but even then I was unable to decipher the tiny print in the weak glow.

What else could go wrong tonight? While I pondered the problem I became aware of a figure across the street. He caught my attention because he was standing still, while everyone else hurried along through the biting cold. He had positioned himself on the very edge of the pavement, facing me squarely, motionless. I couldn't be sure, but I thought he wore a uniform. Suddenly I felt screamingly visible in the booth, glass all around and a light right above the tell-tale crown on my British cap. Too late to do anything about it, I could only hope that he would go away.

After a minute or two I thought of calling up Jacques Maasland, my old Leyden friend who now lived in The Hague. He'd probably die of fright hearing my voice, but he would never betray me. Most important of all, I still knew his telephone number by heart. I would ask him to look up the critical number for me in his directory and then forget that he had ever talked with me. It seemed the only way to reach Peter's contact-girl on whom rested all our hopes of clarification. I fumbled in my pocket for some Dutch coins, provided for this purpose by the C.I.D., and took the receiver off the hook. Out of the corner of my eye I saw the dark shape across the street, facing me, standing like a statue in the cold.

After a while I stepped out of the booth. The man was still there. Now I knew that he had been watching me. Had he recognised my uniform or was he merely curious, unsure of its origin and meaning? I saw no better course of action than to appear unconcerned and carry through the bluff. I crossed the road straight at him. Before I had gone half-way he flicked on a torch and shone it directly in my face. During the next thirty seconds a bizarre scene played itself out.

I walked blindly into the light-cone. He, in his own German-occupied town, saw a British naval officer come at him, gold stripes, cap with crown, unmistakable in the glare. Inside my coat pocket I held my pistol aimed at him, as he no doubt covered me. We waited for each other. Every step brought us closer together. I looked straight ahead, as if I were unaware of the blinding light in my eyes. But he knew that I knew that he had recognised me, and this deadly knowledge existed between us two alone, of all people in the world, binding us together in the silence and the darkness and the cold and the human misery of the war, until the idea of shooting each other dead became unthinkable madness to me.

Only my steps sounded through the hush. The light-cone which pulled me to him shrank and sharpened until my sleeve brushed his uniform. Suddenly the black night lay before me. I must have moved by him like a ghost. The beam flipped around and I saw my shadow on the pavement. Keep going now, don't look back, just keep going.

But no shot, no word, no sound followed me. With every step my shadow lengthened, then the light went out. I walked off the square, down the street, along the Boulevard, across the beach, up the pier and into the dinghy. I never looked back.

(A year later a Dutch policeman escaped to England and joined the Free Netherlands Forces. He told a tale of having seen a British naval officer in Scheveningen, as far back as January 1942. Nobody believed him. Except I. When we met we stared at each other a long time. Then we got drunk.)

The telephone-call, around which the entire sortie revolved, fitted neatly into the general pattern of that night. All call-boxes in the Netherlands had just been rebuilt to take only new, large, worthless, zinc coins. Mine had been the old, silver, tiny ones. They tinkled prettily all the way down and out into the coin-return.

* * *

Peter Tazelaar had fallen victim to a political assignment, which had complicated "Contact Holland" before we were ready for it. He was replaced by agent Ernst, under orders to take over Peter's primary mission: the creation of espionage groups and the development of regular communications with England. A special wireless-operator, agent Evert, was put at his disposal, as were agents Johannes and Fat Willem, still without transmitters. After a month of joint training I took the new team aboard the 320.

This time there were no hitches. In view of recent developments at Scheveningen, we fixed on Katwijk for the landings and reached there easily with time to spare. At 4.20 a.m. I took Ernst and Evert ashore, together with two extra transmitters for Johannes and Willem. Within twenty-four hours they came on the air and confirmed their safe arrival. Johannes and Willem, however, never got the chance to use their new transmitters; they had been arrested by the Gestapo on 13 February in a raid on a house in The Hague. Agent Ernst executed his mission brilliantly and founded one of the most successful espionage organisations of World War II before he was caught and shot. His collaborators continued his work. Then they, together with agent Evert, were caught and shot. Their successors, assisted by new agents from England, built on the infrastructure they inherited and developed it into a nation-wide network. Most of them were caught and shot. But always there were others to take their place, until of the original "Contact Holland" not a trace remained under the successive generations of Dutch agents who gave their lives as the price of freedom.

XVI

"STRAIGHTFORWARD?" SNORTED COLONEL RABAGLIATTI. "IN THIS business there's no such thing as straightforward. Honesty and all that, splendid! But in this game all it does is kill people. It's the only game in which you've got to fool all of the people all of the time. Otherwise you kill people. There cannot, must not, ever be any connection between appearance and reality. Ever." He thoughtfully swirled his brandy.

"Take Van 't Sant." A spark of admiration glinted in his small, hard eyes. "Now when Van 't Sant takes you to lunch, do you know what he would really like? He'd really like to sit at a separate table, with his back to you, and talk through a tube hidden under the carpet." The thought evidently tickled him for he clapped his hands together with little wooden movements, looking like a pleased puppet with a dent in its head.

These few sentences constituted a lengthy, exceptionally candid speech for the Rabbi, and we nodded our heads in appreciation. We were winding up lunch in the Ecu de France, in Jermyn Street, where occasionally he would invite Chris and me for a meal. Observing him I realised that, for someone to whom I entrusted my life several times each month, he had really remained a complete stranger. Of Rabagliatti as a person I only knew with certainty that in spite of his name he was a Scot of aristocratic background, that he handled his expensive Jaguar like a racing-driver, and that in the annals of human conflict he had earned his place as the first man ever to destroy an enemy in aerial combat: on 26 August 1914, the fragile flying-machines side by side like a pair of dragon-flies above the warm summer-green, the pilots aiming hasty shots then dropping their hand-guns to fly the planes, wobbling and tottering, until the German collapsed on the stick and screwed himself into the lush French soil below.

More than this we did not really want to know about him. His sinister anonymity, the dent in his head like a thumb-print of his violent past, the clever eyes, the total self-assurance which radiated from the dapper little figure, even the sudden charm of his smile, like an ambush – all contributed to our fond conviction that when the chips were down Rabagliatti, like Van 't Sant, would be tougher, meaner, dirtier and deadlier than his counterpart in the Gestapo.

"Straightforward? If you want your war to be straightforward you should sign up with one of those harebrain services where they chop each other up with knives, yelling and screaming, or lose their lives to a dumb piece of metal flying through the air." He sniffed disdainfully. "Like the Marines."

Chris and I chuckled. The C.I.D., to which we still officially reported, once again boasted a new chief. We knew him to be busy undermining the unofficial arrangement by which the Mews operated directly with the British. As a result, the Rabbi despised him. I myself had been rather favourably impressed by him at our initial meetings, even though I sensed a threat to the delicate organism of "Contact Holland" which we had nursed to life at such frightful cost. A few days after his appointment on 5 February, he had sent for me. To my surprise his address turned out to be the Netherlands Navy Headquarters, North Row; not as bad as Stratton House but still definitely enemy territory, far from Chester Square. I stepped into his presence very much on guard, but it did not take him long to disarm me. Colonel of the Marines M. R. de Bruyne was idolized by his men and I might have been in the vanguard – had I been a marine instead of a secret agent.

He exuded the attraction of an honest man in a wicked world. He jumped up to greet me, a burly Indies-man with an open, pleasant face, and while we shook hands I knew instinctively, and with very mixed emotions, that he didn't have a mean bone in his body. His ingenuousness charmed me as a person and scared me to death professionally. Before me stood the Perfect Marine: brave, bold and above all – dammit man! – straightforward.

"Well?" Chris asked, when I returned to the Mews from this expedition. He was lying on the couch in his pyjamas, reading the paper.

"I wouldn't go near the place, if I were you. They salute each other in the corridors."

Chris pulled a face. When Peter was still around we would occasionally make a detour for the express purpose of walking by St. James's palace, Corporal Tazelaar with his "banana-peel" on his sleeve and I with my silver second-lieutenant's stars. The guardsman on sentry-duty, confused by the many foreign uniforms in London, never failed to present arms for us in a spectacular, bone-rattling fashion. We would first return the salute in the pompous manner of General Officers, then startle him with a couple of knowing winks. In the end we'd all burst out laughing – silly military nonsense! Furthermore we believed that relations within an intelligence organisation should depend on mutual respect rather than discipline. Both General Van 't Sant and Colonel Rabagliatti would have glared at us suspiciously, had we ever snapped them a military salute. The Marines seemed to take a different view.

"And Colonel De Bruyne himself?"

"A splendid fellow, positively splendid."

"What the hell does that mean?" Chris looked at me uneasily.

"Colonel *of the Marines* De Bruyne," I elaborated delicately.

Chris slowly rose from the couch, as if he couldn't believe his ears. We had just concluded preparations for two North Sea crossings, which we were to execute separately during the next moon-period. With his first independent action looming ahead, he had every reason for concern.

"A marine?" he whispered incredulously. Allowing for his apple-cheeks he looked positively pale. I nodded. I could have added that De Bruyne had come directly from the East Indies, lacked all experience of Holland under the Occupation and knew literally nothing about secret intelligence. Being an honest man he not only admitted this, but had fought his own appointment tooth and nail. However, I did not feel that these revelations would benefit the morale of the Mews.

"Let's leave him strictly alone," Chris advised, sinking back on to the couch to resume the comic-strip adventures of Captain Reillyffoul.

"Amen," I had answered, with feeling. But this time it proved easier said than done.

From that first meeting with De Bruyne I emerged full of hope. The colonel had assured me that the actual intelligence work did not interest him. Consequently he would not interfere with our activities, provided all information from occupied territory reached his desk. I gave him my promise to this effect and walked back to Chester Square, much relieved. Van 't Sant squashed my optimism.

"Don't count on it," he said. We were strolling through the square, walled garden, his arm around my shoulders, slowly and in step along the paths. He gestured cautiously towards the room above his own, where from time to time the outline of Queen Wilhelmina moved behind the windows. "As long as the lady only pays attention to the people back home, the contact with occupied Holland is the hottest thing in London. He'll try and get his hands on it."

"I don't think that's De Bruyne's game," I protested. "He seems an honest fellow. Straightforward."

"Then they'll use him." "They" comprised everybody who failed to put the interests of the Royal Family above all else, or refused to acknowledge that General Van 't Sant had totally identified himself with those interests. "You'll see."

Ten days later Colonel De Bruyne informed us that, on second thoughts, he had decided to take personal charge of all intelligence operations. Consequently he had arranged that, effective immediately, the Mews reported directly to him, not just organisationally but also financially and operationally. As a first step he ordered us to leave Chester Square and find new quarters, preferably around Marble Arch where he maintained his own offices. Clearly "they" had whispered in his gullible ear, as Van 't Sant had predicted.

We said good-bye to our beloved Mews and peevishly rented the most expensive flat we could find, at 23 Hyde Park Place, for eighteen pounds a week. When shortly afterwards the Queen decided to found a club for escapees from Holland, we hired the apartment below ours in her name. She personally opened its doors to the handful of Englandfarers and named it "Orangehaven". In these august surroundings we installed ourselves and viewed the future with suspicion.

*　　*　　*

No sooner did the Marines actively involve themselves with "Contact Holland" than we were headed on a collision course. When Chris and I stepped into the new C.I.D. headquarters for the first time – Chris prudently dressed in civilian clothes – we almost sank through the floor. Officers and secretaries sat around, people walked in and out, and there on the wall before us, in lonely splendour for all to admire, hung three charts showing a lot of sea with a tiny chip of land on each, the three points on the Dutch coast where we were shortly to execute our secret landings: Katwijk, Noordwijk and an experimental corner of Zeeland. There and then we began to look nervously over our shoulders, an attitude which never left us in our dealings with the Marines.

Louis d'Aulnis – P. L. Baron d'Aulnis de Bourrouill – went a step further. He was our most promising agent; during the next moon-period we were scheduled to land him in Holland. Three times a week we laboured together in a bare little room in Hans Place, under the guidance of a purple-nosed genius, struggling to master an exceptionally complicated letter-code. One day Louis failed to turn up; in the evening he arrived unannounced in our mighty flat.

"I'm pulling out," he informed us. "I'm not going with you chaps. This morning I told De Bruyne that I haven't got the guts to see this thing through."

I knew better. The enterprise for which Leydener, Englandfarer Louis d'Aulnis lacked sufficient guts still had to be invented. But behind his noisy joviality functioned a cool, patient brain; he waited more than a year before he parachuted into the Netherlands and survived the war as one of its most successful secret agents.

I poured him a whisky and waited. Louis liked to present his views in unorthodox ways; you had to give him time and room to elaborate. "They are absolutely delightful, these marines," he began. "Marvellous chaps. And the coffee they serve you there in the C.I.D., absolutely marvellous! And then, if you're only willing to listen, they'll tell you everything that's going to happen in Holland. With names. First names, middle names, last names. And cover-names." He roared with laughter, jumped up and paced around the flat.

"Yesterday I went to the Dutch Club. You ever go there? Delightful place, and they gave me an absolutely delightful reception. 'Good heavens, Louis, you still here?' they said. 'We thought you were long since back in Holland. But you're leaving shortly, aren't you? By boat, we hear. Well, have a good trip, old boy. Say hello to the old place for us, while you're still alive.'" He gulped down the rest of his whisky and poured himself another one. He flopped back into his chair, suddenly subdued, barely hiding his bitterness. "Ah, the romance of it all! No wonder it goes to your head. Imagine being a marine – a *marine*, mind you – and all of a sudden you're plunged into all this delicious, secret stuff. How can you possibly keep your mouth shut about it? Well, the point is, they can't. And if you think I'm going to play with these boys, you're crazy. I'd rather stay alive."

My concern about our own safety paralleled my anxiety for our agents under the Occupation, who counted on us to protect them. For in spite of the terrifying situation, we had executed three successful operations in a row. Thanks to the lessons of the past winter, they had become almost routine. In six weeks we had landed five agents and six transmitters, and shortly we would try anew to bring some Resistance leaders out from occupied territory. Now we were ready for it. The future of "Contact Holland" seemed assured. But when after a perfectly executed operation Chris' passenger, agent Jan Maassen, was shot dead at point-blank range in the dunes at Katwijk, I could not get the chart on the wall of the C.I.D. office out of my mind.

A few days later the Marines handed a complete list of our agents in the Netherlands, names and cover-names, to an employee of the Ministry of Foreign Affairs. A diplomatic telegram had arrived from Switzerland, mentioning an execution in Holland. Foreign Affairs encountered difficulties in deciphering the name of the victim, so they turned to the C.I.D. "Could it possibly be one of your chaps?"

"Here's our list, why don't you take a look yourself?"

I learned about it afterwards and violently protested at this breach of security. "But they are good people, there in Foreign Affairs," Colonel De Bruyne reproached me, puzzled by my fury. "Fine people. Good Hollanders, we should trust them." I felt like crying. On behalf of every agent under the Occupation I yearned for the distrustful, muddy safety of Rabagliatti and Van 't Sant.

The critical confrontation came on the day when De Bruyne solved a difference of opinion with the words: "That's an order."

A what?! – He didn't say it in anger or irritation, or even with emphasis. To De Bruyne it was the most elementary thing in the world. He held the rank of colonel, I was a second lieutenant, he gave me an order. Very simple. The thought that I might not obey it probably never entered his head.

I from my side could hardly believe my ears. Not that I disclaimed or resented his authority over me, but in my opinion the highly independent individuals who made good secret agents required – and deserved – intelligent relationships based on mutual confidence, rather than dumb military discipline. The game was the thing, not the rules.

The point at issue was whether or not to put our agents in direct contact with the established Dutch resistance organisations. I objected to it. My experience under the Occupation had shown these to be too large to avoid infiltration by the Gestapo; they posed unacceptable risks for our people. Right or wrong, this was my conviction, and only sound arguments – of which De Bruyne failed to produce a single one – could possibly have budged me from it. But an order? Van 't Sant and Rabagliatti might be ruthless secret service types, yet from them I had learned to regard the trust of an agent behind enemy lines as a sacred responsibility, immune to considerations of primitive discipline. Not for a single second did I consider obeying Colonel De Bruyne's order.

The men whom I had landed in Holland counted on me to protect them in the rear. If the Dutch C.I.D. prevented me from doing so, then back to the Rabbi and his Englishmen. I saw no choice. I shrugged my shoulders and walked out the door, without a word. I never returned – except for a preliminary hearing on 17 April 1942, on the basis of which I was recommended for trial by court martial.

At just about the same time I was recommended for the Knight's Cross to the Grand Cross of the Military Williams Order, the Netherlands' equivalent to the Victoria Cross.

*   *   *

Now the struggle for control of "Contact Holland" exploded at the highest levels in London. The Mews, caught in the middle, paid the price of success. We ourselves had asked for the chance to establish contact with our occupied country and this chance had been given us; we had no grounds for complaint. But every time we "unbalanced adventurers" risked our necks for it in the icy dark, we resignedly accepted the knowledge that we also acted as pawns on the London chessboard. We were wise enough to recognise behind court martial and Williams Order alike the moves and counter-moves of a barren game of power.

Above all else, unassailable, stood the Queen of the Netherlands. Every report from occupied Holland confirmed that the people in their misery had turned to her, and her alone. The cabinet ministers, on the other hand, deprived of parliamentary support, had nothing to fall back on but their force of character, if any, and in this not even the strongest could match their formidable Queen. As a result, Wilhelmina in London wielded more actual power than any Dutch sovereign in history.

Conversely, the Queen's consciousness was entirely concentrated on her subjected nation in the Netherlands. Being a passionate woman she let herself be driven beyond the bounds of fairness in this respect, often barely bothering to hide her contempt for those who through whatever circumstances had missed the Occupation – as she would later be suspicious of anyone who had failed to get arrested by the Germans. The simplest sailor from Sliedrecht commanded more of her attention than the highest functionary in the government-in-exile. Anyone with news from Holland had her ear; anyone who based his arguments on information from occupied territory gained her support. As the war progressed such information became more readily available, but in the spring of 1942 "Contact Holland" was by far the most promising source of this politically powerful commodity.

At this time of undisputed authority the Queen was being counselled and shielded – and, according to his many bitter enemies, used – by the man in whom more than anyone else she had placed her trust: François van 't Sant. Certainly it couldn't be denied that his presence, suave, unobtrusive and always vaguely mysterious, loomed at every intersection of the roads to power in London, blocking the ambitions of determined men. These planned their inevitable counter-attack along the only lines which were certain to penetrate the Queen's consciousness: via Holland. All through the war a steady succession of Englandfarers, unwitting pawns in a dirty game, brought the warning from occupied territory to London: General Van 't Sant, private secretary and advisor to Queen Wilhelmina, is a traitor in collusion with the Nazis.

All Europe lay under German subjection and London became the base of many exiled governments. Intrigues flourished like toadstools in its hothouse atmosphere, and of these the campaign against "the Dutch Rasputin" was the most pernicious. It failed to achieve its goal — Van 't Sant never lost his nerve and Wilhelmina stood behind him like a rock. But the suspicion surrounding the Queen's inner circle, artificially fostered amongst Resistance fighters, lay like a poisonous cloud between the most militant elements of our nation in World War II. For both sides in this unsavoury affair control of "Contact Holland" was of crucial importance —

In the middle of this mess Erik Michielsen, my old pal from the Pieters Church in Leyden, suddenly appeared before me in Orangehaven. "Well," I greeted him. "About time."

He grinned and immediately began to act mysterious. His black eyes darted left and right, although we were quite alone in the clubroom, and he whispered in my ear: "I'm bringing a warning of the utmost importance." He paused, to heighten the tension.

"One guess," I answered. "Van 't Sant is a traitor in collusion with the Nazis." Erik looked stunned. "Come along," I laughed. "You can tell him about it yourself." Half an hour later the three of us strolled through the garden at Chester Square.

"The bastards!" General Van 't Sant exploded, barely raising his voice, after we had viewed the matter from all angles. He thought of little else these days and I knew that he worried about the safety of his wife, daughter and grand-children in Holland. "The bastards, what do they want from me?"

"Where do they get it from?" asked Erik. It rarely took more than a few minutes to demolish the accusation. What had seemed believable in the murk of the Underground, appeared simply ludicrous in the calm normality of the Queen's garden.

"From London," the general answered without hesitation. He stopped and pointed dramatically to the ground between his feet. "From right here. This is where they intend to break my neck. Letters to neutral countries, forwarded from there. Diplomatic mailbags. Very simple." (In fact, German counter-espionage proved to be another source of the rumour, which they had picked up in occupied territory and used to create confusion and despondency among captured agents.)

"And does anybody in London really believe it?"

"Nobody." Van 't Sant swung around to face Michielsen from three inches away. "Except apparently the new head of the C.I.D."

A few days previously De Bruyne had instructed me to break off all contact with the general and deny him access to all classified material. When I informed him of this, Van 't Sant immediately telephoned the Minister-President and demanded a confrontation with the colonel. The meeting took place but De Bruyne refused to retract his order. In effect, the Head of the Dutch Secret Service hereby accused the Private Secretary of the Dutch Queen of being a danger to the Dutch State.

"That must have been one hell of a meeting." Erik struggled manfully to keep a straight face, but finally burst out laughing. "What is this here in London? A mad-house?"

Before I could concur General Van 't Sant distracted me. He was looking away with a strange expression in his eyes. I swung around. The door to his office had opened and on the little balcony above the garden stood Rabagliatti and Peter Tazelaar.

XVII

IN THE MIDDLE OF THE NIGHT THE SHOT THUNDERED THROUGH OUR apartment. I dived out of the blankets, stumbled in the dark across my palatial bedroom into the corridor and switched on the light. I listened — dead silence. Sickening anxiety swept over me: Peter Tazelaar, just back from occupied Holland, lived with us and the shot had come from his room.

With my heart in my throat I pushed the door open. The light flooded in from the hallway and there he stood, in the middle of the sumptuous room, an enormous, blue-steel Browning in his hand. A wisp of smoke curled from the muzzle, just like in the pictures. When I flicked on the chandeliers I saw that the mirror, which covered one entire wall, was pierced by a neat, round hold at about stomach-level. "Oh boy," he said. His tongue seemed to give him trouble. "I'm sorry. I step into this damn room, can't find the bloody switch, next thing I know I see this creep come at me." He pointed with the gun at his own reflection in the ruined mirror and burst out laughing. "Jesus, how much d'you think that's going to set me back?" Well, Peter Tazelaar was back in London. . . .

In the early morning of 19 January, a hundred yards from the little stone pier by the North Boulevard in Scheveningen where Chris and I were waiting for him, Peter had been arrested. Fortunately he had taken the same precaution as for his landing: he wore evening clothes and smelt of alcohol. He also carried a bottle of jenever. The thermometer stood at eighteen below and when they arrived at the guard-post the soldiers did not refuse a couple of fortifiers. In due time their mood improved. Just then a trusted police-inspector arrived, Broer Moonen, at this time thought to be a prominent Dutch Nazi. In reality he formed part of Peter's group and had kept an eye on him for just such an eventuality. He chided the Germans for holding such an obvious reveller and after a few more drinks they let Peter go. Moonen was ultimately arrested and paid for his double role with his life.

During these hours of captivity Peter had looked down the barrels of the firing-squad. In conjunction with the arrest of the two Resistance leaders the previous night he concluded that his presence had become too well known for further usefulness under the Occupation. He decided to get out for the second time. He put his fate in the hands of an anonymous organiser of the early trans-continental escape route via Switzerland, who paired him with a Leyden student, also unknown to him, called Erik Michielsen. After an incredibly smooth passage they reached England three months later. The anonymous organiser turned out to have been my old cut-out, Frits van der Schrieck.

Peter was back, safe and sound, and the joy of our reunion obliterated the grim winter months. We hardly talked about them. We exchanged only practical data of possible use on future trips, such as the undramatic explanation of the mysterious lights on the Palace Hotel: just the lighting of cigarettes by guards, visible three miles away.

But the Mews—the name stuck—was complete again and for a few days it seemed like old times. Pressed and polished we strolled along Park Lane where early daffodils bloomed, we risked our lives jumping on buses, bought wallets on Piccadilly, accepted military homage from the sentry at St. James's palace, guzzled beer and whisky in all the old haunts, descended noisily on La Speranza and the Chinaman and swiped girls from British officers in the Embassy Club and the Suivi. The dark beach at Scheveningen faded like the memory of a nightmare.

On 16 April, three days after Peter's return, a dispatch-rider appeared at 23 Hyde Park Place. He delivered a letter from Colonel De Bruyne instructing me to appear before a special commission to explain why, against orders, I had failed to report to the C.I.D. with Corporal Tazelaar promptly on his arrival. The hearing took place the following morning and resulted in a letter dated 20 April 1942, by which the chief of the Dutch Secret Service informed me that I had been "guilty of a very serious punishable offence", on the basis of which he had recommended me for trial by court martial. At the same time he relieved me, "effective immediately", of my position with the C.I.D.

I didn't pay much attention to all this, for I did not consider myself its prime target. Chris and I had accumulated invaluable experience during the past winter, which was just beginning to bear fruit for the Allied war-effort. It seemed unthinkable to me that any Allied officer, even a furious colonel of the Marines, would knowingly jeopardise a precious commodity like secret contact with enemy-occupied territory for the sake of a purely formalistic transgression. So he must be after bigger game, not just a reluctant pawn on the London chess-board. But the square which I covered, "Contact Holland", promised to develop into a formidable position. In whose hands was it? De Bruyne had decided to find out. It didn't take long; my actions after Tazelaar's return proved clearly that, in spite of all official changes, I had not switched my loyalty. When Van 't Sant requested me – contrary to my orders from the C.I.D. – not to expose Peter to anyone until he had reported to the Queen herself, I unhesitatingly complied. Now De Bruyne knew: the Mews paid no attention whatsoever to the periodic upheavals in the Dutch Secret Service and recognised allegiance only to 77 Chester Square. Damn right! Thanks to Van 't Sant we had established contact with Holland. If in the course of this we had also developed into a sort of personal stronghold for him, we gladly took this as part of the bargain. But not so his enemies. With Colonel De Bruyne as their big gun they went into the attack. The pawns were the first in the line of fire.

As I knew my court martial to be incidental to the real issues, I didn't give it a second thought. If it happened, so be it – but this battle was between the heavy-weights and I put my money on Van 't Sant. I forwarded the letters to Chester Square and blithely continued preparations for our next landing, an action on Noordwijk where we were to meet agent Ernst in a dress rehearsal for the collection of several Resistance leaders.

Our real problems were of a more prosaic nature. In his last letter the colonel had also announced that, "effective immediately", our personal allowances would be discontinued, including the rent for our flat. He proved as good as his word. There we sat again – no money, no income, no place to live. We knew from experience that in financial matters we could expect no help from Chester Square. The pattern repeated itself: my gold cigarette-case, only just redeemed, returned to the pawnshop.

Salvation came from below. Old Mr. Bussey, who with his wife managed the four apartments of 23 Hyde Park Place, lived in a few dark little rooms grouped about the subterranean kitchen. Because we were always forgetting our keys, calling them out of bed late at night, asking them to sew on our buttons or lend us five quid, but particularly since Peter had shot himself in the mirror, they treated us more as sons than as tenants. Now they cleared a room for us between the laundry and the pantry, and from our stately third-floor mansion we descended into the cellar. From time to time they threw in some free food. As Orangehaven above us was meanwhile growing into a lively rendezvous of Englandfarers, we adopted it as our living-room. From here, unpaid, unhoused, fired and under a cloud, we departed on 11 May for our fifteenth landing-action in enemy territory.

In spite of calm seas and lovely weather Chris and I fretted all the way. We sat in the tiny cabin of the 320 and thought of everything that could go wrong. We never mentioned it, but we felt threatened in the rear. Just recently we had suffered obstruction as a result of the conflict amongst competing agencies. We had been deliberately withheld information about Katwijk, where unbeknownst to us the curfew had been extended from four to six o'clock. As a result, on 23 February, we had landed agents Ernst and Evert in the middle of this time-period, and would, but for sheer good luck, have sent them straight to their deaths.

"Do you trust De Bruyne?" Chris finally asked.

"One hundred per cent. And you?"

"Me too," he admitted. "I only wish he hadn't stuck that map of Noordwijk on his wall." An hour later we slowly rowed into the outer surf off Noordwijk.

The purpose of the operation being to meet Ernst and in the process hand him two more transmitters, only three of us were in the dinghy: Bob Goodfellow at the oars, Chris manning the tommy-gun and I to go ashore. The night was dark, the sea calm, everything

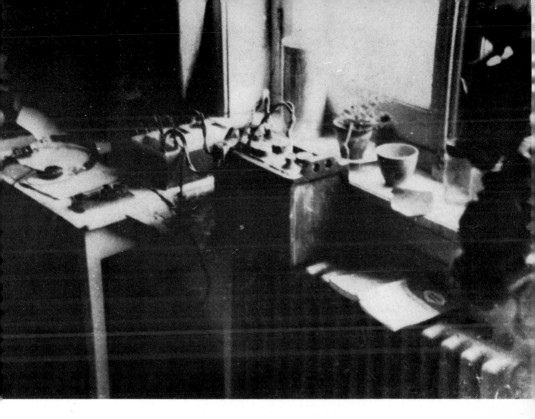

Secret transmitter ready for action under enemy occupation.

German E-boats tracked us down.

DEPARTEMENT VAN MARINE , C.I.D.

No. *C.I.D. 259/1.*

ONDERWERP

Londen, 2o April I942.

<u>GEHEIM</u>.

                In verband met het resultaat van het onderzoek naar Uw gedragingen in de zaak Dogger, heb ik de eer UWeledelgestrenge het volgende medetdeelen:

Ie.   Naar mijn overtuiging hebt gij U schuldig gemaakt aan een zeer ernstig strafbaar feit. Ik zal dit dan ook als zoodanig ter kennis van de bevoegde militaire autoriteit brengen.

2e.   Ongeacht de gevolgen van het ad. Ie vermelde, acht ik Uw gedrag zoodanig in strijd met wat men als de meest minimum eisch van goeden trouw mag beschouwen, dat ik U met ingang van heden onthef van Uwe functie bij de C.I.D.

3e.   Ik neem aan dat gij Ø in Uwe bijzondere positie zelve weet, bij wien gij U thans wederom hebt te vervoegen. Mocht dat niet het geval zijn, dan verzoek ik U mij dit te laten weten, waarop ik den Minister van Oorlog in kennis zal stellen met Uw ontslag uit mijn dienst.

4e.   Den Colonel Rabagliati zal ik mededeeling doen dat door mij de toelagen aan U en dhr. Kredit niet meer zullen worden uitbetaald, aangezien dit sedert I7 Febr. '42 geschiedde op verzoek van dezen Kolonel, daar gij toen met dhr. Kredit direct onder het " Dutch Government " kwam te staan.

5e.   In verband hiermede wordt tevens de door mij gedane toezegging om de huur van Uw flat voor rekening van mijn dienst te nemen bij deze vervallen verklaard.

6e.   Ik verzoek U ten spoedigste (uiterlijk 22 April a.s.) de aan U in bruikleen afgestane pistolen terugtebezorgen bij den Kapt. der Mariniers Lieftinck.

                      De Kolonel der Mariniers,

                      wnd. Chef C.I.D.

                      M.R. de Bruyne.

AAN
den Res. 2e. Luit. KNL.
<u>HAZELHOFF ROELFSEMA</u>.

Met opdracht dhr. Kredit hiermede
in kennis te stellen voorzoover
hem betreft,.

I was recommended for trial by court-martial.

Goodbye to the unhealthy beaches of Holland.

I had the recurrent notion of being one world-war behind.

Robert Bergmann, future Marshall
of the Royal Court.

After everything Erik Michielsen
had gone through,
one fatal moment.

The supernumerary officers comprised eight nationalities.

In spite of everything, we got our wings.

'Little' Cohen, a very honest pilot.

We bounced our bombs in through the front-door.

139 (Pathfinder)
Squadron, R.A.F.
Upwood, 1944.

Ben Hein was
always in the
mood.

De Havilland 'Mosquito', made of pressed wood.

We crowded around the battle-order.

No.139 (JAMAICA) SQUADRON, R.A.F.

SECRET.   RAID SCHEDULE.   DATE: 20.2.45.

DY.
A/C NO. LETT. MARK. PILOT.   NAVIGATOR.

KB.390 'B' XXV   W/CDR.J.CLIFT,OBE.   F/LT.A.DE LA STUA, DFM. (Y)
KB.201 'A' XX   F/LT.G.C OJEEN,DFM.   F/LT.R.C COPER,DFC.   (Y)
MM.200 'E' XVI   F/LT.L.H.WAKEFORD.   F/SGT.R.E.SMITH.   (Y)
KB.482 'G' XXV   F/LT.J.W.T.BOSCH.   F/SGT.J.R.VAN HOUTEN.   (Y)
KB.185 'R' XX   F/LT.A.B.HAMOND.DFC   F/LT.G.A.L.WEST.   (Y)
KB.354 'O' XX   F/LT.M.H. ALLIS.   F/O.F.W.CRAWLEY,DFC.   (Y)
KB.271 'T' XX   F/LT.A.O'GRADY.   W/TM.L.D.GROOME,DFC.   (Y)

KB.217 'H' XX   F/LT.R.O.DAY.   F/LT. .TREBY.   (Y)
MM.131 'J' XX   LT.AAJ.VAN AMSTERDAM,DFC.   S/LDR.H.A.FORBES,DFC.   (Y)
KB.265 'U' XX   F/LT.A.V.SMITH.   S/LDR.M.G.HARRIS,DFM.   (Y)
KB.192 'S' XX   F/LT.W.C.WILSON,AFC.   S/LDR.J.Y.MALLEY,DFC.   (Y)
KB.399 'M' XXV   F/O.A.W.CALDER.   F/SGT.J.D.CRAWFORD.   (Y)

KB.288 'C' XX   Reserve Aircraft.
KB.184 'V' XX   Reserve Aircraft.

            Officers i/c. Operations......F/Lt.E.Hazelhoff.
                                          F/Lt.J.R.Cassels,DFC.
            Officers i/c. Navigation.... F/Lt.J.E.Dawes.
                                         F/Lt.J.Endersby.
                Duty Engineer......F/Sgt.Jones.
                   Duty N.C.O.......Sgt.Ward.
              N.C.O. i/c Radar......Sgt.Brittain.

went along smoothly. I stared ahead, musing about the *Bèbèk* which had preceded us all to England from here, two summers ago. The Huis ter Duin hotel, from which the unsuspecting officers had watched the departure, loomed before us blacker even than the sky. Then I heard a "plop", saw a little rocket shoot into the air and poof! there lay the Huis ter Duin before me bright as day, stairs, terrace, restaurant, windows, balconies, flagpole. The Boulevard, the beach, the surf, the 320, the dinghy, we ourselves – everything was bathed in the light of a parachute-flare. At the same moment tracer-bullets began to flash by overhead, red and white, in low trajectories between the hotel and the M.G.B.

We sat rigid in the brightness as if posing for a photograph, dumb-founded. Bob leant on the oars like a Sunday rower taking a spin around the Serpentine. Chris' expression hovered between laughing and crying, and suddenly I was struck by the incongruity of his presence in the picture: C. Krediet Esq., of Sumatra, Wassenaar and Leyden and more recently the Embassy Club, London W.1, illuminated by enemy flares while sitting in a rowing-boat under tracer-bullets off the beach at Noordwijk, the Netherlands. Then Bob turned the dinghy and started pulling out with all his might. A second, then a third flare burst into a deluge of flat, white light. Two other M.G.B.s, which had accompanied the 320 to gain experience, now opened fire diagonally behind us. Red and white tracer-tracks criss-crossed above our heads like monstrous party streamers, machine-guns and cannon chattered and barked. One single burst would have blown us out of the sea, but nobody saw us. In the middle of the rumpus we bobbed about disjointedly, deserted and lost.

Suddenly a ship cut past from an unexpected quarter, white foam hissing around its razor-sharp bow. It turned away, then came straight at us. "Shoot! Shoot!" I yelled at Chris. It was almost on top of us, I saw men crouching on the foredeck and still Chris with his tommy-gun sat frozen, as in a nightmare. He gave me a strange look; sometimes he forgot that my eyes weren't the best in the world. Of course it turned out to be our boys of the 320. They pulled us aboard without stopping and abandoned the dinghy; the trans-mitters, tied to my wrist, almost yanked my arm from its socket. Then, rearing up under its full power, the M.G.B. roared out to sea.

In a short time we had left the pallid glare behind. The other ships also broke off action, the flares wobbled to earth and all at once it was dark. The night enveloped us, solid and safe. Just as I was beginning to breathe normally again, a dozen specks of light pricked through the darkness in a wide circle all around, followed by two stupendous searchlights between us and the open sea. Our engines stopped and the 320 lay dead in the water. I pushed myself inside the wheelhouse, where Hall and Goodfellow made room for me. "German E-boats," Bob explained. "They all flick on a light at the same time and then keep an eye on each other; if one or more lights disappear, then they know we've come in between. Then they can figure more or less where we are and everybody and his grandmother comes plunging down on us. So we stopped." He counted the E-boats aloud, like a tour-guide. " . . . seven, eight, nine. Those bloody great searchlights are destroyers, two of them."

One of the blue-white beams came slowly sweeping across the water, hesitated, groped back, stopped, then moved on again. As it crept inexorably towards us the 320 started to manoeuvre on its silent engine, very carefully, until it presented the destroyer its narrowest profile, the bow. When the cone touched us we found ourselves in bright daylight for the second time that night. It was so powerful that I could read the spidery scribblings in the log-book on the chart table. At this distance we had felt fairly secure, but the glare seemed to pull us close to the enemy and we cowered in the wheelhouse as if a twitch of our eyelids would give us away. It seemed to last for ever; how could they possibly fail to see us? Anxiously I glanced at Bob. "Bright, isn't it?" he said, with a face like an undertaker's.

At last the beam slid by, but the grim game continued. The sea would seem deserted except for the searchlights while the E-boats changed position in the darkness, then all at once they switched on their lights, nine white dots in a circle, a noose tightening little by little around our necks. During the dark periods we motored westwards as fast as the silent engine could pull us; when the lights flicked on we instantly stopped dead and lay wallowing in the swell, hoping we weren't blocking some fatal line of vision. While moving we nipped through the searchlights time and again, but twice more one grabbed us while we lay motionless in the noose of E-boats, touching and feeling the 320 until, incredibly, the beam passed on. How were we ever to slip through before daybreak?

146

"Couldn't we get air-cover from the R.A.F.?" Chris had stuck his head into the wheelhouse. It was possible now to tell where the sky began, just barely grey against the black sea.

"I suppose so," Goodfellow answered.

"Well?" Chris pressed on, with my wholehearted support.

"We don't need the R.A.F.," said Bob briskly and turned his back on us. Profoundly unimpressed by this display of inter-service pride Chris and I shrugged our shoulders and went below. Whenever things looked bad we would get sleepy and, if possible, go to bed. When I regained consciousness the sun was shining on the green coast of Suffolk over the starboard bow. I asked our English pals how we had finally escaped the German drag-hunt. All they did was smile, but we learned later that one M.G.B. had been finished off by the enemy pack. Ernst, who had witnessed the fireworks from the Noordwijk dunes, sent the following message: "Regret warm reception. When shall we meet?" The answer, had we known it, was simple: "Never again."

The operation of 11 May, led by an officer under his command whom he had previously relieved of all responsibilities, placed Colonel De Bruyne in an untenable position. It left him no choice but to resign as head of the C.I.D. His official objections had been demolished by Rabagliatti's insistence that the Dutch Prime Minister himself had approved my participation. Professor Gerbrandy later denied ever having given such approval. From whom then had the Rabbi received this assurance, which enabled him to carry out our original plan and in this roundabout way so ingeniously removed De Bruyne from the scene? From Van 't Sant, of course, who else?

*   *   *

Queen Wilhelmina took three steps forward, lifted up her right hand until she was bending over backwards and gave Bob Goodfellow a firm smack on the left shoulder. Bob, paler even than usual under his black beard, looked surprised. He was obviously unfamiliar with the ceremony, and while the Queen walked back to the piano where the other two citations lay ready for her, he whispered out of the corner of his mouth: "I say, this party isn't getting rough, is it?"

Bob Goodfellow, thus receiving the royal accolade, had become the first British Knight of the Military Williams Order since the

147

Duke of Wellington after the Battle of Waterloo. The three of us —
Bob, I, Chris — were standing stiffly at attention, lined up between the couch and General Van 't Sant's desk at 77 Chester
Square. It was a grey day, shortly after our last operation. Soft light
filtered through the spring foliage of the lime-tree outside, touched
the leaf-pattern of the curtains and filled the familiar room with a
green glow, like an aquarium. On the Steinway the documents for
the remaining two Military Williams Orders had apparently got
mixed up and the Queen, amiably assisted by her son-in-law, was
busy selecting the ones pertaining to me. Near the window the
guests stood watching silently.

Considering the circumstances, they made a curious group. The
Netherlands Ministers of War and of the Navy were present. I
hadn't seen the former since he threw me out of his office in Stratton
House, assisted by a military policeman. The latter was Colonel De
Bruyne's boss. I could well imagine Van 't Sant's devilish delight in
requesting their presence at this ceremony, on behalf of Queen
Wilhelmina. Between them stood Colonel Rabagliatti, clearly
savouring every minute, with next to him Peter Tazelaar, whose
similar decoration was being blocked by the two Ministers flanking
them. A few British representatives officiated for Goodfellow and
then, as always in the background, there was General François van
't Sant with an expression of such holy innocence on his face that I
almost burst out laughing.

Awarding high decorations for acts of courage is at best an unfair
business. For every man who wears the rare Williams Order there
exist ten who, with a little luck, could have become Knights just as
well. Merely sticking out your neck won't do it. You also have to be
noticed by somebody, ideally a general, who, for whatever reasons,
decides to recommend you for the honour. Amongst the score or so
of Williams Orders awarded in World War II, ours did not cut a
bad figure. But when I remember General Van 't Sant's holy expression I still marvel at the coincidence that they concomitantly
reinforced his own position so fortuitously.

Wilhelmina, documents in hand, stepped forward for the next
presentation. She positioned herself opposite me, waited for complete silence and, with the curious stridency which crept into her
voice at official occasions, read out my citation. Then she advanced
three paces which brought us face to face, and suddenly the

ceremony existed solely between the two of us. She looked into my eyes with the utmost gravity and now it dawned on me that here a Queen, far removed from the petty intrigues represented in that very room, was performing historic rites in order to invest me with the greatest honour for which her status empowered her. My knees began to tremble. The accolade fell, and in that same moment her expression relaxed to a smile, so unexpected, so sweet that tears jumped to my eyes.

After Chris had also been knighted the guests came forward to congratulate us, Prince Bernhard in the lead. "Now every military man whatever his rank has to salute you first," he smiled, digging Van 't Sant in the ribs. "Even generals."

"And colonels, too," Van 't Sant added with a wicked smile —

The demise of Colonel De Bruyne turned into a pyrrhic victory. The wrangle about his successor loosed such discord that finally the government suspended all intelligence activities. Special studies were made and endless reports written; behind every door hid an expert, unknown stars shot up overnight, glittered momentarily and sank back into oblivion, rumours were leaked and documents stolen, innuendo, spying and intrigue flourished on every side.

The next to shipwreck in the pea-soup of exile politics was Euan Rabagliatti. He never knew with certainty who amongst the Dutch authorities, out to isolate Van 't Sant, had managed to sink him with his British bosses.

On 19 June a luncheon took place in a private room at Claridge's, attended by Prince Bernhard, Prime Minister Gerbrandy, General Van 't Sant, Colonel Rabagliatti and myself. Its purpose was to devise a way by which the services of the Rabbi could yet be saved for the Netherlands' war-effort. The Prince offered to take the matter up with Anthony Eden, the British Foreign Secretary. General Van 't Sant revealed that Her Majesty the Queen was willing to discuss the matter with Prime Minister Churchill. Within a week they were scheduled to fly to the U.S.A. together and this would present an excellent opportunity. It seemed the perfect solution.

Bad weather kept Queen Wilhelmina for two days in London-derry, where Winston Churchill was to join her before continuing the journey together in a flying-boat sent by President Roosevelt. At the recommendation of Van 't Sant she had with her as temporary

A.D.C.: Chris Krediet! It was the first flight of her life and she took the delay as a personal affront. "If you refuse to take me up in this weather," she told the startled Americans, "I'll get some of my own Dutch boys. We're used to a little rain in Holland."

When they were finally able to take off, Churchill was not on board. By the time the Queen returned to England, Rabagliatti had faded from the scene. "Tell me," he cracked, when in the end he was transferred, "after fighting each other, do you Dutchmen have any time left to fight the Germans?" We said good-bye and for a moment his warm smile broke through, but the impact of his bitter words lasted many years longer. Then, with a wave of his hand, as abruptly as he had surfaced into our lives a year ago, he disappeared again into the murky world which had spawned him.

Rabagliatti's departure meant the end for the Mews. Until now we had paid little attention to the cabal in the Dutch camp, however vicious the infighting. Amongst the moves and counter-moves my court martial got blocked somewhere, but the C.I.D. was out to get us. Some administrator fired us all over again, although to achieve this he first had to reinstate us in our previous positions. What did we care? In the final instance it was the British who held control, and the Rabbi would never desert "Contact Holland" or us. But when he became the next to succumb to forces which he himself had loosed, in pure classical tradition, then we knew that for us, also, the curtain was coming down.

Besides, I was fed up to the gills. For months now I had moped around London with nothing to do, bored, frustrated, envying Chris in the States surrounded by all that good bourbon and all those slick American chicks. Meanwhile my mother-country, the Netherlands East Indies, was being wiped off the map by the Japs. We had been vaguely aware these past months of another war being fought, half-way around the world in the Pacific, especially whenever one of our Dutch submarines under Admiral "Ship-a-day" Helfrich sank another Japanese transport. But now it hit home: somewhere far away one of my roots had been severed.

Worst of all, with the Rabbi gone I found myself cut off from any information about "Contact Holland". To survive and grow at this stage it needed a constant flow of agents and transmitters, or it would wither through attrition. Was anything being done about it?

Did anybody give a damn? If all they talked about was firing us, should we continue to stick out our necks? Did it serve any purpose? Had I come to England for this, to hang about London day after day, stirring around in this putrid Dutch mess, bickering pettily with my countrymen, letting my love of Holland be eroded by a handful of Netherlanders who had never even seen a Nazi? I had escaped from the Occupation for one reason only: to be free to clobber the Moffen. If this was made impossible for me in Dutch uniform, then any other uniform would do. Hadn't I crossed the North Sea originally to fly with the R.A.F. anyway?. . .

Chris came back from America with a brand-new second lieutenant's star on his lapel. I ran into him at Orangehaven, as if he hadn't been away. "Tell me all about it," I said. "Did you meet any bathing-beauties?"

"Listen," he answered. "The closest I came to a bathing-beauty was Mrs. Eleanor Roosevelt in their pool in Hyde Park, near New York. And that'll do me for a while."

In spite of all his adventures he had surprisingly little to say, as if he sensed how foreign it all sounded there in Orangehaven, how unrelated to London around us, to the war, or even to reality. Queen Wilhelmina had addressed a joint session of Congress in Washington and received a standing ovation, yet the only thing Chris told us about it was that they couldn't get the lectern down far enough. "She looked awfully small standing there," he mused, but then he admitted to having had a fierce hangover that day.

Finally I couldn't contain myself any longer. "Now let me tell you something," I cut him short. "We're going to fly!"

"Splendid idea!" Before his departure Chris had also seen the writing on the wall. "Who with? When? What's it all about?"

We finished our tea and stepped out into the hazy morning. Walking along the park I filled him in on everything which had happened during his absence. At Marble Arch we took a bus to the Air Ministry and from there, a few hours later, to its Dutch equivalent in Arlington Street. The thought of getting rid of us spurred our countrymen to paroxysms of efficiency and before the day was over we had wangled ourselves a transfer to the Netherlands Air Force, for immediate detachment as air-crew to the R.A.F.

Van 't Sant remained behind, alone. Cut off from the S.I.S. by Rabagliatti's removal, left in the lurch by us whom he had so carefully groomed to be his supporters, he rapidly lost his influence in the sphere he loved so well – the Secret Service. After all he had done for us, our defection to the R.A.F. must have been a bitter blow to him. But now that we no longer needed each other, we discovered that meanwhile we had become friends. Our relationship had changed, but then, so had we. The "supercharged particles flung from the cauldron of the Occupation" which had whirled into London a year earlier no longer existed. Our tempers had yielded to their surroundings; we had cooled off. Not the North Sea, not the dark beaches of Holland, but London had in the end subdued us. We didn't have it any more, we were exhausted from fighting bureaucracy, we hankered after a less exacting task – like flying in the R.A.F., simple, honest, straightforward.

But in quiet moments I thought of "Contact Holland" and all we had put into it, and of our Queen's special mission which we had been about to fulfil, and of our agents under the Occupation who counted on us and could not transfer to another service when things fell apart. "Let's go," I said to Chris and Peter one fine morning. For the last time we polished the buttons of our old uniforms, until they gleamed white-gold. Then we walked across the park to St. James's and stepped into the Rabbi's old office. We handed a message to his successor, Major Charles Seymour, with the request that it be transmitted to our boys in Holland. "Can't guarantee it," was his answer, "but I'll certainly try."

The message, which would twitter into a secret agent's earphones during a few deadly moments of contact, read:

"Mews crushed good luck good-bye."

XVIII

I WAS OFF TO A GREAT START. PRINCE BERNHARD BANKED THE flimsy little plane on its ear, pointed to a meadow somewhere in the depths below and rasped through the speaking-tube: "O.K. now, just put her down in there."

With desperate determination I grabbed the stick. The field, surrounded by a fence, looked about as big as a stamp. The Tiger Moth began to buck towards the earth, wobbling and slipping like a drunken camel. The Prince, whose head stuck out of the open cockpit in front of me, looked around unconcernedly as if nothing were wrong. Only when all seemed lost would he give the stick a shove or pull us back on an even keel.

At the very end we had to pass between a tree and a haystack. It was a very tight fit. Frozen with terror I forgot about the fence. This time my tutor also reacted too late. The wheels hit the ground, the nose went up, we bounced over the barbed wire, Bernhard closed the throttle and held the wings level while the aircraft sank to earth like a pudding. The final bang shook my bones, but there we were, right side up in the middle of the meadow.

"I meant to ask you, have you ever flown before?" the Prince inquired, while in true Dutch style we stood side by side emptying our bladders against the haystack. When he had heard that I hoped to be a pilot, he had promptly offered to teach me a thing or two. I shook my head, still trembling with fright. "Well," he went on, laughing, "as you see, there's nothing to it. A piece of cake."

For Prince Bernhard the war was a frustrating business. Born a German, he had after his marriage to Princess Juliana made a conscious and meaningful transition of loyalties to his new fatherland. Because of this, and because of the doubts which his background initially evoked amongst some Britons, he longed more than anyone for a chance to get at the aggressors of the Netherlands. Just turned thirty, by nature no less adventurous than we Englandfarers, he shared with us the zest for battle and revenge from which his royal position excluded him. Instead, he had to burden himself with marginal military affairs such as liaison and representation, which left him unsatisfied. The irritations of the London scene, for us no more than interruptions in a time of action and fulfilment, were his daily diet. Like us, he was separated from his family, but while we blew off steam in cosy bars and nightclubs, often getting blissfully stoned in the process, his situation precluded him from ever entering a public place in London where dancing was in progress.

In his heart he envied the lowliest soldier who saw action against the enemy. As far back as 1940, during the invasion of the Netherlands, rumours circulated that he had fired on German planes from the roof of the royal residence, Huis ten Bosch, in The Hague. "Tell me," I once asked him, "is that really true?"

"Not from the roof," he answered. "From the front terrace. And I missed. But I did hit one from the roof of Noordeinde palace."

Best of all he would have liked to change places with a combat-pilot. Soon after arriving in England he took his training with the R.A.F. and won his wings, ultimately flying every conceivable type of war-plane. From that moment onwards no one, including the Queen, would vouch that he didn't secretly go after the Moffen now and then. In fact he did, and amongst the operational pilots of World War II Prince Bernhard of the Netherlands must be counted, with a number of B-17, B-24 and P-47 missions to his name.

"A piece of cake," the Prince had said, but between me and my dream still loomed the nightmare of a physical examination. Without glasses I couldn't even drive a car and when I strolled short-sightedly down Piccadilly, passing right by my best friends, they laughed at my ambitions. For weeks I stuck to a special diet to strengthen my vision – no alcohol, no cigarettes, pounds and pounds of carrots – but on the eve of the critical day everything fell apart. It started with Erik Michielsen. I literally ran into him, suspiciously

154

close to the entrance of the Wings Club. "What are you doing here?" I asked pointedly. "This joint is for fliers."

"I have also decided to join the R.A.F.," he announced, to my great astonishment. Since his arrival in London he had bombarded Stratton House with one weighty report after another, and I had fully expected him to slide smoothly into a cushy desk-job. Now this. I couldn't very well picture him as a pilot, he simply didn't seem the type, but that was his affair. I was truly impressed. We turned into the Wings Club. Diet or no diet, this called for a drink.

Afterwards I walked him to Orangehaven, just to be sociable, and stuck my head around the door out of pure curiosity. There by the window sat Chris, and Peter, and Louis d'Aulnis whom I hadn't seen for a long time, and Erik's brother Karel from the *Bèbèk*, and Han Doornbos, fresh from Holland, and several more new faces including a girl — such an eminent group, surely one glass of beer wouldn't harm. After an hour or so the conversation turned to physicals and someone suggested a brand-new game: eye-testing, for drinks. I lost to everyone. Did it really matter a damn how much I drank?

At two in the morning we all set out for the Embassy Club. A group of Polish R.A.F. officers were sitting at their usual table above the band. The mood was playful and when we started sniping at them from the back of the room, using little balls of silver paper and an occasional beer-coaster, they went on to the offensive. They jumped over the railing, hurtling a full ten feet down on top of Harry Roy and his band which scattered in a crash of brass and a flood of cockney curses, and stormed our corner where we frantically overturned tables and chairs to throw up a barricade. All I remembered later was Louis d'Aulnis sitting high up against the wall in a flower-pot, but according to eye-witnesses the Polish charge against the Dutch position in the Embassy Club must be counted among the more memorable actions of World War II.

At eight in the morning I got home, just in time to brush my teeth and have a taxi drive me very gently to the R.A.F. Medical Building. Apart from my passing out in the waiting-room, requiring wet towels to be revived, the physical proceeded smoothly; most doctors simply recoiled. Finally I wafted into the eye-section. "Christ!" said the doctor, a huge, shaggy man. He directed me to a chair in the middle of the room. "When I turn the lights out, read the letters."

As soon as he flicked the switch I fell off the chair. Our second attempt achieved a measure of success in that I remained upright, but the letters I couldn't even find. It was almost noon. Without a word the doctor put on his hat and coat and walked me out of the building, down the road and into a pub. Here I made a remarkable recovery. Then, over a light lunch, I told him the whole story, right from its beginnings in Leyden. Back in his office he gave me the highest possible medical qualification, A1B. "Do me one favour," he added. "Fly single-seaters, so you only break your own neck."

On 19 September 1942, I became No. 129282, R.A.F.-VR, cadet aircrew, with the lowest officer rank in existence: temporary acting Pilot-Officer on probation. I dashed to Sackville Street and ordered the most expensive uniform available, complete except for wings. On the black market I located a pair of standard R.A.F. flying-goggles with lens-corrections. In Bond Street I bought six pairs of glasses, three dark ones to wear by day in public, three clear ones to secretly fly with at night. The goggles, which proved to be as true as mirrors in a funhouse, I reserved for occasions when otherwise detection appeared inevitable.

Nine more times I had to pass eye-inspections before finally arriving in the blessed medical indifference of an operational R.A.F. squadron. Eight of these presented no problems. While testing one eye we were required to screen off the other with our hand. For this purpose I had smashed a pair of glasses and selected a number of triangular slivers of lens which fitted invisibly between the base of two fingers. Looking through one of these while supposedly testing the other eye, I could read the charts faultlessly. The ninth time I had to contend with a sergeant who prided himself on his efficiency and screened off my eyes with a piece of cardboard. Prewarned, I had spent hours in a rhododendron bush with a pair of binoculars, learning the letters by heart through the sickbay window.

On the critical day I recited my lesson full of confidence, but the bastard had hung a new chart over the old one. The result was, predictably, startling. He left to inform the doctor of his catch. When they returned they surprised me with my nose on the letters.

With a slimy smile the sergeant put the chart away . . . behind the old one! Now I had the situation under control once again and all he got for his efforts was a verbal kick in the arse.

*   *   *

The Company marched stiffly through the grey dawn. The narrow, curving streets lay deserted in the Sunday silence. A freezing drizzle draped the spires and ancient walls like fog, deadening the alien din of our footsteps. We could barely maintain R.A.F. regulation pace, a ludicrous 117 steps per minute, and still we shivered in our greatcoats. As supernumerary officers we brought up the rear, four Dutch pilot-officers behind a multi-national group of aircraft-men. When we passed a row of giant beeches along the Common, I slipped out of the column and hid behind a tree. Chris Krediet took the next one and Erik Michielsen the tree after that. We made ourselves thin and turned with the movement of the Company to keep the trunks between us and the drill-sergeant in command. Robert Bergmann, who made up the last row by himself, dutifully closed ranks and marched off — left! right! left! right! — with the rest of the cadets into the fog.

We came out of hiding, lit cigarettes and strolled back to St. John's College, hands deep in our pockets, collars over our ears, eyes barely visible under our caps. Through gateways and archways and up a flight of stairs hollowed by centuries of students' feet we reached the tower where we were billeted. Everything around us looked as if the R.A.F. had spared no effort to make us three Leydeners feel at home. And so we did. We ripped off our uniforms as fast as we could and dived back into bed. Cold, early Sunday morning marches did not appeal to the Leyden contingent of No. 2 Initial Training Wing, R.A.F. Cambridge.

An hour and a half later Rob Bergmann came clumping up the steps into our tower, blue with cold. "Trash!" he roared. "Lazy bloody trash! Rotting in your beds again, you're not pulling your weight, damn it! Nobody around here is pulling his weight."

"Robbie," Chris said quietly, sticking his nose one inch out of the blanket. "Do poke the fire up a little bit, will you?"

Bergmann, rumbling and grumbling, raked up the coals in the open fireplace. Then he flopped down with a book on Theory of Flight. In spite of his outburst and flamboyant exterior — smooth black hair, pencilled moustache, gypsy eyes – he exuded an air of patient tolerance. From the beginning he had philosophically accepted his misfortune of being, as a professional soldier and cavalry officer to boot, on the same training course as three Leydeners. Predictably, we took the utmost advantage of our unusual status as foreign supernumerary officer-cadets in the British Royal Air Force, but Rob persisted in executing his duties with painstaking thoroughness. The only thing which would occasionally discourage him, when he came home cold and exhausted from a march or other physical exercise and found us cosily around the fire with a bottle of booze, was that to our English bosses it apparently didn't make the slightest difference.

"Let me explain it to you," I offered, when once it got the better of him. "You're a professional, everything about you is professional. They don't like that in the R.A.F. It's not appreciated. The British are not like Americans. In the Army Air Corps there are lots of blokes who don't smoke, don't drink and do exercises to stay in condition. The Yanks love it if you take them for professionals. In the R.A.F. it's the other way around. Everybody wants to be taken for an amateur – brave, brilliant, but an amateur. Even professionals. It's a pose, like everything else, but the worst impression that you can make in the R.A.F. is that you take it all seriously." Chris and I grinned at each other. It didn't bother us. It's not easy to get excited about a morse test, when a few months earlier you were asking yourself which of your agents might still be alive.

For us the R.A.F. was tailor-made. Formalities were kept to a minimum, so that often it seemed more of a club than a military service. Every aircrew regarded itself as a team of specialists and largely ignored the usual concepts of hierarchy and discipline. The pilot, irrespective of rank, was in charge of his aircraft, with the result that a sergeant might well be in command over majors and colonels. This suited us fine, we thoroughly approved. We were less attuned to the all-pervading effort to familiarise new cadets with death. We had seen the old Reaper swish by too close, too often, to treat him as a big joke.

"They accept your disgraceful attitude only because you're foreigners," Robert defended himself. "Bloody foreigners. Britons only take other Britons seriously. Well, I don't go for that."

Chris and I couldn't care less. Life was a breeze. We just wanted

158

to get our wings, that's all. If it ever got to the point where we found ourselves face to face with the Moffen, we'd make damn sure they'd take us seriously.

"What's more important, Bergmann," Chris cut us short. "I hope to Christ you're good and ready for that navigation test tomorrow. The whole thing is a mystery to us." For the test the next day we carefully positioned Rob Bergmann between us and copied his answers word for word. Our British instructors studiously looked the other way. When they returned our papers to us they had awarded me 86 points for my efforts, and Chris 84. Robbie, fuming, had to content himself with 65.

That evening, as usual, we went to the pubs; the Blue Boar, the Mitre, Joe Mullins', the Bath, the Eagle. The night throbbed with aircraft. Cambridge lay in the heart of "bomber country", a complex of airfields from which the "heavies", Stirlings, Wellingtons, a few new Halifaxes and Lancasters, slowly but surely got the night offensive against Germany off the ground. The bars were blue with R.A.F. Surrounded by wings and D.F.C.s, next to which our unknown decorations meant nothing, we were painfully aware of our insignificance – "kiwis", "wingless wonders". But sometimes in the midst of all the noise and laughter, as if screened off from it by silence which he himself generated, a man in blue would sit, slowly sipping beer. From the stripes on his sleeve – a flight-lieutenant's usually, or a squadron-leader's – our envious looks would slide upward to the wings and the purple/white slashes of the D.F.C., and up. Then came the shock: the schoolboy face, the greyish skin, the acne, the old lines around the eyes, staring vacantly from dark, deep sockets.

When the pubs closed, at eleven sharp, we stumbled out into the black night and felt our way back to the tower of St. John's. Suddenly, in ghostly silence, the sky lit up. It became bright as day. For five, ten, fifteen seconds the streets lay before us, wet and drained of colour, and the drizzle hung like smoke in the glow. In Cambridge everybody knew: somewhere in "bomber country" a plane had crashed on take-off, fully loaded, and just now five or six of us had perished in the blaze. No one spoke. The glare faded to orange, then red and slowly died away. It left the darkness twice as black.

The course concluded with a test in the air. Then we went on leave. In our British uniforms we stepped off the train into the drab, misty, smoky streets and discovered that London was home to us. Just months ago, before we left for Cambridge, it had sheltered us as exiles; but now it was our town and whatever Hollanders it contained were merely part of its eight million citizens. Orange-haven, which that very summer we had regarded as our living-room, now harboured Englandfarers who didn't even know us; we politely introduced ourselves. More and more we drank our bitter in Shepherd's, the traditional meeting-place for officers of all nationalities who had returned to London from afar – Canada, Tobruk, Murmansk, Tripoli, Scotland, even Cambridge. Beyond the Dutch community with which I had been so passionately in-volved, a wider brotherhood emerged and received me with open arms.

Weeks passed, then months, and still we waited for our sailing orders. A green haze touched the bushes outside the windows of Orangehaven, where we gathered in the mornings to drink free coffee and read the *Express*. The news in the papers disturbed us. Montgomery, after endless delays, had beaten Rommel's "Afrika Korps" around El Alamein. At the other end of the Mediterranean American armies fought in Tunisia. The Russians had turned the tide at Stalingrad, in the process destroying the German Sixth Army whose planes had bombed Rotterdam in 1940. Now the headlines proclaimed one Nazi defeat after another, near Rostov, at Rzjev, all along the disastrous retreat to Smolensk. "You know what?" I said to Robert Bergmann, who was glumly reading over my shoulder. "If it goes on like this, you and I are going to miss the boat."

When Holland capitulated I fervently hoped that the Germans would last until my country could have made an honourable con-tribution to their inevitable destruction. Was this the reason for my concern that the war would end before I could take part in it as a pilot? For Holland's "war-reputation", its "share of warfare", or whatever else I used to call it, my lonely exploits at best couldn't make much difference. That wasn't it; in fact, I felt foolish at the memory of my narrow chauvinism. How petty it now seemed, marching side by side with men of a dozen nationalities, sweating through tests together, cribbing each other's answers and blundering through British skies in common fright, misery and exaltation!

What, then, was the reason? I fully understood my desire to clobber the Moffen, but the question remained: for whose benefit? My circle of commitment seemed to be steadily expanding – my family; the limited fraternity of Leyden; then, in the pangs of defeat, the love of country. For this I had gone to war, for the Netherlands. But now, didn't I stand for England as well? And for all other countries with whose sons I served? Or perhaps for all humanity, excluding the Nazis and the Fascists? Circle beyond circle. Surely an ultimate circle must exist, beyond exclusions, beyond strife, beyond war?

Or did I want to fight the Nazis purely for my own benefit, because at my age everyone needs a dragon to slay? What luck, then, that at the right moment Fate had sent one my way, a true ogre at whom I could tilt to my heart's content in the smug knowledge that I was serving Good in the struggle against Evil, everything crystal clear, everything black and white, none of the confusing shades of grey in which less fortunate generations must grope and fumble! —

*　　*　　*

At last our orders came. Aircrew training had been scattered through the Empire and we were instructed to indicate our geographical preference. After endless deliberations we chose Rhodesia, so it shouldn't have surprised us that we were posted to Alberta, in western Canada. On 3 April we reported to No. 31 Elementary Flying Training School in De Winton, near Calgary, where we constituted the last group in the history of mankind to train on biplanes; with my leather helmet on I had the recurrent notion of being one World War behind. After completing the course the Dutch contingent split. Erik Michielsen with four men disappeared to Moose Jaw for twin-engine training; Rob, Chris and I and the remaining Hollanders went on to single-engined Harvards at Medicine Hat. Africa could hardly have been hotter, and the Commanding Officer of No. 34 Service Flying Training School revelled in the reputation of being a slave-driver. This failed to worry the foreign supernumerary officers, now a group of twenty-two from eight different nationalities. Most of us had already seen more action than the other cadets were ever likely to experience, and the British usually left us in peace. Not so Canadian Group-Captain

Ellis. To our dismay he even ordered us to participate in physical training and early Sunday morning church-parade. The officers' quarters hummed in indignation in English, French, Dutch, Flemish, Czech and Norwegian. Robert Bergmann, still performing his duties with exasperating precision, came to the gleeful conclusion that at last military discipline would prevail.

Chris and I thought differently. We promptly professed our allegiance to an imaginary religious creed which, in defiant contrast to the Church of England, we christened "Church of Holland". Clearly this was tricky ground and even the group-captain fell back before the threat of an entanglement with foreign morals. The sect was governed by stringent rules which forbade its members all early morning activities, particularly on Sunday, and when the other nationalities marched off grumbling to church-parade the Dutch had to resign themselves to staying in bed and snoozing a little longer. Spurred by these successes our religious fervour gradually assumed fanatic proportions. Without much effort we converted Han Doornbos, who had meanwhile arrived in De Winton with the next course, after which we proclaimed a series of Holy Days on which, as heads of our respective congregations, we sent each other's commanding officers imperious telegrams. Then all the Hollanders received special leave and departed, with sanctimonious faces and thirsty gullets, to celebrations in Calgary and Regina, followed by the wistful stares of the Norwegians, Czechs and Belgians.

There were other problems. With the end of our training in sight we worried constantly about the tempo of the war and our chances of participating in it, especially as the R.A.F. was turning out too many pilots in relation to the production of operational aeroplanes. As a result, the number of rejects increased alarmingly and hardly a week passed when we didn't say good-bye to another "washed out" pilot standing lonely and miserable on the Medicine Hat railway station. In addition, every so often someone crashed and killed himself, which always left us shaken. Death might be a big joke, but we wanted no part of him. What had gone wrong which couldn't just as easily happen to us? I didn't fly badly, but my technical knowledge remained pure theory. When someone showed me a real engine, with all those little ducts and valves and rods each performing a critical function, it only made me nervous. The general mood was not improved by the practice of always keeping a few newly-dug graves open, ready for the next poor chump. The cemetery lay in line with the runway, and when judging my height in a final approach I found it distinctly disconcerting to look straight down into six feet of fresh red earth.

As far as we ourselves were concerned, we soon learned that Robbie suffered severely from air-sickness, while Chris' heart delivered insufficient pressure to pump enough blood to his head at all times, so that in every tight dive or steep turn he blacked out for some moments. In conjunction with my secret manipulations of six pairs of glasses it was hard to avoid the conclusion that we were more willing than able.

"The answer is teamwork, very simply," Chris tried to cheer us up, when one day we were reviewing our future as fighter-pilots. "Just stay close together. I'll spot those Messerschmitts before they see us, never fear, but I doubt that I'll be much good after the first dive. O.K., then you and he go after them and by the time Rob is puking all over the place, surely you'll be close enough even for you to see them. Well, then all you have to do is knock the bastards down."

On 1 October 1943, we received our wings. It was a great day. To no one's surprise Holland captured the "Prix des Nations", the prize for the best national result in the course, which always amounted to a contest between the Dutch and the Norwegians. On top of this I won the gold cuff-links awarded for the highest individual score. The Wings Parade was one parade nobody missed, except for a Dutch cadet who had got so drunk the previous night that he failed to make it. True to tradition Group-Captain Ellis appeared at his bedside to pin the wings on to his pyjamas.

On the last night, by special permission, I went up one more time. The night was pitch-black; only in the east a crescent moon separated the sky from the black prairies. After circling around for a while I climbed to ten thousand feet, aimed the right wing-tip at the silver sliver, firmly clamped on my glasses, turned the Harvard on her back and let the nose drop. The needle of the speedometer crept up towards the red line. I gently pulled the stick towards me, executing a big vertical curve until we shot straight up into the air on the other side of it. I kept the aircraft vertical, revolved her ninety degrees to the left around her longitudinal axis, pulled her on her back at precisely the right moment and rolled her out to normal flying position. The nose pointed straight at the moon, the altimeter once again read exactly ten thousand feet. I smiled in the darkness — I had learned a lot since that Sunday morning when we marched through Cambridge in the fog.

XIX

"To arms!" the tall lieutenant shouted, as soon as he saw us. He took off his cap, placed it in front of his chest, bowed deeply with chivalrous grace, straightened up and beamed. "Up and at 'em! Victory shall be ours! We shall return to the Fatherland covered with glory, medals, crosses, ribbons, gongs and stars that light up in the dark. Welcome aboard!" Six thousand soldiers swarmed like ants all over the *Aquitania* in New York harbour, and the first we ran into was Van Brero, "Count B" of yore, who had helped carry our dinghy across the dunes at Noordwijk and later escaped with Chris as cook on a coaster, destination England. After making his way through Sweden, Russia, Siberia, Japan and most of the U.S.A. he had halted long enough in Washington D.C., to become Assistant Military Attaché in the Netherlands Embassy. Now at last he was off to war to burn away this stain in the fire of battle. Anyway, he looked pretty sharp in his expensively tailored uniform.

After searching for twenty minutes we found a few square feet free of G.I.s, in a life-raft behind the funnel. We installed ourselves happily, Herman and Chris, Erik Michielsen, Robert Bergmann and I, a little Dutch cell in the apprehensive body of troops about to cross the hostile Atlantic, ready for anything and nothing. We smoked and discussed the incredible coincidence of finding ourselves all together on the same ship, and waited to pull out. Behind us gleamed the skyline of Manhattan, where I had just spent two riotous weeks of leave.

It had been a disquieting experience. The entry of America into the war had not made much impression on me, busy as I was at the time splashing about in the surf off Scheveningen. I had always been convinced of ultimate victory as a matter of faith rather than rationality, long before Pearl Harbour, and therefore failed to appreciate the decisive importance of the event. In this respect our two weeks in New York were hardly helpful. Where was the war? The very generosity which overwhelmed uniformed servicemen seemed to convey a sense of obligation rather than participation, the avid attention we attracted set us apart from our hosts, like bullfighters from their public.

"Aren't you sorry to miss it all?" I asked a young barman in the Biltmore Hotel, after six free drinks.

"Hell," he answered. "Nobody likes to get killed." A thoroughly reasonable attitude, but after Europe it was hard for us to identify with anything less than total war.

Herman departed on an expedition to the bar and returned half an hour later with five bottles of Coca Cola. "No booze," he explained, considerably shaken. "With American G.I.s on board they can't serve it. To nobody, the whole bloody trip long."

Meanwhile tug-boats had towed us down-river and we were passing the Statue of Liberty. The brutal profile of the city shrunk and faded to ethereal loveliness. "By the way," Herman said, "I have a corporal in my unit who claims that he knows you. Tazelaar, his name is. Corporal Tazelaar."

"Peter Tazelaar?" Chris and I stared at him perplexed. "Where is he?"

"Down in the hold." He pointed at the deck under our feet. "Straight down, as far as you can go without getting wet."

We immediately set out for the bowels of the ship, Count B in the lead. Gone was the vision of New York. Row after row of makeshift bunks crowded in all directions, crammed four high right up to the ceiling three feet apart like cells of a honeycomb, iron frames covered with canvas, bulging with hairy, sweaty bodies. This was how I imagined a concentration camp. The deeper we went, the hotter and fouler the air. We had stepped aboard fresh from nights of parties, dinners, girls, music, wine and candlelight. The G.I.s around us, half-naked in the stench, stared sullenly at our immaculate officers' uniforms. It was difficult to realise that

166

we all performed in the same war. And this was where Peter hung out?

In the furthest corner of the bottom hold, where only the ship's skin separated us from unimaginable amounts of cold, black water full of U-boats and our sun-drenched deck seemed a distant memory, Herman stopped at a bunk of which the canvas was tightly laced up. "This is it," he announced, as if we had arrived in the zoo at the cage of the rare, white orang-utan.

"Peter! Hey, Peter!" Chris and I called out. We banged on the sides. I felt the same anxiety I had experienced standing in the hall of 23 Hyde Park Place, the night that he shot himself in the mirror.

"Sod off, all of you," someone inside growled. He seemed to have trouble with his speech. "Everybody sod off." No doubt whatsoever; it was Peter, and he was stewed to the gills —

For Peter Tazelaar everything had gone wrong since his second escape from Holland. On his arrival in London he landed squarely in the middle of our conflict with the Marines. It didn't take Colonel De Bruyne long to bounce midshipman Tazelaar out of the Navy. With the demise of the Mews the reorganisers of the C.I.D., all rank amateurs, considered it prudent to rid themselves as quickly as possible of this experienced Resistance fighter. They offered him a charming choice: either corporal-draftee in the Army or inmate of a camp for British quislings.

But Corporal Tazelaar knew himself to be a respected member of the Dutch Underground, a status which he refused to relinquish. Frustrated at every turn, he broke every rule and regulation, until in the end nobody knew what to do with him. Finally he was bundled off to the Netherlands Army camp in Guelph, Ontario, as far from London as possible. Now he totally withdrew within himself and, unpromoted, undecorated, unbelieved, unknown and bitter, he was generally regarded as a nut. Until 30 June 1943, when Queen Wilhelmina visited the camp.

The royal inspection had been minutely planned, and on the stroke of noon Her Majesty entered the mess to greet the soldiers, assembled for lunch. Dutch, Canadian and American generals fluttered around her and the hall swarmed with lesser officers. But Wilhelmina had prepared her own little plan and knew exactly where to go. To everybody's consternation she walked right through the men straight to a corporal, shook his hand and said: "Good morning, Mister Tazelaar. I'm glad to see you again. I hope that things are all right with you." From that day onwards the officers treated him with nervous respect.

Shortly afterwards the camp was closed and Stratton House, still anxious to keep him out of London, ordered the Netherlands Embassy in Washington to employ him. But now Peter had had enough. He wanted to get back to the war, for which he had twice escaped from the Occupation. After two weeks in the U.S.A. he threatened to give his story to an American newspaper if the next boat to England sailed without him. The Dutch authorities capitulated. The next boat happened to be the *Aquitania*.

Even at this nadir his proverbial luck did not desert him altogether. Discovering one bottle of whisky on board, the commanding officer, an American colonel, decided to raffle it off amongst the six thousand soldiers. No Irish Sweepstake could have aroused greater excitement. Peter won. He locked himself up in his cage and finished the entire bottle before the ship had cleared the harbour. He opened up for no one, not even for us. Once during the journey we ran into each other, but he seemed ill at ease. When we entered Liverpool, standing high up on the sports-deck I saw him way below me on the poop. I waved, but he didn't see me. A few weeks later I heard that he had become a London fireman, in the district of Soho.

We went on leave. For five months I didn't set foot in an aeroplane. By that time I'd had all the leave I ever wanted. London was slowly changing to a semblance of peacetime. No more roly-poly barrage balloons nuzzled the chilly breezes overhead, no crash of bombs shattered the silence at night. The black-out continued, but if ever the guns in Hyde Park fired a round or two everybody went "Aaaaaah!", as at a fireworks display. When the papers printed complaints about aircraft disturbing people's sleep they now referred to the R.A.F., and the hotels dropped their policy of charging less for top-floor rooms of which we had always taken advantage. Where a year earlier the call "taxi!" sounded through every dark West End street, now American voices yelled "cab!" The evacuees had returned, every restaurant and bar was packed and head waiters began to get cocky again. "A few little bombs now and then," I grumbled to Chris somewhere in a queue, "would do this town a world of good."

In Orangehaven we had become strangers. The club-room, which once had seemed enormous to us, now bulged with new Englandfarers. By and large they were a different breed. They drank sparingly, worried about money and called each other "mister". The conversation, which used to consist of inspired nonsense, flying-talk and abuse of Stratton House, now bored us with topics like foreign currency, government insurance and "the future". I felt more at home in Shepherd's.

Some of the newcomers did bring word of old friends and enemies: Frits van der Schrieck had been arrested; Ernst de Jonge had been shot; Paul Renardel was alive in the "Orange Hotel"; the Blubber had been executed by the Underground; my former friend and fellow Leydener, Alexander Rowerth, was fighting in Russia with the S.S.; Jean Mesritz had been moved to a concentration camp in Poland; Jacques Maasland had unofficially passed his final Law exam; Frans Goedhart had been sentenced to death; Dr. Krediet, Chris' father, was performing medical miracles as an inmate of Dachau; Broer Moonen had been executed by the Gestapo; Anton Muller had disappeared. . . . It all sounded so unreal, I couldn't grasp it. Sometimes it seemed as if the war would go on for ever.

Equally incredible was the story of Bob van der Stok, our stowaway aboard the *St. Cergue*. Shortly after the Queen's tea-party in Maidenhead he had been posted on Spitfires. He flew for half a year as a fighter-pilot, until the Moffen shot him down over France in April 1942. He managed to bale out, but was captured and in due course locked up in Stalag Luft III, near the German–Czech border. But Bob had eluded the Nazis before and now he took the lead in the biggest prisoner of war escape in World War II, later published and filmed under the title *The Great Escape*. Eighty-six Allied fliers tunnelled themselves out of the maximum security camp. Ultimately eighty-three were recaptured and some, contrary to all rules and traditions, were executed. The remaining three, two Norwegians and a Hollander, made it to freedom. Bob was the Hollander. Disguised as a slave-labour worker he had managed to reach Switzerland and from there returned to London. I ran into him at Shepherd's. He looked fine. He was back on Spitfires, having a marvellous time.

We waited and waited, and gradually our gang fell apart. Eng-

169

land swarmed with pilots, trained and battle-ready, who would cut each other's throats for a posting to an operational squadron. It was every man for himself and our best chance lay in striking out on our own. To our envious surprise Robert Bergmann beat us all in wangling himself into an Operational Training Unit, the last stop before a squadron; well, at least he had learned something useful from us in Canada! Erik Michielsen, whose chances as a twin-engine pilot were better from the start, departed shortly afterwards. Chris was the next to leave London, and at long last, on 3 April 1944, I myself reported to No. 5 O.T.U. at Condover, near Shrewsbury.

*　　*　　*

I stretched out luxuriously in the warm grass and took a deep breath. It was spring. The sun glowed in the flowering hedges, the scent of hawthorn lay heavy over the meadow. The pale sky arched empty and still, not an aeroplane broke the silence. Bees buzzed, a distant church clock chimed the hour. War? What war?

Before me lay Condover airfield, half a mile away. Beyond it to the east I saw a Miles Master approaching over the brow of the hill, the sound of its engine reaching me simultaneously. As I took my training on the same type of aircraft, half an hour here, half an hour there, I followed the pilot's moves with interest. He flew towards me, banked into his final turn right overhead, lowered his flaps and let down away from me towards the empty runway. I sat up to watch his landing. By the time the little machine touched the ground I could no longer hear its motor. Like a tiny toy it bounced, wobbled into the air and hung there for a moment, hesitating. Next the left wing flipped under, pulling it on its back. It scraped along the tarmac upside-down. Then it lay still. I knew immediately that of the cockpit – and the pilot – nothing could be left.

It seemed such an insignificant incident, such a childish little scene silent in the distance on this glorious day, that at first I couldn't bring myself to take it seriously. I didn't even jump up. The sun felt as warm as before, the bees still buzzed, I could smell the hawthorn. Was this, then, what it all led to, all that love, all those hopes and dreams, to one fragile moment in the sunshine of a lovely afternoon? Could it be?

That very evening Englandfarer Father Monchen called me from

London. Erik Michielsen had been killed. During a night exercise the propeller of another aircraft had torn his tail-plane to shreds. Erik had somehow managed to keep his machine under control long enough to let the crew bale out, but for himself it had been too late. "The funeral is tomorrow," the priest added. "We count on you."

"Forget it, Father," I answered sharply. "I won't be there. I can't afford it." Erik Michielsen had been my friend. We had lived through much together and I admired him. But somehow it seemed of paramount importance to me not to confront death more realistically right now than as a broken toy in the sunshine of a spring afternoon.

A few days later I went back to London again. Why not? Things at Condover were so slow, we could get leave for the asking. Besides, a lot of Dutch fliers would be gathering for a royal reception in Orangehaven, where perhaps I could pick up some useful tips.

The club was jammed. To my surprise they were serving sherry and jenever, and not since Toon Buitendijk's juicy remarks at the Maidenhead tea-party had so much uninhibited Dutch resounded within earshot of Queen Wilhelmina. It didn't seem to bother her at all. With a slight smile on her lips she moved through the noisy crowd, a word here, a handshake there, sometimes all but invisible amongst the tall R.A.F. boys who only at the very last moment would notice her approach and fall back for her, after which she sailed on with the serene dignity of a small battleship in the sea of blue uniforms.

Suddenly I saw little (Robert S.) Cohen. We called him "little" to distinguish between him and "big" (Dr. J.) Cohen. He was the student from Delft who had crossed the North Sea in a canoe. The last time I had seen him he was hanging around London, like me, an unemployed pilot with shiny new wings hunting for a squadron. Now the rumour persisted that he had taken part in the fantastic tree-top raid on the Gestapo headquarters in The Hague. Executed at the request of the Underground it had entirely destroyed the Dutch population records on which the Gestapo based its deportation system. How the hell had he managed that? I had to get the story.

"There were four of us," little Cohen told me in his diffident manner. "Four Mosquitos. We made our bombing-run right over the roof of the Peace Palace, in line of course, Wing-Commander Bateson in the lead. We bounced our bombs horizontally into the place, almost through the front door, and whoosh! off we went, home." I was trembling with excitement. What an experience, especially for him, to help smash the whole Nazi razzia-files to bits!

"My own bombs hung up," he added quietly, with just the slightest suspicion of a tremor in his voice. "When we got back I opened the bomb-doors and there they were, just the way they went in." Robert Cohen, surely the most honest pilot of World War II, received the D.F.C. a few weeks later, just in time before he was shot down and killed over Chartres in France.

"But how did you manage to get on Mosquitos in the first place?" That was what I really wanted to know. He postponed his answer, because the Queen joined us for a chat. She knew us both by name, as she would probably remember most of those present. I found her changed in the two years since we had last seen each other, less tense, as if she felt at home in Orangehaven, pleased to be surrounded by the informality of her Englandfarers. She seemed unusually lighthearted and gave no sign of wanting to leave the party, in spite of the fact that the room was blue with smoke. After a few minutes she moved on. We bowed at each other awkwardly and little Cohen continued as if nothing had happened.

"I packed my bag and hit the road, like a travelling salesman," he said, spreading his hands, palms up. "From airfield to airfield, squadron after squadron. 'Any room here for a pilot? Anybody need a good pilot? Pilot available, able and willing, reliable twin-engined pilot available . . .' Well, at R.A.F. Lacham they needed a pilot."

D-Day had come and gone, Allied armies battled in Western Europe, the Russians were in Poland, but the world of operational fliers remained an elusive Land of Promise. I had almost given up hope; would this approach perhaps offer a last chance?

Full of excitement I called my girl friend Midge and within half an hour we were putting our heads together over a pint of bitter at Shepherd's. For her, also, the world consisted of aeroplanes and flying-men, and since my return from Canada we had been inseparable. "We're going to hit the road," I announced and told her Cohen's story. Outside, Hitler's new V-1s, the spooky, unmanned "buzz-bombs", rumbled through the darkness like distant lorries. As long as we could hear the noise no one in the bar paid the slightest attention to them, although sometimes we had to raise our voices over the din. But as soon as the motor cut, indicating that the projectile had started its steep glide to earth, everybody stopped talking and listened, waiting tensely through about fifteen seconds until the explosion. For several weeks now London had been noticeably less crowded, but Midge had no desire to join the exodus. "Why not Shepherd's?" she countered, powdering her diminutive nose. Just then the glasses rattled on the tables. "Instead of traipsing all around these crumby places, why don't we just install ourselves in here? Sooner or later we'll see every squadron commander in the R.A.F."

Nine evenings in a row we kept our vigil in Shepherd's, before dinner and afterwards till closing-time at eleven o'clock. On the tenth night a short, square wing-commander breezed in. Underneath his wings I spotted just about every decoration obtainable through combat-flying, as well as the golden wings of the "Path-finders". "Hamish Mahaddie," Midge greeted him, as they shook hands. "Just the man we've been waiting for."

I thought, of course, that she'd had too much to drink. The Pathfinder Force (P.F.F.) consisted of a handful of squadrons — fourteen out of the many hundreds into which the R.A.F. had grown — in which the best and most experienced air-crews had been gathered together to lead the night offensive against Germany. Their aircraft were crammed with special radar and electronic gear, enabling them to navigate precisely in any kind of weather. They flew two or three minutes ahead of the main bomber forces, indicating the turning-points along the route with flares, finding and marking the target with Target-Indicators (T.I.s) and generally supplying whatever guidance would improve the quality of the attack. On nights when the weather was considered too fierce for the rest of the R.A.F., they set out on their own.

The handful of Pathfinders, responsible for the precision of attacks carried out by hundreds of bombers, were recruited almost exclusively from crews who had completed a tour of operations varying from thirty to fifty attacks. With their exclusive gold wings, often in tandem with the D.F.C., they represented an *élite* which inevitably had to contend with the envy of other R.A.F. officers. I myself had occasionally eyed them with awe in the Blue Boar or the Eagle at Cambridge, but what possible use did I have for this phenomenon at our table, with his D.S.O., D.F.C., A.F.C. and God knows what else? Pathfinders flew bombers – I had trained for fighters. They required experience – I was fresh from school. Their aircraft were two-engined Mosquitos and four-engined Lancasters – I had only flown single-engine. Their element was darkness – I had just over seventeen hours of solo night-flying to brag about. Midge kept on talking but I barely listened to the conversation, until I heard Mahaddie say: "Well my dear, it is true, in rare instances we do take outstanding pilots with less experience."

"There we are," Midge smiled, kicking me under the table. "Then he's just what you're looking for."

The wing-commander laughed, got up, made his way to the bar and returned with three shots of Scotch, neat, as befitted a Scotsman. "Fair enough," he announced. "I'll get him a posting to the Mosquito Training Unit at R.A.F. Warboys, and if at the end of the course they rate him 'above average', we'll make a Pathfinder out of him."

"Sir," I interjected timidly. "How about first teaching me to fly an ordinary machine with two motors?" Mosquitos had touched down at Condover once or twice, with a landing-speed which gave me the chills, and the idea of starting out on my twin-engine career with a giant Rolls-Royce Merlin on either side of me struck me as a little farfetched.

"My dear fellow . . ." Mahaddie began.

"Cheers!" Midge interrupted, lifting her glass with an innocent smile. "Here's to you, Hamish. And – thanks."

The wing-commander took a big swallow of whisky. "I suppose it could be arranged," he sighed.

For two months I flew Ansons, Oxfords and Blenheims, familiarising myself with twin-engined aircraft of increasing power and complexity, but when I finally transferred to a Mosquito it was like stepping from a family saloon into a Formula One racing car. Somehow I survived, then slowly mastered her intricacies, and after flying her for thirty hours I graduated from the course with the specified "Above Average". Hamish Mahaddie, of course, proved as good as his word.

On 5 September 1944, I reported as Pathfinder pilot to No. 139

(P.F.F.) Squadron, R.A.F. Upwood, not far from Cambridge. The very next morning my name appeared on the battle-order for that night. I walked out of the mess for some fresh air. In the flower-beds around the entrance a few late roses still bloomed. Over neatly-paved paths I wandered into the grey morning, between low, stone buildings, cutting across the parade-ground where an R.A.F. flag fluttered in the misty breeze, along the back of an enormous, camouflaged hangar. The grass verges were trim, the hedges clipped. The few corporals and sergeants I met saluted me good-naturedly, except for a sergeant-major who all but dislocated his arm. The sound of aircraft was everywhere: the flat, stationary rumble of a test-run, close by; somewhere above ten thousand feet a far, smooth drone; the controlled, high whine of a landing-approach; now and then the roar of a take-off. On the other side of the hangar stretched a concrete apron and beyond it, lonely and deserted in spite of all audible activity, the airfield. Mosquitos stood parked in clusters of three in widely separated dispersal areas, their slick lines close to the ground. I tried to locate Q for Queenie, the aircraft I would be flying tonight, and found her on the apron being serviced by the ground-crew; she submitted to their ministrations like a patient horse being curried. From time to time Mosquitos taxied by along the perimeter track, wagging their tails for better vision, pulling to a stop down-wind to run up the engines. Then they swung on to the runway and took off in earsplitting thunder, slender and graceful as soon as the wheels had retracted, skimming the bare, flat land – "bomber country"! Four years since that decision in Wassenaar, two since my transfer to the R.A.F. I sighed deeply. I had made it. Just in time.

A Mosquito landed, taxied on to the apron and switched off engines a few yards away from me. A ground-sergeant came ambling up, opened the nose-hatch, positioned a narrow aluminium ladder into it and handed up an artificial leg. Some moments later the crew, pilot and navigator, came lumbering down the steps. They walked by me, flying-helmets loosened, parachutes across their shoulders, white silk scarves, gold wings, D.F.C.s, a mighty moustache. The navigator, a pale, thin man – South African Squadron-Leader Johnny Day D.F.C. – leaned on a stick and laboriously kicked his left leg before him with every step. We nodded at each other. Squadron-mates, and yet a world apart.

Why? Suddenly I knew why. In spite of my two years in the R.A.F., all the training, the wings, the psychological preparation, the books, the films, the lectures, the stories, the jokes and the anecdotes, I didn't have the vaguest notion what it would be like tonight. He did. He knew exactly. And yet, even had he wished to, he couldn't help me. It was a threshold which every man, when the time came, had to cross alone. What lay behind it was not so much frightening as totally unimaginable. Like the hereafter.

Tomorrow things would be different.

XX

BEN IS LATE. HE'S ALWAYS LATE, BUT NEVER TOO LATE. HOW MANY times now have we been to Germany together? Fifty-eight? Sixty? Still, every time while he's being late, I worry. Actually, it's more a case of my being early. He's a cool one, Ben, he likes to fiddle around until the very last moment with his maps, his pencils and his dividers, his wind-directions, bombing-runs and E.T.A.s, talking to the little computer strapped to his thigh as if the bloody thing were alive. I myself prefer to sit in the cockpit for a while before take-off, nice and quiet. It is so small, even for just two, that you've got to get used to it all over again.

I adjust the harness-straps across my chest, tight but not too tight; wiggle back and forth on the parachute, which fits into the seat, until it feels as if my arse might survive some five hours of continuous contact; reach out to various knobs and levers, first with my eyes open, then blindly, until I can find my way by touch in the confusion around me; then I just sit, staring ahead. After a few minutes I begin to feel better, less awkward. It's very important to me, specially when the weather is bad. The weather is always bad.

Outside, the winter evening huddles over Upwood. Drizzle spots the windscreen, distorting everything; the hangars look like battleships, runway and perimeter lights fuse into a muddled mess. The de Havilland "Mosquito": two Rolls-Royce engines, thousands of horsepower, revolutionary super-plywood construction, radar, the latest in electronica, but simple ordinary windscreen-wipers – forget

M

it. That's the R.A.F. for you. The most sophsticated aircraft of World War II, Ben and I swear by it, but we never leave the ground without an ample supply of rubber bands and chewing-gum for all kinds of essential little repairs in the cockpit.

Darkness reaches down from the sky. It's cold, you can be sure there's ice up there. How low would the cloud-base be five hours from now, on landing? Bloody met. officers, always painting a rosy picture! Night-fighters, flak, rockets, I'll take them all in exchange for some decent weather. But I suppose we'll manage. If you get through the first five operations you'll be all right, they say. Maybe so, but after my first one – to Hamburg some six months ago, with F.O. Ray Snelling D.F.C. – I never thought I'd make it to five.

We have a gadget in the cockpit called the "boozer". It's secret. It starts to glow when the jerries pick us up in their radar: red when they track you, bright red when you're locked into the aiming mechanism of a heavy flak battery, yellow when you've got a night-fighter on your tail. We're very happy with it, particularly since we ourselves are unarmed. Mosquito Pathfinders are supposed to survive by being smarter and luckier, as well as fast.

From the moment we crossed the Dutch coast the boozer glowed. Every time it jumped to bright I yanked our Mozzie wildly off her course and when once the yellow came on, probably just because of static electricity in a thunderhead, I threw her into such a steep diving turn that she almost didn't come out again. All this in solid cloud, pitch black, hour after hour. It was a miracle that we ever found Hamburg, or even England on the way home. At de-briefing we reported having seen no trace of the enemy, but when the next morning we turned up for flight-check we found our baby – Q for Queenie – under repair in the hangar, with seventeen fist-size holes in her wooden fuselage.

There's Ben. I can tell from here that he's all set to go, looking for action, ready to clobber them. Ben likes big, fat targets and tonight it's a juicy one. Navigation-board under his arm, chin stuck out, he strides pugnaciously across the dispersal, around Mosquitos which stand silently in clusters of three and four, slender as wasps. He stops at T for Tommy, where Dave Groom and "Rosie" O'Grady are about to climb the steep little ladder to the hatch in the nose. They move clumsily like bears, in their parachutes and Mae Wests. They laugh, jab Ben in the ribs and hoist themselves up the steps and through the hole. The ground-crew slam the hatch-cover and lock it. Now they are no longer Dave and Rosie, only T for Tommy.

"Hello Hazelsnout!" Ben's head sticks up through the floor of the cockpit, round and smooth in the leather helmet except for the ear-phones. Other pilots are addressed as "captain" and "skipper", I have to make do with "Hazelsnout". He squirms through the hole like a giant beetle, into his seat to the right of me. We both face forward, shoulder to shoulder in the mass of instruments. While he struggles into his harness, cursing contentedly, I switch on the wing-tip-lights. The ground-sergeant holds up his thumb and shuts the hatch. He scurries off, wheel-chocks in one hand, pitot-head cover in the other. I look at my watch – from now until we have marked the target with our T.I.s, our target-indicators, as aiming point for the bomber-fleets behind us, we live by the second-hand. Two minutes and twenty seconds until take-off. It's almost dark now outside, all around glow the little red and green lights. Ben sits silently beside me; everybody and everything seems to be waiting and it's very quiet everywhere, very quiet. . . .

Behind us an engine sputters, immediately followed by two, three more; one catches and roars, then another, then four, six, a dozen, all of us, and within seconds the whole dull, dismal evening, the bleak field and miles of sleeping English countryside have sprung to violent life. All around engines thunder, flames blast from exhaust-pipes, propellers whirl, tail-planes shudder, aircraft tremble, and now they move, nosing left and right, little red and green lights stopping, starting, Mosquitos like black shades turning and twisting towards the perimeter track, then running straight for the starting post as if eager to get off. I move in behind T for Tommy, the noise swells dramatically and there goes the first one, dimly lit by the run-way-lights, carefully feeling for direction, then faster and steady, roaring down the field and up, away into the gloom. Now the next, and the next, and the next, every thirty seconds. T for Tommy, off and gone. Our turn. "Check petrol-cocks." "Petrol-cocks SET." "Check booster-pumps." "Booster-pumps ON." The green flash hits my eyes, hurry, hurry! We swing on to the runway and instantly, miraculously, the muddle of lights resolves itself into a wide avenue leading straight into the dubious night. I slowly push the throttles forward all the way.

"Ice," I inform Ben, as soon as I have a moment. Barely off the ground and already we're in the soup — cloud, rain, hail, ice. Queenie feels sluggish and wobbly. Outside the dim little cockpit it's blind-dark.

"None of my business," Ben cheerfully announces. I turn up the volume of the intercom, the better to hear him. "You're the bloody pilot, it's your job to keep the bitch in the air. That's what they pay you for." I grin. I suppose he'll never quite forgive me the one time that I stuck my nose into his navigating —

After eight or nine operations with Ray Snelling I ran into Ben Hein, in the Blue Boar in Cambridge. He patted me approvingly on the chest, where underneath the Military Williams Order my brand-new Pathfinder's wings gleamed. "Hazelsnout," he declared, "with you I'll fly. We may fall flat on our arses, but at least we won't turn back when the going gets sticky. There's more of that in this war than you might think, and I've had a bellyful of it." Spoken like a true descendant of the Dutch pirate and naval hero Admiral Piet Hein; which he was and sometimes had trouble forgetting.

My desire to fly with Ben was based on less heroic considerations. As a lieutenant in the Netherlands Navy air services he was bound to be a superior navigator. Also, we had been to school together, in The Hague, which should make for a happy team. He requested and obtained a transfer to Upwood, but our first trip together — to Berlin on 12 October 1944 — almost resulted in the end of our friendship. And of us, too.

To begin with, we couldn't understand each other. With both Dutch and English at our disposal we never knew what language to listen for. Over a weak intercom the mixture of multi-lingual flying terms proved unintelligible. Confused and unhappy we flew to Berlin, where Ben dropped our "Christmas trees". We were in cloud all the way and failed to observe any activity whatsoever over the target — no reflection of searchlights, no night-fighter flares, no flak, nothing. Under those circumstances it takes a lot of nerve to mark an aiming point for hundreds of approaching bombers.

But neither was there any trace of our own squadron. After several minutes on the way home I looked back once more: our cluster of red flares still hung above the clouds in solitary splendour, while underneath them silent flashes of light reflected the bomb-bursts of the main force behind us, dropping their block-busters . . . on what? A meadow somewhere? Killing a few luckless cows? Could it really be that we were the only Pathfinder who had found and marked the target that night? Ben maintained a surly silence. Finally I couldn't stand it any longer. "Ben," I said, "are you sure that was Berlin?"

This time he heard me perfectly. "Christ almighty!" he exploded. "Now you can kiss my arse." He grabbed his maps and flung them through the cockpit. I suppose the trip had affected me more than I suspected. I just couldn't take it. "Fair enough," I shot back, letting go of the steering column. "And you kiss mine."

There we sat, two stubborn Dutchmen side by side, grim and furious, as if we had never heard of Germans. From 38,000 feet we tumbled down. Of course, out of Ben's sight I kept my left hand on the trim-wheel and my feet on the pedals, but even so the Mozzie fell like a stone. Every so often Ben cast a sidelong glance at the altimeter and when we whizzed by 18,000 feet without let-up, he snatched a map out of the air. "Aw hell, let's go," he mumbled sheepishly. I was more than happy to comply.

But it was just the beginning. We had forgotten about the jerries. After levelling off we found ourselves smack over Magdeburg at 15,000 feet; ten seconds later we felt a sharp blow and our starboard engine was on fire. It didn't blaze, but the flames were bright enough to reflect frighteningly in the clouds around us. I quickly feathered the prop, closed the petrol-cock, switched off the ignition, increased power on the port engine, re-set the trim, pushed the extinguisher-button and hoped the fire would go out. Ben, the microphone pro-truding from his round head, stood out against the glare like some weird pig. He looked unhappy.

"Did you press the tit?" he asked peevishly.

"What tit?"

"The whipped-cream tit."

"Naturally."

"Then why isn't the fire out?"

"Look Ben, I didn't invent the bloody thing, I only pressed it. If you let me fly, I'll let you navigate. O.K.?" And that's the way it's been ever since.

The fire did go out, but we still had to fly home on one engine. With difficulty we maintained an altitude of 12,000 feet. Having lost the generator we ran out of juice, which knocked out all the lights and the wireless. At the last moment Ben found a torch somewhere. Increased petrol consumption forced us to take the shortest route and everyone along the way celebrated our unannounced arrival by blasting away at us: the Germans in the Ruhr, the Americans around Aachen, the Canadians near Antwerp and lastly, with particular gusto, the British Navy off Sheerness. When at long last we rolled to a stop at the end of Upwood's runway 2, we had pretty well jelled into a team. And you had to give him credit: only Ben that night had found and marked the target.

*   *   *

"Set course zero nine three."

"Zero nine three. O.K." I set the new course on the gyro-compass and slowly start to turn on instruments. Ben, double-checking his calculations, doesn't even look up from the navigation-board on his lap. Everything calm, everything under control. We're old hands now, too experienced, too formal almost for such childish outbursts and fits of temperament. Ben has been promoted to lieutenant senior grade, I am a captain; we have completed our first tour of operations, we wear British D.F.C.s and Dutch Flying Crosses and gold Pathfinder's wings, we form a unit about which nobody worries any more. "Q–Queenie? No word from Q–Queenie? Isn't that Ben and Hazel? Oh hell, no panic. They'll be all right."

R.A.F. Upwood was a peacetime station – central heating, hot and cold water, spacious mess, well-stocked bar, batwomen, all the comforts of home. Before the war, the roses in the garden won prizes in the local flower shows. Here Ben and I led a bourgeois existence, very quiet, very smooth, no emotions. We shared our own room with bath, and if ever the hot water ran out, we snorted with indignation. A W.A.A.F. corporal woke us in the morning, made our beds and kept the place clean. Well, what of it? We didn't bat an eyelid when the squadron lost forty per cent of its crews in two months, but all this manly stuff in tents and draughty Nissen huts – no, thank you. Even the daily routine suited a Leydener: plenty of activity during the night and long, lazy mornings. And when around eleven we sedately made our entrance into the bar for an early sherry, we were greeted with respect by the new boys – just like Seniors in Minerva.

Furthermore, no one had to sleep at Upwood unless he wanted to. My girl, Midge, had found herself a room in St. Ives, six miles away, and many nights I bicycled through the soft, silent countryside, still high on oxygen while the residual roar of flights to Munich, Hamburg or Cologne lingered in my ear. Midge had fresh eggs and Guinness and a mattress of goosedown. And when we lay under the covers, safe, warm and happy, I thought about the next day and hoped my name would be on the battle-order again. It happened often enough. We flew three or four operations a week, weather permitting, and what with flight-tests and briefings we barely managed an occasional pint at the Pike and Eel. Even on New Year's Eve Ben and I and several others quietly slipped away from the mess, shortly after midnight, champagne glasses in hand. Most of 139 Squadron and their ladies were standing around the piano, and when we got back we happily plunged into the same old song — "roll me o-o-over, in the clo-o-over" — and nobody except Midge had missed us. Yet in the interim we had clobbered Hanover.

Zero nine three, due east. We're on course now, levelling off at altitude, 36,000 feet. I adjust the trim until Queenie all but flies herself, make sure that the exterior lights are out and stretch my legs comfortably beyond the rudder-bar. It's pleasantly warm in the cockpit, almost cosy; outside, the temperature stands at minus fifty and Ben reports winds in excess of eighty miles an hour. The cloud is solid, but just as I resign myself to yet another blind journey we burst breathtakingly from the gloom. We have outclimbed the setting sun and caught the day in its last golden moments.

First I quickly look around — as usual, there's not another aircraft in sight. We all take off together, fly the same route at the same height to the same target to arrive at the same moment, but we hardly ever see each other. Except when one of us is caught in enemy searchlights; then everybody sees him, often for the last time. Still, they must be around us somewhere, eight times two friends packed tightly in wooden boxes brim-full of fuel and dynamite, covered in ice. Behind us follow hundreds of bombers, Mosquitos and Lancasters, invisible also, to aim their loads at our "Christmas trees".

Ben, figuring out the time for the first route-marker, is talking to his computer again, a sure sign of well-being. I nudge him and point outside. We seem to be sailing in a scarlet sea crested by

183

golden waves. Behind us Queenie's tail-fin stands like a dagger against the sunset. Pink curtains of cirrus hang daintily beyond the brute profile of our port engine and through a gash in the clouds below I glimpse a rose-coloured abyss. Dead ahead, most majestic of all, comes the night in steely shades of purple. There, below, in the darkness, lies the Third Reich in its final agony.

They were lasting a long time, the Moffen. Americans across the Rhine, Russians across the Oder, bombers pounding from the sky around the clock, and still they fought on like tigers. You had to respect them, but pity? Impossible. They had wronged too deeply, gone too far. Now the rest of humanity was at their throats in outraged fury. For England the day of retribution had come. Like a giant aircraft-carrier she lay on the fringes of the European war, which had now moved entirely to the Continent. In daylight endless fleets of Flying Fortresses and Liberators, packed with Americans, took to the air; at night the English skies throbbed with Lancasters, Halifaxes and Mosquitos of the R.A.F. Now provincial towns like Cambridge and Peterborough formed the centres of military activity, bursting with aircrews from Bomber Command and the Army Air Corps. London awaited the soldier's leave like a City of Joy – not even New York could touch the gaiety of the British capital which had suffered so much, so recently. All our old West End haunts fell to the Yanks; we couldn't afford them any more and moved our action further out, to pubs and clubs in Knightsbridge and Chelsea. The buzz-bombs had meanwhile been licked and no one paid much attention to Hitler's second secret weapon, the V-2. Not that they were ineffective, but there was nothing you could do about them. They fell out of the stratosphere and when you heard them it was all over, one way or another; so why worry? Air-raid shelters, mostly deserted, regained a measure of popularity for unforeseen sex encounters, now that the black-out was being less strictly enforced. One night, dropping from the clouds after a mission to Stuttgart, we could hardly believe our eyes: circles of little white lights twinkled around the airfields of "bomber country" and red beacons showed us the way home. No doubt, victory was in the air.

I was playing a role in that victory, and in that agony. It was impersonal, I didn't get excited any more. For the British I rejoiced with all my heart; as far as the Nazis were concerned, they had signed their own death warrants when they placed themselves at the triggers of the firing-squads, the levers of the gas-chambers. That sentence was now being carried out not because of Holland, not because of Europe, but on behalf of all humanity. Circle beyond circle. Like a snake shedding its skin you outgrow one circle after another, ever wider, until the last ring bursts asunder and you belong to everything. Where would it all lead? What would the future bring? In war life is simple. But wars come to an end, the taut horizon recedes and there lies Life. . . . endless. . . .

XXI

"New course. zero eight four." ben's voice comes through metallic over the intercom.

"Zero eight four. O.K." I take a look at him. We're so close, I have to turn my head almost at right angles. It's dark now, the little light clipped to the navigation-board casts an eerie glow on his formidable chin. Out of the corner of my eye I see the boozer come to life, glowing red; we must have crossed the Dutch coast. I peer down through the blister in my window, past the blue exhaust-flames of the port engine. Obliquely below us – Wassenaar? Scheveningen? – an orange speck appears, hovers indecisively above the low cloud for some seconds, then streaks suddenly up in jerky gusts of speed and disappears at stunning heights: a V-2 rocket on its uncertain way to London – more work for Peter and his fire-brigade!

To the south, where Allied armies are sloshing ahead, I can follow the front from the Dutch rivers through the Ardennes well into France, a line of flickering light-reflections below thin cloud. From time to time vicious streams of tracer-bullets break through the cloudcover, red, orange and white, whizzing back and forth. Chris operates down there somewhere, on Spitfires no less, dodgy heart and all. So does Robbie Bergmann, hunting tanks in a Typhoon, airsick no doubt, puking all over Germany. Still, he got himself a D.F.C. the other day. I wouldn't change places with them – all that bloody mud and cold and stand-up latrines. I've recently discovered that our batgirl, if adequately smiled at, will serve tea in bed.

It's time for the route-marker. Ben peers at his watch, finger on the trigger of the Verey pistol. Plop! For a split second I see our wings, ghostly grey, as the flare shoots up and away. I bank the aircraft and look back at the red ball hanging motionless in space. Not without pride I imagine the main force behind us wheeling at full tilt to line themselves up with our signal and follow our lead. A second ball suddenly floats in the dark, out of nowhere, to port and slightly lower, then two more to starboard, very close, and another. A minute ago we were alone beneath the hard brilliance of the stars, now I sense the presence of our squadron all around me. It's a good feeling.

We're barely over Germany when the boozer jumps to bright. I nudge Ben. "Christ, what are you pulling on me now?"

"Osnabrück," he answers calmly. "We're just a teeny bit close to Osnabrück."

I can't fool around, we've got to get to the target on time, two minutes before the main force. If the Pathfinders are late the entire attack falls apart, bombers milling around in the searchlights and flak without an aiming point to drop their cookies on – very bad show. I decided to ignore the boozer; the gunners of Osnabrück aren't the greatest anyway, in our experience. Soon it returns to a dull red. That's how it stays, because from now on the entire German Air Defence tracks us every foot of the way, trying to guess tonight's target in time to crank up their guns and put the night-fighters in the air. We try to fox them; we are routed to approach a city menacingly, turn away at the last moment towards another, then veer off again suddenly to pounce on the unsuspecting victim – we hope. Sometimes it works, sometimes it doesn't, but this little game we and the jerries play every night.

We're approaching the heart of Germany. The weather has turned clear, right down to the ground. All around us lie the fat, juicy targets, legendary, awe-inspiring names that seem to have bounced around in our subconsciousness ever since we put on air-force blue. Now they're getting it, by day from the Americans, by night from the R.A.F. This morning it was the Flying Fortresses. To starboard the sky glows, below it rivers of fire run into four orange pools: Brunswick. Far to the north a tiny trickle of amber sparks

187

drips down, then more, hundreds, thousands, a rain of golden illuminating-flares which quickly knit themselves into a brilliant canopy over the unfortunate city below: Hamburg. Elsewhere, also, the big boys are on the prowl, Lancasters and Halifaxes; in several places I see the lacework of heavy flak spattering delicately. Here and there near the ground climb the leisurely tracers of light anti-aircraft fire. Everybody's in the act tonight.

The boozer flicks to bright. Now it's serious, this is Hanover and here they know their business. "Have we time for evasive action?" I ask Ben.

"What kind?"

"Slalom."

"Plenty of time." If he had answered in the negative, we would have ploughed straight on. It's as simple as that.

I wait for the first shell-burst; they rarely score first go. There it is, an innocent-looking little black cloud to the left of us, slightly high. Now the jerries below start correcting the error. I know that it takes a shell about twenty seconds to get to us, so after fifteen seconds I change course five degrees to the left. If they are efficient down there the change will have occurred after they fired the next round, but before it reaches us. . . . Poof! There it is, on schedule, to the right of us where it ought to be. Below they're correcting again. Meanwhile I change course to the right, ten degrees this time to make up for the previous deviation to the left. Poof! Very nice, to the left of us. Ten degrees to the left. . . . Poof! To the right of us. And so on, occasionally combined with a gain and corresponding loss of a few hundred feet of altitude. In this way we maintain our original direction of flight while staying alive. All you need is a reliable gun-crew down below.

"Hey Hazel, what time do you make it?" I almost jump out of my seat. I recognise the carefree, "down-under" accent of Rosie, somewhere out there in the dark, but he sounds so close that instinctively I glance over my shoulder. We always maintain radio silence, except for emergencies and irrepressible Australians. I tell him the time, that's all. I'm acutely aware that hundreds of Germans are listening to these two enemy voices deep inside their country. They all know the game. It can't be long now. Ben is immersed in calculations.

"Last course into target," he announces curtly. Everything now revolves around Ben and his radar-box, and the accuracy with which I follow his instructions. We know our stuff, we want to be the best. "Course one four eight. First lose two and a half minutes. We're early."

"Two and a half minutes. Course one four eight. O.K." I carefully put Queenie into a specific turn; exactly two and a half minutes later the circle is complete, we are at the same spot. "One four eight ... now!"

Ben, staring at his watch, grunts with satisfaction and shoots off a route-marker. Before sticking his head back into the radar-box he pulls a stopwatch from his pocket and pre-sets it with the duration of the bombing-run. Since our radar will be useless over the actual target, we have to fly the final, critical miles by dead reckoning: course, speed, height, time, all determined beforehand. Bombers weave into the target-area and fly straight and level no longer than it takes to drop their loads accurately, but Pathfinders must maintain an absolutely steady bombing-run for up to several minutes in order to produce the basic requirement of a successful attack: a valid aiming point. Sometimes I wonder if it's worth the little gold wings we wear.

I lower my seat and turn up the instrument-lights. Whatever happens outside, from here on in there's little I can do about it. We have penetrated so far east, surely by now the jerries must know what it's all about. . . . Ah, there they are, and they're ready for us. Dead ahead, wholly unreal but with cold, defiant menace, hundreds of searchlights pierce the cloudless sky, rigid, motionless, like quills of an enormous porcupine. "Come and get it," they say. We're coming. Here goes for the juiciest target of all: Berlin.

Someone has entered the frozen forest of searchlights and magically it comes alive. The blue-white beams begin to weave slowly, each in its own section, long, slim fingers feeling their way, touching the inside of the transparent black dome above, unhurried, hesitating, but always moving on, searching. . . . Over to port I see a speck of solid matter in this rarefied world. On the ground they have seen it also — ten, fifteen beams whip over to it and cross each other where the Mosquito holds them together like a clasp. White lacework begins to spatter around him. Undaunted the little ship presses on, straight as a die — one of ours, 139 Squadron. Suddenly

I find myself staring at some tiny cracks in the paint of our own engine nacelle, which a second ago was invisible in the dark. As I look over the side an unblinking, glittering eye meets mine, bitterly hostile, so blinding that I quickly pull back my head. Wham-wham-wham-wham . . . four more beams smack in on us, then half a dozen more. We're tightly coned, down below pools of violet light surround us. Even Ben looks up from his box. I can see every hair on his unshaven chin. "This is what they pay us for," he says soothingly.

"How much longer?" We're well into our bombing-run now.

"Ninety-six seconds . . . ninety-five . . . ninety-four. . . ."

I drop my seat all the way, only the top of my head sticks out above the cockpit. Don't look, just keep going. We are droning along inside a light-ball of incredible intensity. Course, height, speed, everything steady, just the way Ben wants it: like a train on rails. Next to me, parallel to Queenie and only a shade higher, five or six black puffs burst into existence. I can't help seeing them out of the corner of my eye. Twenty seconds until the next lot. No slalom this time, straight ahead, level and steady. Just keep going.

"Sixty seconds coming up . . .' Ben never takes his head out of the radar-box, he wants that Christmas tree in the right place. ". . . now. . . . Fifty-nine . . . fifty-eight . . ." Poof! There they are, corrected for height, still to the left but close enough to hear. Keep going . . . Crrrack! Very close, smack in front. We sail through the black clouds, I can smell the cordite. At the same moment a cluster of three yellow flares pops out of nowhere, right above us; German night-fighters. They are signalling to the gunners below: "Hold your fire. We're here. This one is ours." Just keep going.

"Thirty seconds. Open bomb-doors."

"Bomb-doors open." Actually we're not carrying any bombs tonight, only target indicators, reds and greens. I must remember to call them out to the main force, to offset the dummy T.I.s which jerry is shooting up from the ground. Final check: course – exact; speed – exact; height – exact; we should produce a fine aiming point, if we make it. It's ominously quiet around us. Where is the flak? Then suddenly the yell in our earphones: "Fighters! Look out! Fighters!"

"Steady . . ." Ben has one eye on the radar, one on the stop-watch and his thumb on the bomb-release. Does he give a damn that we're lit up like a show-case, visible for miles, an unarmed, sitting duck for every night-fighter around? The yellow boozer flicks on, here they come! "Steady . . . steady as you go . . . it's moving in beautifully . . . ten seconds to go . . . steady . . ." What can I do? Just keep going . . . "Five . . . four . . . three . . . two . . . one . . . T.I.s gone!"

"Q–Queenie. T.I.s gone. Reds and greens. Reds and greens!" Shouting my message to the main force I yank the Mozzie into a vertical turn, dropping the nose steeply. "Hit them, you peasants," Ben growls to himself. We are diving, twisting, turning, climbing. The boozer goes out. The searchlights lose us. Suddenly we're in darkness, safe. In a warm, exulting wave life floods over me.

We're heading west, weaving lightly, out of the target-area. We watch the eerie activity behind us, to our right. The attack is in full swing. The Pathfinders have done their job, now it's up to the main force. Six cones of light move slowly over Berlin, each holding a bright little Mosquito in its apex, surrounded by flashing white dots. Clusters of red and yellow fighter-flares hang all over the sky and there, motionless amongst the weaving beams, float our Christmas trees in deadly splendour, brilliant red, luscious green, while a late one cascades between them like a lazy, golden waterfall. Underneath the T.I.s, blockbusters crash into Hitler's capital, billowing into fiery mushrooms.

A mile to the north a stream of tracers shoots through the night to the focal point of a cone. At its tip a little orange speck appears, gradually increasing in size, but not much. Then it begins to spiral down in tight turns, slowly, ever so slowly. The searchlights won't let go, from all sides others join in the kill and follow the stricken Mosquito down. It takes a long time. Finally the beams are almost horizontal, a vivid sea of light in which the Mozzie blows up with a puny flash. Now the beams sweep the sky in exultation, up, down, up, down, up, down. . . .

Suddenly I was bicycling along the road to St. Ives. How soft the English countryside, how fragrant, even in winter, even in the rain. Forty thousand feet high, what horror, but now I was riding my nice old bike, close to the friendly earth. Would Midge have managed to get fresh eggs, I wonder? What was that I smelled? Honeysuckle? Here? This time of year? God, life was stupendous! A couple of fried eggs, maybe, once over lightly, with a strip or two of bacon, and then to bed. . . . What would it be like to spiral down from

191

forty thousand feet above Berlin in a burning Mozzie? And then to bed. What a lovely evening it was, soft and gentle. What would it be like? How great to trundle through the night to St. Ives . . . three . . . two . . . one more bend in the road. The door stood open. . . .

"You're five degrees off course," Ben snarls. I jerk back to reality. He has a right to snarl; if I don't steer his courses, he can't navigate. Behind us the attack is over. The remnants of one burnt-out T.I. still glow in the target-area, an orange glare here and there shows some scattered fires. Save for a score of searchlights sticking up motionless into the sky, widespread and dismal, Berlin lies in darkness. How did we get so far, so quickly? Don't ever let them tell you that an attack, any attack, is "a piece of cake". It gets to you, it wears you out. When it's over you're so bloody tired and relieved, it's hard to concentrate. You feel you've had your share for the night, but there's the weather over England still to come, always the bloody weather. . . .

André van Amsterdam told me a good one the other day. The Chief of the Pathfinder Force, Air Vice-Marshal Bennett, is a bit of a stickler. He insists, for instance, that while in the air his pilots express themselves in dignified, professional terms. Even his car is stuffed with radio-gear, so that at all times he can tune in to their wavelengths. "Jesus Christ, chaps, I must be nuts, farting around up here in this bloody weather!" an anxious voice came down one particularly nasty night.

The A.V.M. switched to his transmitter and barked into the mike: "This is Bennett speaking. The airman who made that vulgar and unprofessional remark, report your name and serial number."

After a short silence the same voice came back: "Sir, I may be nuts, but I'm not that nuts." Great chap, old Amsterdam, superior pilot, one of the best of the seven Dutch Pathfinders in the R.A.F.; or six, now. What in God's name could have happened, that he failed to return from Hamburg last night?

"You can start losing altitude," Ben advises. We're taking a bee-line home and have just plunged into a massive cloudbank, choppy as hell. This is where it gets sticky. You drop the nose down and stare yourself blind on the instruments, sometimes for an hour or more. The hands of the altimeter turn, turn, knocking off the thousands of feet, slowly, inexorably. The speedometer creeps ever

It was strictly forbidden to photograph briefings.

If Ben got knocked off, I still had an emergency-map in my boot.

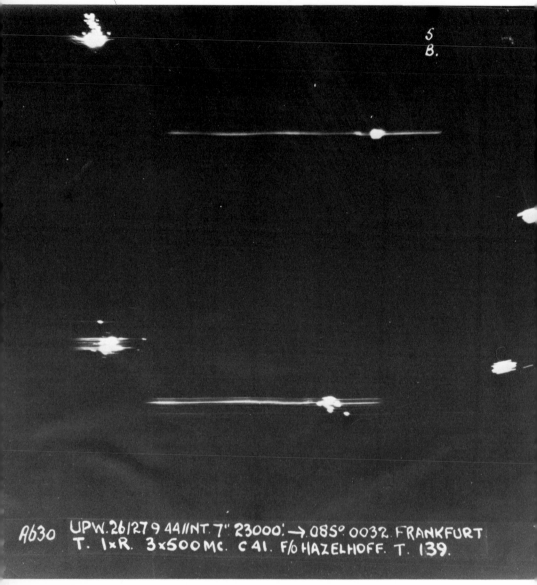

The aiming-point photo showed a steady run over the target.

DATE 1	TYPE OF AIRCRAFT 2	AIRCRAFT LETTER 3	SORTIE No. 4	TARGET 5	6	REMARKS, including reasons for :— (i) Failure to complete sortie ; (ii) Ceasing to operate in, or leaving, current squadron (e.g. missing, posted, killed, etc.) 7
MAR. 7	Mosquito	Q	53	Berlin	C	
" 11		Q	54	Berlin	C	MASTER BOMBER
" 13		Q	55	Berlin	C	
" 14		T	56	Oldenburg	C	
" 15		V	57	Erfurt	NC	STARB. ENGINE SHOT AWAY OVER COLOGNE
" 17		W	58	Berlin	C	
" 20 a.m		Q	59	Berlin	C	MASTERBOMBER
" 20 p.m		S	60	Berlin	C	DAMAGED BY FIGHTERS
" 22		Q	61	Berlin	C	
" 24		Q	62	Berlin	C	
" 26		Q	63	Berlin	C	FORCED LANDED AT WOODBRIDGE; PORT ENGINE U/S.
" 30		L	64	Berlin	C	
" 31		V	65	Berlin	C	DEPUTY MASTERBOMBER.
APR. 19		Q	66	Kiel	C	
" 22		Q	67	Kiel	C	

POSTED FROM THIS SQUADRON ON (Date).................................... TO.....

If the sheet is completed in respect of a pilot, insert a star in column (4) against sorties as second pilot.
In column (6) insert C if sortie was completed.
NC if sortie was not completed.

ADD 5 MULTIPLE OPS.: TOTAL: 72

Some weeks we hardly saw the 'Pike and Eel'.

'Mozzie', R.A.F.-Pathfinder.

The first step back on Holland's soil, leaning on another?
Unthinkable!

At first we gazed out impressively over the multitudes.

SUPREME HEADQUARTERS
ALLIED EXPEDITIONARY FORCE
MISSION (NETHERLANDS)

PERMIT TO ENTER RESTRICTED ZONE   NO. 948

FULL NAME __Capt. Erik HAZELHOFF-ROELFZEMA__

NATIONALITY __Dutch__

NO. & TYPE OF IDENTITY CARD __R.A.F. 1250   No. 129282__

DESTINATION __All parts of NETHERLANDS (including Restricted Zone).__

REASONS FOR JOURNEY ____

__As Aide de Camp of H.M. Queen WILHELMINA__

THIS PERMIT IS VALID UNTIL __indefinitely__   ~~FOR ENTRY ONLY~~
                                               FOR ENTRY AND EXIT

DATE OF ISSUE __21 May__ 19 __45__

TRAVEL PERMIT OFFICER
2 1 MAI 194
SHAEF   G-2 SUB/SECTION.

Richard A. Ken
Capt.

A SHAEF pass opened all doors.

Two generations of Queens turned on me.

Slowly the big Packard rolled into my old stomping-grounds.

higher, surreptitiously, no matter what you do. All those vital, intent little faces stare right back at you, until you get the feeling that they, not you, are flying the aircraft. Outside, cloud hugs the ship like black cotton wool, until it seems to seep into the cockpit. Increasing air-pressure crackles in your ears, the roar of the engines gets louder and louder, and all the time the hands of the altimeter keep turning. . . .

Ben and I fell on our arses, a few weeks ago. It was more weird than serious. I had bought myself a sharp-looking pair of black flying overalls, and every time I wore them something went wrong, little things, but enough to abort our operations. Four successive times we were forced to turn back, then Ben asked me to leave them at home. I insisted on one more try. Dressed in black I set out for Berlin. We marked the target, flew home and touched down at Upwood in perfect weather. I was just about to heave a sigh of vindication when the Mozzie – S for Sugar, Queenie being under repair – suddenly swung to starboard. They never determined the cause, but I simply couldn't hold her. At eighty miles an hour we went into a ground-loop, tearing off the undercarriage in a cloud of dust and sparks. On the frozen earth the wooden aircraft disintegrated like a matchbox. The "blood-wagon" came tearing down the field and, despite our protests, took us to the sickbay. We were just arguing our way out when the doctor walked in, greatcoat over his pyjamas and accompanied by an enormous dog. Both eyed us sourly. Then the doc rummaged in his desk and gave us each a pill.

"I don't want a pill," Ben said. "I'm fine." He spoke for both of us, we didn't have a scratch.

"Do as you're told," the doctor snapped. Now that we had got him out of bed, he was bloody well going to do something. "Regulations. You have a prang, you get a pill." As he held the rank of squadron-leader, the pills disappeared. Then he concentrated on filling in lengthy forms.

"What did you do with your pill?" I asked Ben after a while, in Dutch. "Did you eat it?"

"Are you crazy?" he answered, in the same language. "I gave it to that damn dog. He loved it."

"Oh Jesus, so did I."

At this moment the creature fixed us with a long, reproaching look and keeled over. We later heard that he had slept for two days and two nights. The doctor glared at us suspiciously when we finally saluted him across his snoring pet and got the hell out of there. The black overalls came to a fitting end that night in the roaring flames of the heating-furnace —

A bolt of lightning suddenly flashes all around us through the darkness, almost giving us heart-failure. For several seconds I'm completely blinded. When I can see again, eerie blue flames dance on the propeller-tips. Next we are caught in a net of static electricity, which runs across the windscreen in fiery, crackling rivulets, harmless but alarming. Then again we seem to be underwater, as a thick layer of ice covers all the windows instantaneously. Queenie wobbles under my hand, she flies like a pudding. At the same time we bounce around in a series of drops and sickening lurches, and all the time the altimeter keeps turning . . . 28,000 . . . 27,000 . . . 26,000. . . . Would we be over Holland yet?

Holland. How in God's everloving name was it possible, how could it conceivably have occurred that the whole world was free from Germans, liberated, France, Poland, Belgium, even our own southern provinces below the rivers, but that this tiny corner of Europe, north-west Holland, the heart of my country which held everything, everybody I loved, was caught in a trap, a hell of hunger, terror and death to equal the worst miseries of World War II anywhere? Admittedly, I myself had been late in realising it. When the British airborne assault on Arnhem failed in September 1944, and the Nazis ensconced themselves defiantly north of the rivers in what used to be called "Fortress Holland", anybody could foresee that the inhabitants of the area were in for a rough winter. But not that it would be this gruesome. Living my self-satisfied little life in the R.A.F., pleased with the fact that I risked my neck now and then, I had paid scant attention to the news from the Netherlands. Until one afternoon in London, when I had nothing better to do and decided to drop in at 77 Chester Square.

It so happened that I followed the same route along which Peter Tazelaar and I had walked to our first meeting with Van 't Sant, more than three years ago, loaded with sherry and very little else. The guardsman in front of St. James's gave me the same spectacular salute, which I returned gravely, without a wink this time. The Royal Standard waved above Buckingham Palace; the King was at home. I bet he felt pretty good these days – only a short time ago the Moffen were still trying to dive-bomb him. Chester Square looked as shabby as I remembered and the house in the corner still needed a paint-job. The Mews was all locked up, dark, overgrown by the lime-tree. I slipped into the garden by the side door. Van 't Sant was standing on the balcony. Only the bluetit was missing.

"What do you hear from Krediet?" the general inquired, as soon as we sat down in the old, familiar room. He had immediately made time for me. I told him that Chris was hale and hearty, whizzing about in a Spitfire over France.

"And what about Peter?" I asked him.

"Doing the best he can," came the smooth answer. As far as I knew Peter was knocking around Soho as a fireman, but from Van 't Sant's innocent face I might have known that he was up to his old tricks.

"And the Prince?"

"In Holland." That didn't surprise me. Prince Bernhard had at last obtained a position which suited his temperament: commander-in-chief of the forces of the Interior. Now he spent most of his time in the liberated part of the Netherlands, south of the rivers, happy to be with all the Resistance leaders and former Underground fighters, a wild bunch if there ever was one.

"And the Queen?"

"She's upstairs. I'll let her know you're here, she may want to see you." In retrospect I realised that the general had his reasons. Queen Wilhelmina had obviously received information from occupied Holland, which she might wish to discuss with one of her Englandfarers.

"Have you heard?" she exclaimed, the moment I stepped into her room. The Queen was sitting in a small armchair, wrapped in some sort of blanket. For the first time in my experience she didn't rise to greet me. An aura of great agitation emanated from her. "Have you heard? They're dropping dead in the streets." It came so unexpectedly, I stared at her bewildered. "The people," she explained, with a gesture of impatience. "The people are dropping dead in the streets."

I hardly knew what she was talking about and could be of no help. Furthermore, I was so shocked by her horror and grief that I thanked God when our meeting ended. This time something made me pause at the door and bow in her direction, but she had already forgotten about me. She sat staring out of the window into the grey afternoon, huddled in her blanket like a wounded bird.

"Holy Christ, what's going on?" I pressed Van 't Sant, who stood waiting for me in the hall. We went back to his room, where he told me everything which was then known in London about Holland's infamous "Hunger Winter", when for six months Europe's most densely populated corner, without food or fuel and racked by terror, became like one, huge concentration camp—

"Ten minutes to the Dutch border." Ben reaches across me. He has picked up a radio-beacon from England and sets the final course on the compass. He folds his maps, switches off the navigation-light and, grunting and snorting, makes himself comfortable. His job is done, but not mine . . . 20,000 . . . 19,000 . . . 18,000 . . . Pitch black outside, like under a blanket. I'm beginning to get desperately sleepy . . . 17,000 . . . 16,000 . . . 15,000 . . . Every so often, when I don't pay attention, those dim little instrument-faces around me slyly change position. I sit bolt upright, rub my eyes and meekly they slide back into their places. 14,000. . . .

Alexander Rowerth, my former friend and fraternity-brother who joined the S.S., is alive. One day an ordinary postcard lay by my plate in the dining-room. The postmark said "Kiev", but the stamps were Turkish. It read: "Wish you were here. Cordial greetings. Alexander." I had to laugh. It didn't surprise me that Sturmführer Rowerth was fighting on the eastern front, but how on earth had he managed to get something mailed from Turkey? It was addressed to me, c/o R.A.F., England. From the crumbling German armies in the Ukraine: "Wish you were here." Oh shades of Leyden!

"Interesting people you know," laughed the wing-commander opposite me. I turned the card over. It showed an idealized S.S. officer, arms folded, legs astride half the world, against a background of a gigantic swastika. Yet it had been properly delivered by the British Post Office and the R.A.F. Civilised. Alexander would appreciate that. Several times lately I've had the gnawing feeling that if I had gone to stay with him when he invited me, back in 1940, or shown the slightest friendship or understanding, Alexander might well have been sitting next to me now, in R.A.F. uniform, instead of being a doomed Nazi in the slaughter on the Russian front. Too late . . . 12,000 . . . 11,000 . . . too late . . . 10,000. . . .

Suddenly my senses tell me that we're flying upside-down, my heart pounds in my chest. But one of the little faces assures me that it's not so. 8,000 . . . 7,000 . . . 6,000. . . . Why, then, am I jammed crookedly in my seat? Or am I sitting level, while my seat is at an angle? We're flying on our side! No, the little face says, you're all right. I look at the wings, what I can see of them – the starboard one points right up, the port one straight down into an abyss. I absolutely must pull the aircraft level. No, the little faces say, you *are* level. I obey, gnashing my teeth with the effort it takes. 5,000. . . . Nothing but inky blackness, I suppose this is going to be another one of those blind approaches, all the way down on instruments until your belly scrapes the ground. Did I re-set the altimeter? Should I? What are we flying towards, a high or a low? Bloody Met. blokes. 4,000. . . . Suddenly a voice shouts in my ear; I almost jump out of my skin. Some other pilot calling his control-tower; you'd swear he's hurtling through the dark right alongside us – perhaps he is. Ben nudges me and points ahead. I lift my eyes from the instrument-panel – it's clear outside! We're over the North Sea, the clouds have disappeared as if by magic and before us stretches the most beautiful, wonderful, heart-warming sight ever to greet the night-flyer of World War II: England, but not just England – an England cloudless, fogless, hazeless, clear as crystal. Safe and solid it beckons from behind the hedge of coastal searchlights, familiar, dear, our very own for these few years.

As far as the eye can see, hundreds of airfields, almost overlapping, cover the ground with perfect circles of soft-white lights, like strings of pearls on black velvet. Scattered through them, little red beacons wink their welcome. Let's see – dot-dash-dash, that's the W of Wyton, and there, dot-dot-dash, is the U of Upwood.

Between Upwood and Wyton lies the road to St. Ives.

XXII

THE DC-3 LANDED ON THE AIRFIELD OF GILZE-RIJEN, BETWEEN Tilburg and Breda, in the liberated part of the Netherlands, south of the rivers. Peter Tazelaar and I jumped on to the wet grass, assisted in placing the steps and positioned ourselves on either side. Queen Wilhelmina appeared in the door of the aeroplane. She sniffed the moist breeze with obvious approval and looked down the stairs. They were steep and had only one hand-rail, on the left, where Peter stood in stiff salute. I put out my hand to help her down. She ignored it pointedly. The first step back on Holland's soil after five years of exile, leaning on someone else? Unthinkable! I experienced the historic moment with one hand outstretched and the other at my cap, like a doorman expecting a tip. Peter, facing me five feet away, could barely contain himself. Suddenly I saw him leaning on his coal-shovel, half naked, black and sweating, and heard our laughter bouncing around in the iron bowels of the *St. Cergue*, when together we escaped from the Netherlands. Together we had returned, as A.D.C.s to the Queen.

I had learned the news in the small hours of 23 April, after a misson to Kiel. I sauntered into the dining-room for the usual post-operative ham-and-eggs and beer, and next to my plate lay the telegram, signed by General Van 't Sant. The following day I reported at 77 Chester Square, and there sat Peter. I could hardly believe my eyes – instead of wearing fireman's togs he was decked out in a

smart military uniform, purple beret, paratrooper's wings, lieutenant's stars and . . . the Military Williams Order. "What in hell
has happened to you?"

"It appears that I am A.D.C. to Her Majesty the Queen," he
answered. "How about you?"

"Well, bugger me gently," I replied in complete amazement. "So
am I!" We looked at each other and burst out laughing. What else?
Inevitably that misty morning in Schiedam came to our minds,
with Sjakie tottering above the precipice; and the day they threw
us out of Stratton House, and the suits for which we landed Prime
Minister Gerbrandy with the bill; and the Mews, and the little
cabin of the 320, and our dark walk hand in hand through the surf
off Scheveningen; and the mirror in 23 Hyde Park Place, and the
battle with the Poles in the Embassy Club; and our last, dismal
meeting aboard the *Aquitania*. . . .

Meanwhile we hadn't exactly dawdled. While I flew seventy-two
operations on Germany, including twenty-five on Berlin, Peter had
first continued his improbable career by becoming a fireman in
Soho. Nobody else wanted him, it seemed the end of the road. But
Van 't Sant hadn't given him up, and when in the summer of 1944
Dr. Van Heuven Goedhart was appointed Minister of Justice, the
general at last had an ally in the Dutch cabinet. Englandfarer Van
Heuven knew Peter personally from secret, top-level meetings in
occupied Holland during the winter of 1941 and was indignant to
find him back, not without difficulty, as a mere hose-carrier in the
fire-brigade. Within a few weeks Peter had been rehabilitated,
commissioned and knighted, all long overdue. No victory, except
perhaps our appointments as A.D.C.s to the Queen, can have
tasted sweeter to Van 't Sant.

Now they had to find something for Peter to do, but about this
he had his own ideas. He wangled himself on to a parachutists'
course, got his wings and managed to persuade someone to drop
him into occupied territory. Flying scared him rigid and he later
assured me that he had jumped out over Holland with a sigh of
relief. As a secret agent he once again proved himself more than a
match for the Gestapo. When in April 1945, the Canadians entered
Friesland he missed his own liberation by being asleep on the effects
of a somewhat premature celebration.

"I must say," he grinned to Van 't Sant, as we were taking our leave, "she has a lot of nerve, the old lady, to plonk herself down in that mess over there with us as A.D.C.s."

"We can't hold her back any longer. You know how she is," the general answered. Then some final doubt crossed his mind. "Now, please, don't forget," were his last words to his protégés, "you've got to behave. What the Queen says, goes."

It started off badly. Peter and I arrived early at the airfield. It was cold, so we hurried inside for a cup of coffee. From the restaurant we had a clear view of the runway, so we relaxed and took our time. Suddenly a Dutch general burst in and remarked, with icy sarcasm: "If perhaps the gentlemen would care to finish their coffee, the Queen and the Princess have been waiting in the plane for fifteen minutes." We had kept our eyes on the wrong runway.

We ran on to the field. Around the DC-3 stood all the highest Dutch authorities in London, waiting in the cold to witness the historic departure. A snort of indignation went up from the group, followed by an audible sigh of relief when we raced up the steps, no doubt in part because at last they were rid of us forever. Inside the cabin Princess Juliana smiled at us. The Queen was sitting in a special armchair way up in front; she didn't look around when we clumped aboard behind her. The total immobility of the small figure had an ominous effect and I prepared for the worst. I really didn't know what to expect, but when we reported to her she smiled. "I know, I know," she said. "I suppose you were having a little nip to celebrate our return home." The DC-3 bounced along the runway, pilot Captain Rijkhof opened up and seconds later England – and the war – lay behind me. It was 2 May 1945, five years almost to the day since the German invasion of the Netherlands.

*   *   *

In the woods of Ulvenhout, a few miles south of Breda, stood a country house named "Anneville". One came upon it unexpectedly at the end of a row of beeches, a square villa, modest but dignified, it's drive curving around a trim lawn, where stone steps led up to a small portico. Five rooms upstairs, an equal number plus veranda below, a dozen steps and you were across it and looked through high, glass doors on to the gardens at the back and the Brabant countryside. Here, where the low wall round the terrace crumbled and moss pushed up between the flagstones, the little mansion could not hide the neglect of five years of Occupation; and settled comfortably amongst wide lawns, magnificent trees and mounds of rhododendrons clustered around a pond full of croaking frogs. Queen Wilhelmina entered the front door and Anneville became the centre of the Netherlands.

Here we lived, the five of us: the Queen, Princess Juliana, our female counterpart Rie Stokvis, Peter Tazelaar and I. A handful of military police, whom Van 't Sant had sent over from England, set up their quarters above the garage. Together we constituted the entire "Court" which accompanied the Royal Family home from five years of exile. World War II was grinding to a close in Europe. The gigantic vice from California to the Urals was about to snap shut. Somewhere amidst the German rubble Americans and Russians had embraced each other. There was fighting in Berlin. Rumours circulated that in north-west Germany the Moffen had finally ceased their heroic resistance. In Holland above the rivers, still occupied and on the brink of total ruin, food-packages were being dropped to the famished population by the R.A.F. and the A.A.C., without enemy interference. Tremendous events were in the air, in the midst of which Peter and I struggled manfully with problems varying from the acquisition of toilet paper to the safety of the House of Orange.

A few years before, the thought of living in a modest villa with the formidable and legendary Queen Wilhelmina of the Netherlands would have made our blood run cold. But from that very first morning Peter and I felt at home in Anneville. This was due to our relationship with the Queen, which over the years, imperceptibly, she herself had moulded. Her demands were clear, simple and few: do your best and tell me the truth. This suited us fine. It was only natural that we hoped to acquit ourselves adequately of our honourable assignment, but if we failed we would make room for others without resentment or regrets. We loved being A.D.C.s and assisting Her Majesty, but we knew ourselves well enough to realise that in the long run the personal restrictions and discipline of a Court were not for us. We had no axe to grind. As a result our relations with our royal employer were those of free men, unencumbered by ulterior motives—in contrast to the dignitaries who sometimes emerged trembling from an audience with Wilhelmina, pale around the nose, and grateful for the snort of gin with which we quickly fortified them on the veranda. From us she always heard it "like it was", and many a time I had to report another minor disaster resulting from our honest efforts. Then, with a gesture of despair, she would exclaim: "Captain, you make it impossible for me to reign" — and smile at my discomfort.

On this basis we tacitly arrived at certain ground-rules to ease the closeness of our day-to-day contact. She allowed us to contradict her, as long as we didn't quibble or mope. On the other hand, her orders had to be executed, even if we disagreed; we could, however, register protest, provided again that it never led to even the slightest hint of "I told you so". Of course, a measure of tact was essential. A young Resistance man who helped us out temporarily had the bad judgement to admonish the Queen, in a moment of righteous conviction: "But Majesty, you simply cannot do that." His successor, a Leydener, told a joke in her presence leading up to the punch-line: "The Liberation? As far as I'm concerned, you can keep it." Leyden humour did not appeal to Wilhelmina. She called me to her study and declared, with a vicious chop of her right hand for emphasis: "Captain, as far as I'm concerned, that gentleman has *had* it." And once you'd had it with her, you'd had it for ever.

Immediately on arrival at Anneville the Queen installed herself upstairs and plunged into the business of reigning the country. For everything else — food, security, communications, transport, mail, laundry and all the household details — Rie, Peter and I were responsible. Somehow we managed, but she didn't always make it easy for us. Generous farmers from the area had filled our cellar with wholesome foodstuffs, but when Rie produced strawberries for the very first dinner the Queen refused to touch them, protesting that she did not intend to eat anything which wasn't also available to "the people". The following morning application forms for our ration-cards arrived, which she insisted on filling out personally: Name — Wilhelmina; Occupation — Queen; etc. The meagre diet which this initially supplied seemed insufficient to me from a health standpoint. After all, I was responsible for the Queen's welfare. So one night I ordered a steak to be placed in front of her. Deep in thought she munched on one or two bites, then suddenly she froze: "Captain, this is steak."

"Yes, Your Majesty."

"Is everybody in Holland eating steak tonight?"

Although the whole country had by then been liberated, this was a statement I dared not make. While I pleaded how hurt the farmers would be if she refused their offerings, Her Majesty kept a furtive eye on the juicy filet mignon. I would not venture to guess which one of us finally persuaded her.

The other occasion at which I raised her ire also involved "the people". The news of her return had spread far and wide, and from miles around the Dutch hiked to Ulvenhout to pay their respects. Throughout those early days endless lines of silent men, women and children shuffled down the drive of Anneville, past the portico and out the other gate. At first Peter and I revelled in the processions, standing behind the Queen in our beribboned uniforms, gazing out impressively over the multitudes. But soon it palled. It was all too intimate for bravado, too sad. From the eyes of the people, often sunken deep in wan, pallid faces, something spoke which put our cheap vanity to shame, something between "the people" and their Queen from which we were excluded. Besides, standing there for hours on end was just too tiring. Not for Wilhelmina. I knew her desk to be piled high with urgent matters of State, but the people came first. Once, when I saw how close to exhaustion she was, I instructed the M.P.s to speed up the pace. Immediately I was called to task. "In my garden nobody gets pushed around," she snapped, although she could barely keep herself upright. "And don't you *ever* forget it."

From the moment we set foot in Holland and saw the confusion of war all around us, I worried about the Queen's personal safety. Shortly after our arrival at Anneville one of the M.P. sergeants warned me that the gardens might still be mined. The report came from the local Forces of the Interior, who advised that only the paved walking-areas should be considered safe. Consequently I requested Her Majesty to stick to the paths until the entire garden had been checked out with mine-detectors. That very same evening I saw her walk to the pond, right across the lawn. With my heart in my throat I ran out of the house, after her, restraining an urge to shout a warning. I'm glad I didn't. She heard my footsteps down the path and watched with unconcealed amusement as I tiptoed the final yards through the grass. "Oh come now, Captain," was her answer to my urgent plea. "Do you really believe I'll suddenly blow up? BOOM, just like that?" Queen Wilhelmina blow up? BOOM, just like that? Not under my responsibility! The next morning the garden was swarming with sappers from a near-by Canadian regiment. They found no mines.

Wilhelmina's reaction to personal danger need not have surprised me. On the evening of 20 February 1944, she had miraculously escaped with her life when a German bomb exploded five feet outside her cottage in South Mimms, north-east of London. Two M.P.s on guard at the door were killed. General Van 't Sant later told me that the Queen had retired for the night, but had just left her bed again to put away a bracelet, a present from her daughter Juliana. The blast ripped a heavy beam from the ceiling, which fell on the bed and lay squarely across the pillow where a few moments before Wilhelmina's head had rested. "The bracelet saved her life," Van 't Sant said. "No doubt about it." After several hours in a bomb-shelter she was driven through the suburbs of London, under heavy attack that night, to Stubbings House near Maidenhead, which she reached in the small hours of the morning. Yet she kept all her appointments the following day, including a cabinet meeting. None of the ministers present noticed anything unusual about her—

Slowly we walked back from the pond. I felt uneasy. Apart from the land-mines I was acutely aware of the presence, a mere dozen miles away, of the German S.S. division which occupied the northern banks of the rivers. Even now, I didn't consider it beyond them to make an attempt at kidnapping the Queen of the Netherlands, perhaps as a hostage. Hadn't they snatched Mussolini from under the Allies' noses? I thought of the fatherly sergeants above the garage, to my knowledge our only protection. Involuntarily I glanced over my shoulder. Dusk lay across the land. Under the trees and rhododendrons black shadows lurked. Why had the frogs suddenly ceased their croaking? Who had turned off the light on the terrace? Abruptly the Queen stopped in her tracks, head high as if she were listening. I felt goose-pimples rising under the hairs in my neck. "Ah!" Wilhelmina sighed, breathing deeply. "Nowhere does it smell the way it smells at home."

For the first time during that long, confused day it sank in. I was back in Holland. I was home.

XXIII

"Best of all i would have liked to come back to the Netherlands and then in the evening just ring a door-bell somewhere, at an ordinary house, or a farm perhaps, and then have asked the woman who opened the door: 'May I spend the night here with you?' — I have often thought about it. That's how I would have liked to come home best of all." A shy smile touched Wilhelmina's lips; she did not easily disclose such matters of the heart.

We had just finished dinner. Most meals we took together, usually with four or five or more if we had guests, on rare occasions — like now — just the two of us, the Queen and I. The food was always placed on the table in advance; we helped ourselves, there were no servants. Afterwards, over coffee or a beer, we would talk. The subjects pressed themselves upon us: the peace, the war, future and renewal, liberation and home-coming, the people. . . . This time we discussed the Liberation, which had just freed the north. A spring night, barely dark, enveloped Anneville in silence. The only sound came from the frogs, croaking in the pond.

The armistice, which became known on the evening of 4 May, had surprised me in Tilburg. Peter, with his usual luck, was on duty at Anneville and so goes down in history as the man who told Queen Wilhelmina that, as far as Holland was concerned, World War II had ended. "Man, what a scene!" he described the great moment. "I barged into the salon without knocking and we shook each other's hands like mad, endlessly, and with her other hand she was banging me on the shoulder."

In Tilburg the people ran out of their houses with the news, shouted it around and wrote it on walls and the sides of trucks. My immediate reaction was a desire to be alone. In no time the streets were packed and to escape the crowds I took a room in a hotel. I left the lights out and opened the door to the balcony. An enormous full moon stood above the town, long lines of revellers, arms around each other's shoulders, ten, twenty abreast, bounced along the street below. I lay down on the bed, fully clothed. I so vividly remembered my emotions at our own surrender, five years before, that now I wanted to find out exactly how it felt to be on the winning side. The moon poured its rays into the shabby room, while from below rose the rhythmic, inhuman din of revelling Dutchmen. — I didn't feel a thing. I fell asleep, that's all.

Wilhelmina wanted to enter the newly liberated provinces immediately, but the Allied security authorities would not allow it. She was furious. In the general confusion rumours abounded about fully armed German units still roaming the countryside and quislings sniping in the cities, but she dismissed all such reports as part of an exaggerated concern for her personal safety. To pacify her I proposed that I should go to Amsterdam in her name and place a wreath on the spot where in the final days a last, large group of Resistance fighters had been executed. When after my return I reported to her about this sortie, she became somewhat more resigned to the necessity of remaining below the rivers for a while.

We could only get across the Rhine at Arnhem, from where the driver and I decided to take the old road to Utrecht. After buying a wreath locally we would then continue to Amsterdam, very simply. The roads were ruined and packed with military traffic, until suddenly in a wooded area between Oosterbeek and Amersfoort I noticed that we were driving all alone along the deserted highway. At the same time I saw troops swarming amongst the trees on both sides.

"Captain," the driver said. He was one of the M.P.s who had spent the entire war in England. "Now what kind of uniforms are those?"

"Pay no attention, just drive on," I answered reassuringly. It was too late to turn back, I had to keep him calm. From where I sat

I could distinguish the skulls and crossbones on their S.S. caps. "Must be one of those newfangled units from Stratton House."

The wrecked tarmac slowed us down. Groups of soldiers gathered by the wayside to watch our approach, their Nazi insignia depressing me as never before. They were fully armed and still looked hard and sharp. To my surprise some waved at us and here and there a desultory cheer went up. I could think of only one explanation: we were sitting in a large, grey, unmarked car and neither of us wore his hat – it must be that they took us for the last of the *Herrenvolk* to be driving around in a decent automobile. I might have waved back, if I hadn't been so scared. In Utrecht we were told that the road from Arnhem was still in the hands of an S.S. division, which up to now had petulantly blown up every Allied vehicle trying to get through.

The final stretch also brought its problems. We hit the remnants of a tank-trap, which tore two tyres off our wheels. Having alerted the Amsterdam authorities to my imminent arrival, I simply had to press on. Draping the outsize wreath around my neck I put out my thumb to hitch a ride and shortly snared a laundry-van. At the city limits a large delegation of notables, headed by the Burgomaster, awaited Her Majesty's A.D.C. With obvious alarm they watched him emerge from a mountain of dirty linen, wreath and all.

The Queen couldn't help laughing at the story, but quickly regained her composure. "Anyway, did you make it quite clear who you were?" she asked urgently. "Did they clearly realise who you were?"

I nodded. I knew the reason behind the question. During her years in England Queen Wilhelmina, on the basis of information brought out by Englandfarers and secret reports from occupied territory, had become ever more convinced that she would be going home to a profoundly changed people, a nation purged through suffering, unified and "renewed". Of this "renewal", which developed into the corner-stone of her post-war expectations, Rie, Peter and I were symbols. We possessed the proper qualifications: Englandfarers, active war-records, young and of common birth and background. Nothing about us recalled her former, highly formalistic and class-conscious surroundings, against which she nursed a bitter resentment. For in the course of her lonely exile Wilhelmina as a human being had undergone a dramatic transformation. She had so passionately identified with her people under the Occupation that the desperate suffering of the Netherlands became her own. She suffered for everybody, she suffered the most. This empathy had awakened a humility incompatible with any concept of class, status or rank. Always she had towered above the people, now she wanted to be part of them. Everything "old", which in the past had prevented and in the future might endanger such union, she now opposed implacably. It was finished, over and done with, a waste of time, and she jettisoned it with chilling ruthlessness. She, too, was "renewed".

"You and your R.A.F. missed your targets often enough," she once reproached me in bitter jest, many months later. We were standing in the ballroom of Noordeinde, one of her palaces. No other royal building contained so much of her life – here she had been born, had given birth to her only daughter and stood at the biers of both her father and her husband. "So often you have missed the mark" – she waved to indicate the stately halls around us – "surely you could have dropped one inadvertent little bomb on this old place."

Another time, drinking tea in the veranda, I saw three generals standing in the garden of Anneville. They were obviously in confusion. I went over to them. First they mortified me by pulling themselves to attention and formally saluting my Military Williams Order. Having forgotten my hat, as usual, I couldn't even properly accept the ceremony and mumbled foolishly "thank you, thank you". Then they introduced themselves; the names sounded vaguely familiar. Before the war they had been the commanders-in-chief of the Dutch army. Now, after five years in a prison camp, they had come directly to report to their Queen.

"I'll announce you immediately," I offered, as a matter of course.

"That has already been done," came the answer. "We were told that Her Majesty cannot see us."

"Surely that must be a mistake, don't you think?" one of the generals added. He had tears in his eyes. I helped him out of his dream. Like three old men they tottered down the drive. They were the past, the Queen had only time for the future. When at lunch I had the temerity to voice a protest about the incident, she looked at me irritably. "Now really, about that sort of thing I *really* can't bother myself any more."

A few nights later we were visited by a baron. After his departure Queen Wilhelmina commented, not without a certain conspiratorial air: "What did you think of him, Captain? Don't you find his kind just a little too pompous for us?" — Pompous or not, I thought of Baron Louis d'Aulnis de Bourrouill at his secret transmitter, and Jonkheer Ernst de Jonge on the dark beach of Katwijk, and the many others of noble birth who, side by side with us commoners, had fought and died for their country. But the passionate convictions which buttressed Wilhelmina's strength seldom left room for nuances. Nobility represented the past, it was guilty by association, it was finished. For the Queen a new era had dawned, the era of the Resistance fighter and the Englandfarer, "noblemen" — as she herself put it — "in the true sense of the word". With them she chose to associate as *prima inter pares* —

It was getting late. Even the frogs were silent at last. Wilhelmina looked at her watch. "If you are going to have another beer, I'll have one with you," she said pleasantly. "And then to bed. So much to do tomorrow. . . ." I fetched three bottles of beer from the pantry, and four glasses of which I put three in front of me and one by the Queen. Now came the beer-ceremony. From each bottle I poured a mouthful into one of my glasses and tasted it carefully. Wilhelmina followed my ministrations attentively. When I had found what seemed to be the least gassy one, I pretended a moment's hesitation. "This one," I declared, pointing with great finality, and poured the rest of that bottle into her glass. While I watched with an expression of expectancy she took a swallow and nodded, as always, approvingly. The clock in the salon tick-tocked through the quiet house.

*   *   *

From liberated Holland problems without end whirled towards Anneville. Roads, bridges, transportation, telephone, everything was kaput, and in this chaos the Queen somehow had to re-start the machine of State. Gerbrandy and his cabinet had automatically resigned; now she had to select a new Prime Minister. It became part of our task to deliver the candidates for this office safely to her door. From all corners of the country we hauled them to Anneville, in cars, trucks, delivery-vans, on the back of motor-bikes, in row-boats across the rivers and once even in a spotter-plane which landed in a meadow outside Amsterdam to pick up an aged city-councillor. After a hair-raising flight through storm and rain he staggered into our veranda, pale and shaking. Unfortunately it soon appeared that the Queen was expecting a totally different person of the same name.

We worked hard, but no harder than Wilhelmina. When she was in good spirits she would whip us along to a pace of cheerful frenzy, but whenever she felt tired or nervous her irritability seeped into the farthest corners of the villa. Then everybody tiptoed around, whispered and lost his temper. "What's she like today?" we asked each other every morning. Sometimes the answer had to be: "Quite impossible."

There was usually a good reason for her moods, such as the invasion by a dozen British press-photographers for whom, under pressure, she had agreed to pose in her new surroundings. News-papermen made her nervous, she couldn't stand them. She never referred to them as "the Press", but always as "press-mosquitos", sometimes harping on the word as if she hoped to exorcise them with it.

"Do you think we should offer these press-mosquitos something to drink?"

"I would think so, Majesty."

"What do you think these press-mosquitos drink? Tea?"

"I think whisky, Majesty."

"Whisky? Do press-mosquitos drink whisky in the middle of the day?"

"If they can get it, yes, Majesty."

We had made seating arrangements on the terrace, where the Queen and Princess Juliana installed themselves. The photographers complained to me that the scene looked a trifle bare. Could I per-haps dress it up a bit with some documents? I grabbed a handful of papers and envelopes indiscriminately, and was about to place them on the table when the Queen unexpectedly turned to me and snapped: "Oh for heaven's sake, Captain, why don't you get out of here." Apparently I looked so surprised that Juliana burst out laughing. At this moment of confusion, centred around me as the butt of two generations of Dutch Queens, the shutters clicked. The picture appeared in magazines the world over, mostly with reference to the weighty matters of State being attended to at that precise moment.

After a hard day we often sought the company of Princess Juliana. She herself kept busy as Head of the Dutch Red Cross, but spent as much time as possible at Anneville to be with her mother, who adored her. On warm spring evenings, reminiscent of the radiant invasion-month of May, five years before, we would sit on the lawn drinking sherry — Juliana, Rie, Peter and I. Never had I known someone who blossomed forth so surprisingly in a small, familiar company. When we had overcome our mutual shyness — which took us considerably less time than it did her — our pleasant chats gradually grew into warm, gay and often intimate occasions. Juliana enjoyed teasing us "courtiers", particularly when one of our periodic blunders had embroiled her mother, but the gist of her mischief was always to encourage us not to take it all too seriously. At first she rarely formed the centre of the conversation, but let her devastating humour flash in and out until every subject, shorn of its frills, lay clean and clear before us. I relished the thought that she, also, was a Leydener — year 1927 — and more than once we found each other in the bizarre sense of humour of our alma mater. Once she got going, she threw herself into the fray with fire and candour, and in the heat of discussion the inevitable distance between us melted away. In matters which lay close to her heart she displayed all the passion of her mother. Of these, the most important ones were, of course, her little daughters, the Princesses of Orange.

"My children have a right to a normal, happy childhood," she once exploded, thinking no doubt of her own formal, sequestered and lonely youth. "But I'll have to fight for it." The desire to be part of the people, new to Wilhelmina, had been born into Juliana. In this her husband, Prince Bernhard, was her staunchest ally, and in that spirit they raised their children. Later that year the two eldest returned from Canada, where they had spent the war, and on 3 August 1945, I accompanied them home from England. We flew in an antique Dakota with ventilation-holes in the windows. The girls were five and seven years old, and it seemed natural to address them by their first names. Irene sat quietly by the window, eating sweets. Beatrix kept asking every few minutes: "Are we over Holland yet? . . . Are we over Holland yet?" At last I could answer "yes". Irene was just about to throw another sweet-paper through the ventilation-hole, but Beatrix stopped her. "We are over

Holland," she said severely to her little sister. "You mustn't make a mess any more." When we arrived at Gilze-Rijen a strapping major of the Marines jumped to attention and gave the Princesses a military salute. Irene looked at him as if he were mad. Beatrix ignored him completely.

Our warm contact with Princess Juliana created one predictable problem — more and more we looked on her as a personal friend. One evening I overheard Rie call her "Jula". I promptly took her aside. "Rie, you can't do that."

"She told me herself that I could," Rie answered.

"Then you'll just have to decline the honour. You can't call her Jula." The crux of the matter did not lie between Rie and Juliana — if Rie Stokvis ever overstepped the bounds of propriety, which I did not for a moment anticipate, Princess Juliana would undoubtedly put her firmly back in her place. The real problem revolved around the fact that, in spite of all fervent hopes of "renewal", a distance did continue to exist between the Royal House and the people. If we reduced that distance in our own case, we automatically put ourselves above the people, at least in their eyes. And the Queen hadn't brought us over from England for that.

Rie did not give in lightly, but agreed to abide by the judgement of Van 't Sant in London. Via the military I sent him an open telegram which, it seemed to me, capsuled the question in a few words unintelligible to outsiders: "Who may say Jula?"

I don't know what alarming conclusions the general drew from the message, but a few hours later came his answer: "Not you."

*   *   *

The small procession halted at the city limits of The Hague. Queen Wilhelmina and a lady-in-waiting stepped out of her car and proceeded to the open Packard, in which she was about to make her official entry into Holland's centre of government. They installed themselves on the ample rear seat.

The Queen acted as if she just couldn't get comfortable. "I know," she finally said. "It's much too draughty here." As the temperature hovered around eighty-five and furthermore we were standing still, we all waited for what would come next.

I might have known that she had something up her sleeve. The previous day she had suddenly asked me, out of the blue: "You're from The Hague, aren't you?" Immediately after our arrival from the Indies we had made it our home. I studied in Leyden, true, but The Hague had always remained home territory, the place where my friends lived, where I had gone to school, where I played football and where I dated, the place where I grew up: my home town.

The two old ladies got out again. Her Majesty pretended to study the situation. "I know, we'll sit on the little folding-chairs," she announced next.

When she and the somewhat bewildered lady-in-waiting had finally arranged themselves on the folding-chairs, she still didn't appear entirely satisfied. She glanced over her shoulder at the wide, empty back seat and ordered: "Captain, you sit on the back seat behind me. Otherwise the whole thing looks ridiculous."

Otherwise the whole thing looks ridiculous? I knew better. The gesture of letting me come home in the Queen's car, in the place of honour, but even more the elaborate act to mask her generosity, was pure, undiluted Wilhelmina of Orange–Nassau.

I took my place on the back seat. Up front the M.P.s composed their faces. Slowly the big Packard rolled into my old stomping-grounds. As soon as she saw people waiting to welcome her Queen Wilhelmina, on the little chair in front of me, began to bow energetically, back, forth, back, forth, bouncing off the backrest, waving to the crowds, back, forth, the crowds growing into multitudes, back, forth, amongst the pennants and the flags and the flowers and the bows, orange, everything orange, back, forth, into the storm of cheers, long live the Queen! long live the Queen!, back, forth, the mass of humanity breaking through the lines of police pouring into the streets, pressing closer, ever closer, waving, laughing, crying, cheering, the Packard all but submerged, Wilhelmina barely visible, smiling, bowing, waving, bowing, back, forth, back, forth, like a little wind-up toy. . . .

I wished I could wave back at the crowd myself, especially when I saw a small boy half-way up a lamp-post.

XXIV

The first to get restless was Peter. After the German capitulation the war raged on in the Far East—what, then, was Lieutenant Tazelaar still doing in the Netherlands? Furthermore, the position of A.D.C. to the Queen required the not inconsiderable talent of playing second fiddle, an instrument for which neither of us had ever shown much aptitude. More and more often I saw him wander through the gardens of Anneville with a face like a thunder-cloud or found him sitting morosely in our veranda with a crock of jenever. Evenings he usually disappeared and at night he rarely came home at all. Prince Bernhard, who occasionally whirled into our little household like a fresh breeze from the outer world, only made matters worse. He brought with him the smell of adventure and when he roared out of the gate again in one of his powerful cars we stared after him longingly. Especially Peter, who now began to abscond across the rivers to the north, where the breath of war still hung raw in the streets.

"If they tell me one more time how they hid under the kitchen table when the Gestapo came to the door, I'll throw up," he said on one occasion. He was honouring us with his presence after a foray to Rotterdam. We were sitting in the veranda, the stone crock much in evidence.

"Well, and how about you? Didn't you regale them with your adventures on the beach of Scheveningen and in the polders of Friesland?"

"Like hell. I kept my mouth shut. The hell with it."

"Yeah, you know why? Because you don't *have* to tell them. It's damn easy to be modest, when all the time you sit there with a bloody great Military Williams Order poking everybody in the eye."

We never expected a hero's welcome, but the chasm between us and those who had stayed in Holland proved alarmingly deep, particularly in the cities of the north, still reeling from the "Hunger Winter". After the shock of the Liberation the people shivered with nerves. Every town throbbed with frenzied celebration, but underneath the boozing and the singing the times were sad. There had been too much suffering, too much destruction, too much death. Under the shrill flags everything was drab and grey.

Into this dismal scene burst the Dutch from England, well-fed, sharply uniformed and beribboned. They wore stripes, wings, stars, insignia, and each sported at least one fascinating decoration. Those who had survived the horrors of the Occupation had nothing to show for it, nothing to fall back on but words, words, words. We nodded, and nodded, and nodded.

The Canadians and British and Americans who had liberated the Netherlands constituted the new *élite*. They had houses, cars, liquor and money at their disposal, and little else to do but give parties. And why not, had they not just won a war? To these festivities we got invited, but not the Hollanders of the Occupation, unless they were young, willing and female. The former Resistance fighter bicycled home in the evening past mansions resounding with music and gaiety and sparkling with lights and uniforms – on his home-made, wooden tyres.

Bars and night-clubs sprouted like weeds. The Dutch from London possessed British pounds, and so they could afford them. The girls, even the most stalwart, were tired to exhaustion of all the drabness, all those years. They, too, wanted to go dancing, and on to bed, with a smart uniform spiced with bright ribbons and stars. But the Underground hero, who had risked his life countless times under the Occupation, stood outside in the cold and gnashed his teeth.

"Had a nice war?" they taunted us.

"You were in the Underground too, I suppose?" was our snide retort.

But the wounds went deeper than this. Our nerves, also, had been racked by the Liberation. No matter how much we had outgrown our past, one dream had never left us for a single day of the war: our home-coming to the Holland of our memory. We did come home and the memory was crushed by reality. The dream exploded. Our country lay before us unrecognisable, emaciated like a wretch from a concentration camp. We couldn't cope, and so we refused to accept it. We turned away as from a leper, sickened and uncomfortable. We felt more at ease with our Allied buddies, with whom we had fought the war in freedom, than with our old friends who carried the mark of the Occupation. Paul, Jacques, Frits, Anton — names from a vanished world. We got together long enough to establish that we had nothing to say to each other. Leyden? I carefully avoided it. Of course, it was only a matter of time. But how long? Too long for me. The greyness repelled me, the narrow borders pressed me like prison walls. The war was over, a life suddenly stretched out before me. I wanted to live it, growing, expanding, fulfilling. I needed room, air, light, warmth, colour! Peter was not the only one who was getting restless.

Most of Queen Wilhelmina's dreams, too, remained mere dreams. In Anneville we lived and worked together side by side, like ordinary people. But Holland was no Anneville. Rie, Peter and I didn't know any better, and the Queen didn't want it any other way. The old days were over, this was the Renewal. But the people resented it.

Wilhelmina set the tone; we performed our jobs accordingly, without regard for traditions and bugaboos. Through the endless corridors of Noordeinde Palace I whizzed around on a motorbike, just missing the occasional old retainer. Rather than give up, I had arrived in Amsterdam on a heap of dirty laundry. No antiquated inhibitions held us back. The Queen whole-heartedly approved. But the people resented it.

Sometimes I was caught in the middle. "For God's sake, make it a real good show, next week in Amsterdam." I heard it left and right. It was a time of Freedom festivals and official entries. On 29 June it would be the capital's turn. "For Her Majesty's own good, see to it that there's something for the people to gawk at. If only a good, long line of shiny cars. They have waited for this long enough."

"Captain, don't forget. Under no circumstances do I want more than four M.P.s in the procession." That meant one car!

Wilhelmina wanted simplicity and humility, in tune with the reality of the present. The people were sick of reality, sick of the present; they longed for the pomp and splendour of the past. My cautious efforts to bring the matter to discussion were met with frosty silence. In the Renewal the past had no place. I obeyed her order, of course, but I did stick each M.P. in a separate, shiny Cadillac.

Meanwhile Wilhelmina's hopes of a constitutional rebirth of the Dutch state, nurtured in the solitude of her exile, died a cruel death in the political arena. The struggle for post-war power killed off her illusions one by one, and proved unmistakably that the unity of the Dutch nation under the Occupation, on which she had based her belief in a national "renewal", was nothing more than a temporary fusion of Holland's traditional diversity in the heat of oppression. After very few months it became clear that everything would remain as of old. Wilhelmina had identified with a dream, and when it faded in the light of reality she could not, or would not, relinquish it. She abdicated in 1948, in the fiftieth year of her reign, in favour of her daughter Juliana. She gave as her reason considerations of the mind; but then, Wilhelmina did not easily disclose matters of the heart.

To her own "renewal" she remained faithful. Never again did she recognise the concepts of class and rank. To every Netherlander she offered her hand in equality; but the Netherlanders continued to bow. Queen Wilhelmina, after reigning for half a century, had in the end become too democratic for them. To the proverbial *"plus royalist que le roi"* she had added a historic counterpoint; more democratic than the people. Thus the distance persisted. And when I watched her walking through the gardens of Anneville, step by little step, dwarfed by the chestnut trees, my thoughts sometimes wandered to an inscription she had ordered carved in stone: "My dearest and most faithful friend". It stood on the grave of Blackie, a dog.

*   *   *

At last the land across the rivers was declared safe; the Queen could come. She left Anneville with regret, having clearly enjoyed the intimacy which the snug villa had forced upon us. Only once had the house seemed too small. One evening I saw Her Majesty approaching along a corridor in her dressing-gown. I opened the nearest door and dived out of sight, landing in a narrow cupboard full of cleaning equipment. With a broom in my hand and my nose against the inside of the door, I barely fitted. But evidently the Queen was also on the prowl. Suddenly she opened the door. We stood face to face, perplexed.

"Good evening, Majesty," I finally said, for want of anything better.

"Good evening, Captain," Wilhelmina answered with a startled glance at the broom – and slammed the door closed again!

We moved to Apeldoorn. Driving out of the gate for the last time I looked back once more. Anneville had played its unique part and over the stout little mansion at the end of the sun-dappled drive there already lay that quiet which is an echo of historic events.

Apeldoorn meant the beginning of normal times, the beginning of the end. Queen Wilhelmina installed herself in a modest town-residence, not far from her palace Het Loo. I moved into a hotel around the corner. Ministers plied back and forth without risking their necks, Her Majesty ate steak without pangs of conscience, for informal talks or the beer-ceremony there was neither time nor occasion. Anneville seemed a mirage, the war a page of history. I myself began to feel like a relic of romantic times.

The first to disappear was Peter, enveloped in his usual cloud of mystery. He sneaked off to London and wangled himself into a commando unit bound for the Far East; but he altogether neglected to inform the Queen. "I hear that you have meanwhile left my service," she greeted him, when he turned up in Apeldoorn to arrange his departure. Even now she showed no sign of irritation. One day it struck me that I hadn't seen Peter for a while. He had left, whither or even exactly when I never knew. Years later he was spotted on his belly in a rice-field near Sukabumi, Java, during a violent dispute with an Indonesian guerrilla – in sharp contrast to Chris Krediet, who by that time had peacefully retired to an island in the Caribbean with his old friends Kant, Kierkegaard and Will Durant.

Now I had also come to the end of my tether. As temporary A.D.C. my assignment had included the proposing of "renewed" candidates for the Queen's permanent staff. Gradually the organisation had taken shape, until only one more post had to be filled – the office of aide de camp, my own successor. I knew the perfect candidate: Captain Robert Bergmann. About Robbie's "renewal" I had my doubts, but his professionalism, which had plagued him in the R.A.F., would make him a great A.D.C. One more appointment and I was free to leave. Even the Army could not stop me; the pre-war records showed that I was officially 4F.

I waited a little too long. One afternoon the Queen and I strolled through the garden of Het Loo, I half a step behind her, hands behind my back, exactly like Van 't Sant along the paths of Chester Square. We were discussing possible A.D.C.s and I was just about to mention Bergmann, when she said: "You may put yourself at the top of the list."

What now? The Queen of the Netherlands asked me to stay – could I refuse? The answer was "yes". She herself had taught us always to put our cards on the table, always to tell the truth. Even so, I kept my fingers crossed. "Your Majesty, I have other plans. In a little while I would like to leave your service."

She didn't answer. Gravel crunched under our feet. The grass, newly mown, smelled warm in the sun. From an open window somewhere a typewriter clattered. Finally I added: "I hope you're not angry with me."

Queen Wilhelmina pulled herself up to the full height of her small stature. Walking behind her I could not see her face, but her voice was barely audible. "No," she said. "I'm not angry. It's been very kind of you to string along with an old woman for so long" —

First I took my leave of General Van 't Sant. Once again he had manoeuvred his protégés into positions of influence, once again we left him in the lurch. He took it philosophically, but he didn't get at it all. "Now tell me honestly," he said. "What is it that you want for yourself out of this?" After all these years, he didn't know.

"Nothing," I answered, feeling suddenly foolish.

I saw Queen Wilhelmina one more time after Apeldoorn. She had moved to a little house in Scheveningen, right on the street. I came to say good-bye; in a few days my ship would sail for America. She served tea. We didn't talk much. I sensed that the war was on both our minds, all the way back to that other tea-party the first time we met, in Maidenhead, when the only thing missing was the Dormouse. Close by the window a tram rattled by – line 8, the one which had curved by me on that deadly winter morning in 1942.

At last I got up to go. She walked me to the front door, like any Dutch housewife. While we shook hands she suddenly smiled, the same unexpected smile I had seen once before – in the solemn hush when she had just knighted me. "Anneville . . ." she said. They were the last words I ever heard her speak. "Anneville . . . that was our fairytale."
Amen.

* * *

I stood on a dune near Wassenaar. In the distance I heard music, in waves on the dark, wet wind. Where does music come from in the night over the dunes? – Memorial service on the Waalsdorp execution-grounds.

It was for those who stayed, who were cut down. I went away and grew on. But one grows, ring after ring, from a core. One grows outward in every direction, but the core stays. The core holds. Somewhere in that music I detected my core. They are dead, I am alive, but in that music we are one.

We are one because together we believed in something. If we had not believed in it, we would not have fought for it – not I, anyway. Each according to his conscience. But if you believe in something, you must fight for it. Always. Once in our lives we believed in something strongly enough to kill for it and to die for it. We have reason to be grateful. Even they. They perhaps most of all.

The music comes to me in shreds through the night. Somewhere it is whole.

EPILOGUE

as of January 1st, 1972

Queen Wilhelmina	died 27 November, 1962
Princess Juliana	Queen of the Netherlands
Prince Bernhard	Prince Consort
Princess Beatrix	Crown Princess; married Prince Claus von Amsberg; Holland
Princess Irene	married Prince Juan-Carlos of Bourbon-Parma; Spain
Chris Krediet	retired airline executive (K.L.M.); Holland
Peter Tazelaar	oil-tester on tankers; Rotterdam, Holland
Paul Renardel	Netherlands Ambassador; Baghdad, Iraq
Alexander Rowerth	killed in action; S.S.; Ukraine, U.S.S.R.
Jacques Maasland	judge, Superior Court; The Hague, Holland
Erik Michielsen	killed in training; R.A.F.; England
Karel Michielsen	oil executive (Broken Hill); Melbourne, Australia
Van Brero	restaurateur; Connecticut, U.S.A.
Anton Muller	judge; Haarlem, Holland
Carel Kranenburg	killed in action; Netherlands Army; Java, Indonesia
Frits van der Schrieck	oil executive (Shell); Holland
Lodo van Hamel	executed by Germans
Blubber	executed by Underground
Toon Buitendijk	watchman; Rotterdam, Holland

Bob van der Stok	physician; Hawaii, U.S.A.
Jan Plesman	killed in action; R.A.F.; France
Taro Bosch	killed in action; R.A.F.; France
Louis baron d'Aulnis de Bourrouill	marketing executive; Holland
Johannes Terlaak	executed by Germans
Ernst de Jonge	executed by Germans
Evert Radema	executed by Germans
Aart Alblas	executed by Germans
Peter Loasby	captain, Royal Navy; Australian waters
Bob Goodfellow	oil executive (Shell); England
Robert Cohen	killed in action; R.A.F.; France
François van 't Sant	advisor to Royal Family until his death at eighty in 1966; Holland
Euan Rabagliatti	retired insurance executive (Lloyd's); Cannes, France
Pieter S. Gerbrandy	died in 1961; Holland
M. R. de Bruyne	General of the Marines (ret.); Holland
Broer Moonen	executed by Germans
Frans Goedhart	member of Parliament; Holland
Wiardi Beckman	died in concentration camp; Germany
Gerard Dogger	tea executive; England
Han Doornbos	colonel, Royal Netherlands Air Force (ret.); Holland
André van Amsterdam	missing in action; R.A.F.; Germany
Robert Bergmann	Marshal of the Royal Court; Holland
Hamish Mahaddie	aviation consultant; England
Ben Hein	manufacturing executive; Holland
Rie Stokvis	died in 1970; Holland
Jean Mesritz	died in concentration camp; Germany